BONNIE S

SIMPLY
HEARTSMART
COOKING

RANDOM HOUSE
TORONTO

HEART
AND STROKE
FOUNDATION
OF CANADA

CONTENTS

This book is for my good friend Maureen Lollar
who has worked with me for fifteen years.
I am in constant awe of her work ethic, her understanding and
compassion for those in need, her eclectic sense of humour
and her incredibly acute taste buds.

ACKNOWLEDGEMENTS

The Heart and Stroke Foundation would like to thank the following people for reviewing the introductory chapter of *Simply HeartSmart Cooking*. Their expertise was invaluable in helping to present the most current, relevant information to provide you with an understanding of healthy eating.

Members of the National Nutrition Advisory Committee:
Gail Leadlay, RD; Suzanne Mahaffy, P.Dt.; Bretta Maloff, M.Ed., RD;
Rena Mendelson, M.S., D.Sc., RD; Laura Sevenhuysen, M.Ed., RD.

Program Development and Review Subcommittee Workgroup:
Johanne Carrier, APR; Gwen Dubois-Wing, R.N., M.A.; Gerald Gray, Ph.D.;
James C. Welsh, Ph.D.

Members of the Canadian Dietetic Association Review Committee:
Barbara Anderson, P.Dt.; Kathryn Camelon, B.A.Sc., RD; Doris Gillis, M.Sc., M.Ad.Ed., P.Dt.;
Donna J. Nadolny, M.Sc., RD.

Elaine Chan Fabiano, B.Sc., RD; Carol Dombrow, B.Sc., RD; Susan Fyshe, M.H.Sc., RD;
Richard Lauzon, Ph.D., M.B.A.; Doug MacQuarrie, M.Ed.; Bonnie Stern;
Lysanne Trudeau, M.Sc., Dt.P.

A special thanks to

- the Cookbook Task Force who spent many hours providing input on all the aspects required to provide you with the best cookbook yet: Bonnie Stern, Shelley Tanaka, Richard Lauzon, Ron Bradley, Lilianne Bertrand, Beverly Tobin, Kasia Czarski, Elissa Freeman, Niki Guner, Leah Reynolds, Linda Samis, Doug Pepper, Pat Cairns, Alan Terakawa, Carol Dombrow, Rick Gallop.
- Denise Beatty, RD, for writing the wonderful introduction for this cookbook and for always being available to answer questions.
- Barbara Selley, RD, Consulting Associate, InfoAccess (1988) Inc., for providing nutrient analysis for recipes and for keeping everyone on track.
- Elaine Chan Fabiano, RD, for expert assistance in organizing all of the components of the book; Susan Finkelstein and Lynn McAuliffe for assistance with the final editing.

The Heart and Stroke Foundation gratefully acknowledges the generous support of Becel in helping to make this cookbook possible. The financial support received from our sponsor does not constitute an endorsement by the Heart and Stroke Foundation or the author for the sponsor's products.

The Canadian Dietetic Association has reviewed *Simply HeartSmart Cooking* and acknowledges its contribution to promoting the nutritional well-being of Canadians.

AUTHOR'S
ACKNOWLEDGEMENTS

My father always says that the harder you work the more luck you have. And although I work very hard, I know that I am also a very lucky person. The love and support from family adds to my good fortune immeasurably. It is through their understanding that I can take on the projects that I do. Loving thanks go especially to my husband, Raymond Rupert, and Anna, Mark and Fara; Meredith, Charles, Jane and Wayne Krangle; Max and Ruth Stern; Bruce and Hedy Felstein; Jack Rupert and Shawn Duckman. My extended family includes Daphne Smith, Tina Lastima and Dely Balagtas.

A project like this is a huge undertaking and I consider it to have been sixteen years in the making. There have been a lot of people who have influenced the material, and I appreciate their input and support very much.

My staff at the cooking school make it a pleasure to come to work every morning. They tackle new projects with enthusiasm and put up with my last minute recipe changes with good humour. Warm thanks go to Anne Apps, Lorraine Butler, Robert Butler, Rhonda Caplan, Sadie Darby, Letty Lastima, Julie Lewis, Maureen Lollar, Sandra Madour, Jacques Marie, Francine Menard, Melissa Mertl and Linda Stephen. In addition, I must thank Brian Campbell and Wendy Craig for their computer expertise — without their help this manuscript may have been submitted in longhand!

It was a great opportunity to work with the Heart and Stroke Foundation of Canada on this project. Not only was it a wonderful learning opportunity for me, but they have also given me the chance to contribute to a very worthy cause. I want to thank everyone connected with this project at the organization and especially Denise Beatty, Lilianne Bertrand, Kasia Czarski, Carol Dombrow, Elaine Chan Fabiano, Elissa Freeman, Rick Gallop, Niki Guner, Richard Lauzon, Ruth LeBar, Lynn McAuliffe, Leah Reynolds, Linda Samis, Barbara Selley and Beverly Tobin.

Once again it was reassuring to have Random House as my publisher. They have taken another of my manuscripts and translated it into a beautiful cookbook. There are many people there to thank along with the creative artists, editors and designers they engage to complete the project: Mary Adachi, Pat Cairns, Sarah Davies, Joseph Gisini, Diane Hargrave, Sheila Kay, David Kent, Kathryn Mulders, Doug Pepper, Andrew Smith, Lorraine Symmes, Alan Terakawa, Wayne Terry, Olga Truchan, Robert Wigington, Tanya Wood and Lorella Zanetti.

Very special thanks go to Marian Hebb, without whom this project would never have got underway. And also to Shelley Tanaka, my meticulous editor, without whom this project may never have been completed. It must have been all those early morning, late night and Sunday conferences.

I have been influenced in many delicious ways by many talented chefs, teachers and friends who have shared ideas, techniques and recipes with me: Elizabeth Andoh, Fran Berkoff, Gwen Berkowitz, Giuliano Bugialli, Hugh Carpenter, Jim Dodge, Bernie Glazman, Barbara Glickman, Simone Goldberg, Marcella and Victor Hazan, Andrea Iceruk, Madhur Jaffrey, Madeleine Kamman, Diana Kennedy, Susur Lee, Patti and Earl Linzon, Nick Malgieri, Lydie Marshall, Bob Masching, Christopher McDonald, Mark McEwan, Alice Medrich, John Moscowitz, Jacques Pépin, Joel and Linda Rose, Nancy Lerner and Richard Rotman, Lynn Saunders, Nina Simonds, Sharon Sobel, Heidi Steinberg, Irene Tam, Susan Weaver, Edward Weil, Lynn and Barrie Wexler, Carol and Jim White and Cynthia Winc.

I am also most grateful to my colleagues and members of the press who give me the chance to promote good cooking and reach many more people through radio, newspapers, magazines and television than I could possibly do through my school: Elizabeth Baird, Debbie Bassett, Vyvyn Campbell, Ed Carson, Wei Chen, Bonnie Baker Cowan, Anita Draycott, Lin Eleoff, Carol Ferguson, Margaret Fraser, Ruth Fremes, Alison Fryer, Randy Gulliver, Peter Gzowski, Gerald Haddon, Deby Holbik, Mildred Istona, Adele Ilott, Mary Ito, Patricia Jamieson, Marion Kane, Loni Kuhn, Bob Lawlor, Anne Lindsay, Samantha Linton, Dan Matheson, Keith Morrison, Peter and Margie Pacini, Norm Perry, Dini Petty, Valerie Pringle, Daphna Rabinovitch, Mary Risley, Monda Rosenberg, Paula Salvador, Liz Stocks, Pamela Wallin, Robin Ward and Judy Webb.

And thanks to the Toronto Star, Canadian Living Magazine, CFTO'S Eye on Toronto and CTV's Canada AM, where some of these recipes may have appeared before.

And last but certainly not least, a significant tribute goes to my wonderful, inquisitive and faithful students, who are my built-in taste panel. Of all the different things I do, my very favourite is teaching my classes because I can communicate personally with other cooks. My students keep me ahead of the game by their constant interaction, so that I am always aware of what people need to know, what people want to know and how best they want to learn it. Their questions enable me to include the answers within my recipes so that I can help you have great results when you spend your precious time and effort to cook. Thank you, thank you, thank you.

BONNIE STERN
TORONTO, 1994

PREFACE

It sounds so simple: eat low fat, high fibre foods! But, you ask, "How can I do it?" Over the past six years, the Heart and Stroke Foundation of Canada has addressed the "how" for you by publishing three cookbooks:

- *The Lighthearted Cookbook*
- *Lighthearted Everyday Cooking*
- *Heart Smart Cooking on a Shoestring*

Each book took a different path to heart healthy eating. The continuing popular demand for these books reinforced our belief that we helped to satisfy a need for those millions of Canadians who wish to cook heart healthy.

Simply HeartSmart Cooking caters to making heart healthy cooking simple. Our renowned author, Bonnie Stern, has responded successfully to the challenge. We are confident that this book will become a valued resource in your home library. The meal preparation tips alone are worth it! But that would be overlooking the introductory chapter and body of the book.

The introduction allows the Foundation to present some of the latest developments in the prevention and control of heart disease and stroke. Feature writer, dietitian Denise Beatty, neatly covers a variety of topics: active living, risk factor updates, antioxidants, healthy eating, and Canada's Food Guide to Healthy Eating. She discusses fat intake among children and includes some common questions and answers on healthy eating. There's also some startling information on women, heart disease and stroke.

The book's format was employed to make heart smart cooking simpler. The use of colour inside and special side bars help you focus on the essentials. Menu planning compliments the recipes themselves. In the end, I am certain that you will enjoy both the messages and the meals in *Simply HeartSmart Cooking*.

FRANCES M. GREGOR, RN, MN
PRESIDENT, HEART AND STROKE FOUNDATION OF CANADA

INTRODUCTION

**WHO'S THIS
COOKBOOK FOR?**
This cookbook is primarily
for healthy people who want
to eat better in general.
Whether it's a Monday night
supper or the dinner party of
the year, you'll find delicious
but healthy recipes and
menu ideas for those who
love food and love to eat.

It will also be useful to
people with diabetes
who will find it easy to
incorporate the recipes
into personal diet plans
using the Canadian Diabetes
Association Food Choice
Values in Appendix page 291.

Heart patients, too, will
enjoy the recipes, although
some may have to be
reduced even further in salt,
fat and dietary cholesterol.
The tips in Appendix,
starting on page 285, will
help you do this.

HEALTHY EATING FOR HEART HEALTH

No one would be surprised if after a quick glance at these introductory pages, you skip right over to the recipes. After all, it's the
recipes you're usually after when you buy a cookbook.

But then again, this is no ordinary cookbook!

In this cookbook, the Heart and Stroke Foundation of Canada
has teamed up with well-known cook Bonnie Stern, who has
created two hundred, heart-healthy recipes with a flavour and
flare for which Bonnie is renowned.

What's more, there is this introductory chapter that explains
what's important in healthy eating today.

It's entirely up to you on how to proceed from here. You can
continue reading and learning about healthy eating or jump right
in, so-to-speak, by making one of Bonnie's delicious and healthy
recipes.

Just as I am sure you will turn to Bonnie's recipes time and
time again, you can return to this introductory section to refresh
your memory on what healthy eating is all about.

HEALTHY EATING—WHAT'S IN IT FOR YOU?

If you're tired all the time and feel dragged out at the end of the
day, chances are that poor food choices, erratic eating habits and
lack of regular physical activity are partly to blame.

You'll feel better, look better and enjoy having more energy
when you eat in a healthy way and become more active.

Healthy eating and being active will:

- provide you with all the essential nutrients in adequate amounts
- help you avoid the energy highs and lows associated with hit-
  and-miss eating because you'll be eating *regular* meals and snacks
- help keep your immune system in top-notch fighting form,
  ready and able to fight off common cold viruses, bacteria and
  other foreign invaders that make you sick
- give you a better chance of achieving and maintaining a healthy
  body weight
- reduce your risk of diet-related health problems such as heart
  disease, cancer, obesity

A HEART-TO-HEART TALK WITH WOMEN

As a society, Canadians tend to associate heart disease with middle-
aged men. But it's not only men that suffer from heart disease and
stroke. It is time for women to listen to their hearts too.

Heart disease and stroke is the most common cause of death among women. Yes, surprising as it may seem, heart disease and stroke accounted for 41% of all female deaths in Canada in 1992. Women must recognize the risk factors and act positively to control them.

RISK FACTORS

Women, just like men, are at increased risk for heart disease if they:

- smoke
- have high blood pressure
- have elevated blood cholesterol and triglycerides
- are physically inactive
- are overweight
- have diabetes

As well as the additional risks of using oral contraceptives and the onset of menopause, women seem more at risk than men if they suffer from high blood pressure, elevated blood triglycerides and diabetes.

HEART ACTION FOR WOMEN

What can women do to have healthier hearts? Women, like men, need to be aware of the lifestyle factors that put them at risk and make changes where necessary.

Here are five key actions to promote heart health:

- If you smoke, quit. Smoking doubles your risk of heart attack and if you both smoke and take oral contraceptives, your risk doubles yet again.
- Become more physically active every day.
- Know your blood pressure. If it's too high, get help right away. Normal blood pressure should fall within these ranges: a systolic pressure (upper number) of 100–140 over a diastolic pressure (lower number) of 70–90.
- If you suffer from excessive stress, anxiety or depression, get some help. Changes in your lifestyle such as eating more healthfully, being more active, engaging in relaxation therapy or stress management courses can help you cope in healthy ways.
- Follow a healthy eating pattern that is lower in fat and higher in foods rich in complex carbohydrates and fibre (whole grains, vegetables, fruits and legumes). The information and the recipes in this cookbook will get you off to a good start.

WHAT IS HEALTHY EATING?

At its most basic level, healthy eating is a way of eating that provides you with all of the essential nutrients and at the same time reduces your risks of developing nutrition-related diseases like heart disease, cancer and being overweight. It's also much more than this.

GETTING PHYSICAL
Being active every day goes hand-in-hand with healthy eating.

What you do to be active is not nearly as important as doing it!

The best physical activities are ones you enjoy doing and are easily worked into daily routines.

Walking and gardening are two very easy and enjoyable ways to be active. Of course organized sports★ such as baseball, basketball, exercise classes and leisure-time activities such as biking, skiing, hiking, tennis, swimming, skating, golfing all count, too.

★ *Some types of physical activity may not be suitable for everyone.*
Before engaging in new types of strenuous activity, check with your doctor.

Q: *What can you suggest for a safe and healthy way to lose weight?*

A: Weight loss is a complex health issue for which there is no simple answer. It has become abundantly clear that low-calorie, starvation-like diets fail to help most weight losers achieve and maintain a healthy weight for any length of time. What's more, losing and gaining weight, time and time again isn't healthy either — physically, emotionally and psychologically.

Current thinking on weight loss favours a moderate approach that involves healthy eating, not dieting, and being more active. You can use the information and recipes in this cookbook to adopt a lower-fat and sensible approach to eating that may help you reach a healthier weight.

Healthy eating also means having a healthy relationship with food and eating. Healthy eaters use food in a sensible way; they neither overeat nor feel the need to completely eliminate foods they enjoy. They respond to their bodies' internal cues that tell them to eat when they're hungry and to stop when they've eaten enough.

When you adopt a pattern of healthy eating it frees you up to enjoy food and eating, to take pleasure from it without feeling any guilt.

HEALTHY EATING YOUR WAY

There is more than one way to be a healthy eater. Whether you eat meat, are vegetarian or are restricted by a special diet, there are some basic principles that are common to all healthy eating patterns.

In Canada, the tool that helps many people establish a healthy eating pattern is Canada's Food Guide to Healthy Eating, shown on page 12. Although some details of this food guide are unique to Canada, the basic healthy eating principles that it promotes are much the same as the Food Pyramid used in the USA and the food guides of other Westernized societies.

GETTING A HANDLE ON THE FOOD GUIDE

If you're not already familiar with the Food Guide, take a few minutes to scan it on pages 12 and 13.

The Food Guide is exactly what it claims to be…a guide to healthy eating. By showing what foods are important and recommending a range of servings, it takes the guesswork out of eating nutritiously.

To build on, rather than repeat the information already given in the Food Guide, this section of the cookbook discusses in more detail the key, heart-related principles of healthy eating.

UNDERSTANDING THE FOOD GUIDE BETTER

WHAT SHOULD YOU EAT?

The goal of healthy eating is to shift the way you eat from the traditional Canadian diet that is based heavily on protein-rich, higher-fat foods to one that includes more complex carbohydrates, fibre, key vitamins and minerals.

This shift is promoted visually in the Food Guide by the rainbow design. The larger outside arcs encourage you to eat proportionally more grain products, vegetables and fruit; the smaller inside arcs represent the smaller amounts needed of milk and meat products.

Free copies of Canada's Food Guide to Healthy Eating and the more detailed consumer booklet are available from the nutritionist at your local or provincial health department.

Health Canada   Santé Canada

CANADA'S Food Guide TO HEALTHY EATING

Enjoy a variety of foods from each group every day.

Choose lower-fat foods more often.

Grain Products
Choose whole grain and enriched products more often.

Vegetables & Fruit
Choose dark green and orange vegetables and orange fruit more often.

Milk Products
Choose lower-fat milk products more often.

Meat & Alternatives
Choose leaner meats, poultry and fish, as well as dried peas, beans and lentils more often.

Canada

Different People Need Different Amounts of Food

The amount of food you need every day from the 4 food groups and other foods depends on your age, body size, activity level, whether you are male or female and if you are pregnant or breast-feeding. That's why the Food Guide gives a lower and higher number of servings for each food group. For example, young children can choose the lower number of servings, while male teenagers can go to the higher number. Most other people can choose servings somewhere in between.

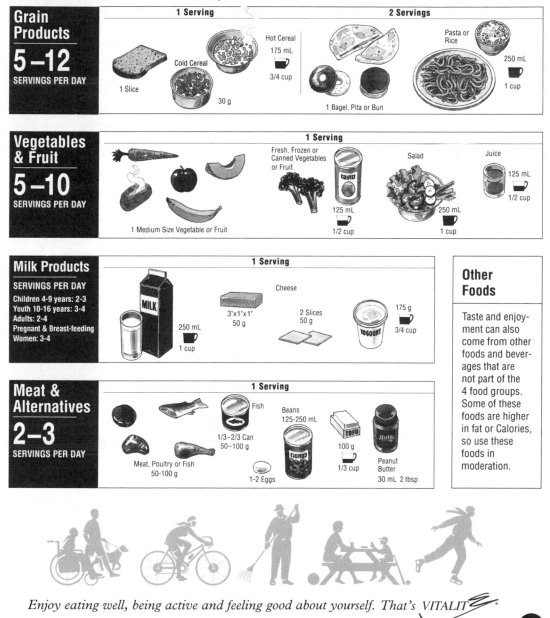

Grain Products
5–12
SERVINGS PER DAY

1 Serving
1 Slice
Cold Cereal — 30 g
Hot Cereal — 175 mL — 3/4 cup

2 Servings
1 Bagel, Pita or Bun
Pasta or Rice — 250 mL — 1 cup

Vegetables & Fruit
5–10
SERVINGS PER DAY

1 Serving
1 Medium Size Vegetable or Fruit
Fresh, Frozen or Canned Vegetables or Fruit — 125 mL — 1/2 cup
Salad — 250 mL — 1 cup
Juice — 125 mL — 1/2 cup

Milk Products
SERVINGS PER DAY
Children 4-9 years: 2-3
Youth 10-16 years: 3-4
Adults: 2-4
Pregnant & Breast-feeding Women: 3-4

1 Serving
MILK — 250 mL — 1 cup
Cheese — 3"x1"x1" — 50 g
2 Slices — 50 g
175 g — 3/4 cup

Other Foods

Taste and enjoyment can also come from other foods and beverages that are not part of the 4 food groups. Some of these foods are higher in fat or Calories, so use these foods in moderation.

Meat & Alternatives
2–3
SERVINGS PER DAY

1 Serving
Meat, Poultry or Fish — 50-100 g
Fish — 1/3–2/3 Can — 50–100 g
1-2 Eggs
Beans — 125-250 mL
TOFU — 100 g — 1/3 cup
Peanut Butter — 30 mL 2 tbsp

Enjoy eating well, being active and feeling good about yourself. That's VITALIT

HOW MUCH SHOULD YOU EAT?

Like many people, your first reaction to the Food Guide may be that it recommends too many servings of Grain Products and Vegetables & Fruit.

It doesn't. You'll find that as you cut back on higher-fat foods, you will eat more of the lower-fat grain products, vegetables, legumes and fruit to satisfy your hunger.

Besides, the number of servings needed by you each day depends on your age, sex and how active you are. Children and women, for example, may need only 7 servings of Grain Products and 6 servings of Vegetables & Fruit. But athletic people, very hungry teenage boys or adults who work in physically demanding jobs may need to eat more of these foods to get their daily calories.

The serving sizes may fool you, too. The sandwich you eat contributes two, not one serving of Grain Products; a big glass of juice is two, not one serving of fruit; the plateful of pasta may amount to 2 or 3 servings of Grain Products.

WHAT IF YOU'RE A VEGETARIAN?

Canada's Food Guide to Healthy Eating can be used as a guide for vegetarians who eat milk products and/or eggs.

The main difference will be that instead of meat, alternatives such as legumes and eggs will be used. There is no need to combine legumes, vegetables, grains, nuts and seeds in any particular way to get sufficient protein. As long as milk products are used in recommended amounts, the diet will be sufficient in protein for both growing children and adults.

There are recipes in this cookbook that will help you learn how to prepare healthy, meatless meals.

THE FOOD GUIDE'S BASIC PRINCIPLES OF HEALTHY EATING

Now that you have some familiarity with Canada's Food Guide to Healthy Eating, I will focus on the key underlying principles of healthy eating on which the Food Guide is based.

They are:

- Enjoy a variety of foods

- Eat more grain products, vegetables, fruit and legumes

- Reduce the amount of fat you eat

- Limit salt, alcohol and caffeine

Q: *Should I cut out high-cholesterol foods such as eggs?*
A: There is no need for relatively healthy people to completely avoid high-cholesterol foods such as eggs and liver. According to Canada's Food Guide to Healthy Eating these foods can be eaten in moderation. This means you might include high-cholesterol foods in your diet a few times a week but certainly not every day.

The advice is different for those with a diagnosed blood cholesterol problem, however. If your blood cholesterol is elevated, a dietitian or doctor may advise you to restrict consumption of these high-cholesterol foods. Even though the cholesterol in food does not affect blood cholesterol as much as dietary fat, particularly saturated and trans fat, it does have some effect in some people.

Whether you're looking to prevent blood cholesterol from getting too high or you're trying to reduce already elevated blood cholesterol levels, the most important dietary strategy is to cut back on dietary fat, particularly saturated and trans fat. What's more, when you do this, your intake of dietary cholesterol is automatically reduced since sources of saturated fat and food cholesterol are usually one and the same.

Enjoy A Variety Of Foods

Eating a variety of foods is important because no one food is
perfect. Foods vary in nutrient content — rich in some nutrients,
poor in others, high in fat or low in dietary fibre. By eating all
kinds of different foods, you blend the various positives and
negatives in foods to achieve a healthy balance.

How do you eat a varied diet? It's simple.

Eat foods from each of the four food groups every day as
recommended by the Food Guide. In addition to choosing foods
from all food groups, vary your choices from each group so that
you're not eating the same foods day-in and day-out.

Eat More Grain Products, Vegetables, Fruit And Legumes

Grains, vegetables, fruit and legumes are the cornerstones to healthy
eating today because they are sources of complex carbohydrate,
dietary fibre, key vitamins and minerals.

In countries where people naturally eat a diet high in complex
carbohydrates and fibre, there is a lower incidence of diseases such as
heart disease and cancer. It's not entirely clear whether this observa-
tion is due to the complex carbohydrate and fibre content of the diet
or to the fact that these diets are naturally low in fat.

The important point is that these foods are clearly beneficial
and that's why Canada's Food Guide to Healthy Eating puts an
emphasis on eating more of these foods.

What's more, grains, vegetables and fruit are the main dietary
sources of the antioxidant vitamins C, E and beta-carotene.
(Dietary sources of vitamins C, E and beta-carotene are in
Appendix page 290.) It is thought that antioxidant vitamins help
to stabilize and render harmless a highly reactive form of oxygen.
If not stabilized, this form of oxygen sets off harmful reactions in
the body that may play a role in the development of heart disease
and certain cancers.

FOCUS ON FIBRE

It's been known for a long time that dietary fibre is good for
health. It keeps your bowels in good working order, it may
reduce your risk of certain cancers and it plays a role in regulating
blood sugar and lowering blood cholesterol.

Fibre is found only in foods of vegetable origin — whole grain
foods, brans (wheat, oat, rice), vegetables, fruit and legumes.

Adults should be aiming for a daily fibre intake of 25–35 grams.
This amount is easy to get if you follow the advice of the food
guide, eating plenty of whole grain foods, vegetables, fruit and
legumes.

A FIBRE-SURE DAY

Getting enough fibre every day is easy with this three-point fibre plan! Eat at least:

- One serving of a high-fibre cereal★ or 125 mL/½ cup legumes
- Six servings of fresh, canned or frozen vegetables and fruit (not juice)
- Four slices whole grain bread or 2 slices whole grain bread + 2 servings other whole grain food (brown rice, whole grain pasta)
- ★ *Suggestions:* Any favourite cereal mixed with 50 mL/¼ cup of any very high-fibre cereal; Cooked oatmeal or oatbran plus 30 mL/2 tbsp. wheat bran or 50 mL/¼ cup dried fruit

Reduce The Amount Of Fat You Eat

If there is one nutrient that's been linked to poor health over and over again, it is dietary fat. The average Canadian adult eats too much fat which partly explains why heart disease, cancer and obesity are so common in this country.

WHAT SHOULD YOU DO ABOUT FAT?

The main goal of healthy eating is to cut back on all fat. Although some fats are better for heart health than others, the overriding consideration is to eat less fat in total.

For more information on the various types of fat in food and their effects on health see Appendix page 288.

HOW SHOULD YOU CUT BACK ON FAT?

Once you know where fat is generally found in food, you can make changes in the types of foods you choose and the way you prepare or cook them. As you'll learn from Bonnie's recipes it's easy to cut back on fat without sacrificing good taste.

A FAT-CUTTING TOOL FOR HEALTHY EATERS

I'm going to give you just two simple numbers — one for women and one for men that will help you make lower-fat food choices. Let me explain. Canada's Nutrition Recommendations advise Canadians to cut back on fat so that only 30% (instead of the current 38%) of the day's calories come from fat. This is good advice but what does it mean? It doesn't mean much to most people and with good reason. The fat in food is measured and reported on food labels, in brochures, in food magazines and in cookbooks as grams, not percentages. So what you really need to know is what this 30% figure means in grams of fat.

That's where my two numbers come in. I've calculated what 30% of calories from fat works out to be in grams of fat. Put these two numbers to memory because you'll use them time and time again to make healthier food choices.

DON'T BE PERPLEXED BY COMPLEX CARBOHYDRATE

Complex carbohydrate is the same thing as starch.

Anything made with flour (white, rye, whole wheat) or grains such as rice, barley, cracked wheat, cornmeal will be high in complex carbohydrate. Legumes and a few vegetables such as corn, peas and potatoes are also good sources of complex carbohydrate.

Contrary to long-held beliefs, it isn't these starchy foods that are fattening. Quite the opposite is true since these foods are naturally low in fat and calories. It's what you combine with the starchy food — *the butter* with bread or toast, *cheesy cream sauce* on the pasta, *the hot dog or sausage* on a bun — that is the source of higher calories and fat.

HOW MUCH FAT SHOULD YOU EAT IN A MEAL?

There is no one rule. And of course, no two days are likely the same. However, you can use these rough guidelines to help you plan the fat content of meals.

- Breakfast and morning snack: 10–15 grams
- Lunch and afternoon snack: 25–35 grams
- Dinner and evening snack: 25–40 grams

THE MAIN SOURCES OF FAT IN YOUR DIET

- Table and cooking fats: butter, margarine, shortening, lard, vegetable oils, regular salad dressings, mayonnaise
- Foods made with or fried in table and cooking fats: cookies, cakes, crackers, many convenience foods, snack foods like chips, many fast foods
- Milk products unless they are skimmed milk products★
- Meat, poultry, fish and eggs

★ *The recipes in this cookbook have been analyzed using 2% lower-fat milk. Fat intake can be reduced even further by using skim or 1% milk.*

Q: *I just discovered that margarines contain either hydrogenated oil or palm oil. Aren't these ingredients just as bad for me as butter?*

A: In this matter, quantity is everything. While the so-called health margarines do contain some saturated fat (palm or palm kernel oil) or trans fat (from the hydrogenated vegetable oil), they contain far less than the amount of saturated fat you get from butter. Use as little as possible.

HEALTHY FAT INTAKE FOR A DAY

(In Grams)

For the average man age 19–74 who requires between 2300–3000 calories a day	90 grams or less
For the average woman age 19–74 who requires between 1800–2100 calories a day	65 grams or less

KEEP NUMBERS IN A HEALTHY PERSPECTIVE

These numbers are just a tool to help you choose lower-fat foods for healthy eating. Since a healthy fat intake is linked to caloric intake, more active people who have higher caloric needs may be able to handle a little more fat than less active people.

HOW TWO NUMBERS CAN MAKE A DIFFERENCE

You can use these numbers as a benchmark against which you can judge the fat content of foods as these real-life situations illustrate.

Shopping

- You're in the grocery store choosing frozen fish.
Two pieces (about 100 grams) of a breaded product provides 16 grams of fat; the same amount of plain, frozen fillets provides less than 1 gram of fat. If you choose the breaded product you know that it's a lot of fat for just one part of a meal.

- You want a microwave entrée for a quick dinner.
Although serving sizes vary slightly, chances are you'll eat all of a single-serving portion. When you compare the various entrées you see quite a range in fat content. What you choose may depend on what else you plan to eat and what you've already eaten throughout the day.

Product	Serving Size (grams)	Fat in Grams
Vegetarian Chili	(350 g)	4.9
Lasagna	(286 g)	12.0
Shepherd's Pie	(270 g)	18.0
Macaroni & Cheese	(340 g)	26.0
Spinach Soufflé	(335 g)	30.0

Eating Out

At a sandwich bar you're asked to choose the type of bread or bun you want. From reading labels at the grocery store you know that a small croissant has at least 12 grams of fat whereas 2 slices of whole wheat bread or a bun contribute only traces of fat. Choosing bread or a plain bun instead of the croissant will spare you 12 grams of unnecessary fat.

FAT AND YOUR CHILDREN

When it comes to nutrition, children are not just small-size adults! They have different nutrition needs, especially for fat. Children, especially young children in the pre-school and early school years, can't eat large quantities of food and will likely need the concentrated calories of higher-fat foods to support proper growth and development.

Health Canada in consultation with the Canadian Paediatric Society has recently concluded that adult goals for fat intake should not be applied too strictly to children.

Childhood years should be seen as the step-down period between the higher-fat diet of infancy where 50% of calories come from fat to the lower-fat diet advocated for adults. During these growth years, children can be learning to enjoy lower-fat foods and meals as eaten by the rest of the family and promoted in these recipes. But at the same time they can be including more of the higher-fat foods such as cheese, peanut butter, nuts, seeds and ice cream that their older siblings and parents might eat less often.

As children approach the end of physical growth — around age 14–15 for girls, 17–18 for boys, fat intake should be gradually lowered to the level currently recommended for adults. Lower-fat foods and meals would be chosen more often and higher-fat foods would be used more sparingly.

Limit Salt, Alcohol And Caffeine

Issues around the use of salt, caffeine and alcohol are frequently a source of confusion. Let it be said that all of these dietary substances can be used by most healthy people without harm, as long as they're used in moderation.

However, some or all of them may be restricted when you're on a special diet as prescribed by your doctor or dietitian.

SALT

Salt is used widely in the food supply providing most people with a sodium intake far in excess of need. And since sodium may promote high blood pressure in some people, the public is advised to cut back on salt intake.

Q: *What are the best margarines to buy?*

A: The best margarines are :

- low in saturated or trans fat. However, since current laws do not allow for trans fat to be listed on the label, it's not practical to use these criteria for selecting a margarine.

- high in unsaturated fat. This information is on the label and can be used, as described below, to choose a good margarine.

- always sold in a tub — not in foil-wrapped stick or brick form

- always labelled with nutrition information.

To select a good-quality margarine, use the information on the nutrition label. Add up the grams of polyunsaturates and monounsaturates only. The best regular margarines will contain: 6 grams or more of unsaturated fat in a 10 gram (2 teaspoon) portion. A good quality light margarine will contain 3 grams or more of unsaturated fat.

Q: *I've heard olive oil is the best oil to use. Is this true?*

A: Cooks like Bonnie love the taste that olive oil imparts to food. But aside from taste, olive oil is a good oil because it's high in monounsaturated fat and naturally contains the antioxidant Vitamin E. However, good oil or not, the bottom line is always to use as little oil as possible.

- coffee: 108–180 mg per 6 oz cup/200 mL, filter drip
- tea: 78–108 mg per 6 oz cup/200 mL strong tea
- cola soft drinks: 28–64 mg per 12 oz/355 mL can
- chocolate, especially dark chocolate: 40–50 mg in a 56 g/2 oz bar dark chocolate
- cold remedies and headache relievers: 15–30 mg per tablet

USE FOOD LABELS★ TO SHOP FOR HEALTHY EATING

Food labels can help you shop for healthy eating. All packaged food must have a List of Ingredients. Use this information to reveal if the product is made with whole grain ingredients, what kinds of fat it's made with and sources of salt or sodium.

In addition, some packaged food will also be labelled with more detailed nutrition information listing such things as the calories, fat and fibre content of food. As shown in the shopping examples on page 17, you can use this information to compare products and make healthier choices.

....

★ *For more information on understanding food labels, contact your local Heart and Stroke Foundation office.*

ALCOHOL

Although there have been studies showing some cholesterol-lowering benefits from wine, there are too many other health risks, like liver disease and certain types of cancer, associated with excess alcohol consumption to endorse its use for this purpose. If alcohol is used, use it in moderation. This means no more than one drink per day or seven drinks in a week. One drink is 1 bottle of beer (5% alcohol); 150 mL/5 oz. of wine (10-14% alcohol); 50 mL/½ oz. spirits (40% alcohol).

CAFFEINE

According to Canada's Nutrition Recommendations, most healthy people are not put at an increased risk for heart disease, high blood pressure, poor behaviour or adverse effects on pregnancy by moderate intakes of caffeine. A moderate caffeine intake is up to 400-450 milligrams a day, an amount you might expect from four, 6 ounce (200 mL) cups of drip coffee or strong tea.

TIPS FOR SHOPPING, PREPARING FOOD AND MEAL PLANNING

Healthy eating may begin in your head and your heart but it's the decisions made in the grocery store and at home in the kitchen that can make or break your desire to eat more healthfully.

To help you put these basic principles of healthy eating into action, here are some tips about planning for meals, shopping for and preparing foods.

HOW TO ENJOY A VARIETY OF FOODS

Shopping Tips:
- Buy foods from all food groups
- Try new foods, new products

Preparation and Meal Planning Tips:
- Try new recipes
- Try new ways to prepare and cook foods: braise in broth or tomato juice instead of frying; replace the butter normally used on bread or toast with some apple butter (recipe page 231) or yogurt cheese (recipe page 228); use a low-fat pressed cottage cheese instead of cream cheese to make cheese cake; mix lentils with rice

HOW TO EAT MORE GRAIN PRODUCTS, VEGETABLES, FRUIT, LEGUMES

Shopping Tips:

- Buy plenty of these foods to provide recommended number of servings
- Choose whole grain breads, brown rice, higher-fibre breakfast cereals, low-fat muffin mixes, whole wheat flour for baking, lower-fat crackers and cookies
- Vegetables and fruit can be fresh, frozen, canned or dried
- Select lots of dark green and orange vegetables and orange fruit, important for folic acid and the antioxidant vitamins beta-carotene and vitamin C. Generally, vegetables are more nutrient-rich than fruit.
- Canned legumes are more convenient to use than dried; look for legume-based soups, stews and in dried mixes combined with rice or noodles

Preparation and Meal Planning Tips:

- You want to fill up on these foods so it's okay to serve pasta with potatoes or both bread and rice at the same meal
- Aim for 2-3 vegetables or fruit at each meal
- Include more legumes in your diet by adding green peas to rice; putting chickpeas in salad; adding a can of lentils or kidney beans to canned soup
- Keep the naturally low-fat quality of these foods by using very little, if any, butter or margarine on bread; by not adding oil to cooking water of rice and pasta; by using lower-fat recipes for homemade baked goods
- Rinse canned vegetables (when possible) and legumes to remove some of the salt before using.

HOW TO REDUCE THE AMOUNT OF FAT YOU EAT

Shopping Tips:

- Use Nutrition Information on food labels to help choose lower-fat foods
- Buy fewer potato chips and cheese-flavoured snacks and rich, dessert items such as ice cream, pies, cakes, danishes and donuts
- Buy lower-fat milk products such as:
  - skim, 1% or 2% milk, yogurt, cottage cheese
  - block or spreadable cheese with 20% or less butter fat (b.f.)
- Choose lower-fat frozen desserts such as:
  - sherbet or non-dairy sorbet
  - frozen yogurt with 3% or less butter fat
  - ice milk with 5% or less butter fat
  - light ice cream with less than 7.5% butter fat

WHAT'S A LEGUME?

Legumes are the mature, edible seeds of peas, beans and lentils. They are particularly valued as sources of complex carbohydrate and dietary fibre and for being naturally low in fat. They're also important vegetable sources of protein, calcium and iron.

SOME LEANER CHOICES OF MEAT, POULTRY AND FISH

Beef: Eye of round, inside and outside round; sirloin tip, sirloin roasts and steaks; rib eye steaks; stewing beef; tenderloin; flank steak

Pork: ham; leg roasts and cutlets; tenderloin cuts; centre cut chops and roasts; picnic shoulder; shoulder butt

Lamb: leg roast; loin chops

Veal: all cuts

Poultry: all cuts without skin

Fish: most fish *

Deli meats: ham, turkey roll or pastrami, beef pastrami

....

* *Although some fish such as salmon and trout are higher in fat, these types of fish are used in the recipes because most of the fat is omega-3 polyunsaturated fat, a type of fat that is heart healthy. See Appendix page 288 for more information on the various types of fat in food.*

- Since recommended portion sizes of meat are smaller than they once were, buy smaller quantities of meat
- Buy the leanest meat products; also plan to use more of the lowest fat protein choices such as fish

Preparation and Meal Planning Tips:
- It's at home where food is prepared that a lot of fat gets added. Use all fats and oils sparingly as Bonnie has done in the recipes and at all stages of food preparation, from buttering bread to making cookies.
- Use higher-fat milk products like cheese in moderation
- Prepare smaller portions of meat per person
- Use legumes instead of meat more often; make a meatless meal by having baked beans for dinner; enjoy a tomato sandwich with a bowl of split pea or black bean soup for lunch; replace the ham or chicken in a salad with chickpeas or kidney beans; try the recipes in the meatless main courses (page 115) and pasta chapters (page 97)
- Still hungry? Choose extra servings of grain products, vegetables, fruit and legumes instead of seconds of meat and cheese-based entrées

HOW TO LIMIT SALT, ALCOHOL AND CAFFEINE
Shopping Tips:
- When possible, buy foods claiming to be lower in salt; this doesn't mean the product is low in salt but it is at least lower in salt than the original
- Avoid regular use of highly salted foods such as: most canned and dried soups; casserole, rice and noodle mixes; processed cheese food; condiments such as soy sauce; frozen meals and entrées
- If caffeine is a problem for you, use decaffeinated or light coffee (partly decaffeinated) or switch to drinking weak tea

Preparation and Meal Planning Tips to Cut Back on Salt
- Like fat, it is at this stage that much of the salt you eat gets added to food, so be mindful of using the salt shaker
- Don't salt the cooking water of pasta and vegetables and use just a little, if any, when cooking rice
- Don't salt meat when cooking — add garlic, onion, pepper or other favourite spice instead
- Reduce the salt called for in recipes
- Remove the salt shaker from the table; use lemon pepper, Thai seasoning or an herb- and spice-based seasoning. Steer clear of salt-based seasonings such as celery salt and garlic salt
- Get creative with herbs and spices — Bonnie's got some great ideas to try. For more tips on cutting back salt, see Appendix page 285.

CONGRATULATIONS ARE IN ORDER!

If you feel overwhelmed by what you've just read, it's understandable. I condensed a tremendous amount of information into this one chapter of the cookbook.

My advice to you now is to leave the healthy eating facts for a while and get on to the fun part of healthy eating — the cooking and eating!

As you become familiar with Bonnie's recipes, you will see how she's incorporated the basic principles of healthy eating into them. She has used a wide variety of ingredients to create new and different dishes; she shows you how to include more grains, vegetables, fruit and legumes in your meals; she shows you how to reduce the amount of fat in preparing and cooking foods; and she keeps salt to a minimum and makes good use of salt-free herbs and spices to create delicious meals.

In time, you will shop, prepare foods and plan meals based on the principles of healthy eating without even thinking about it. Once learned, these healthy eating skills are much like the skills of tying your shoes or riding a bicycle. You never forget them. They're with you for life.

DENISE BEATTY, RD
CONSULTING NUTRITIONIST

ABOUT THE
NUTRIENT ANALYSIS

Nutrient analysis of the recipes and menus was performed by Info Access (1988) Inc., Don Mills, Ontario, using the nutritional accounting component of the CBORD Menu Management System. Sidebar recipes have not been included in the analyses.

- The nutrient database was the 1991 Canadian Nutrient File supplemented when necessary with documented data from reliable sources.
- The analysis was based on:
  - the Imperial weights and measures,
  - the smaller number of servings (i.e., larger portion) when there was a range, and
  - the first ingredient listed when there was a choice of ingredients.
- Canola vegetable oil, 2% milk and homemade unsalted stocks were used throughout.
- Specific measures of salt were included in the analyses but "salt to taste" was not. In all recipes you will want to use the least amount of salt that you find acceptable.
- When previously prepared dried legumes, rice or pasta were called for they were assumed to have been prepared without salt.
- Optional ingredients and garnishes in unspecified amounts were not calculated.

NUTRIENT INFORMATION ON RECIPES:

- Nutrient values have been rounded to the nearest whole number. Non-zero values less than 0.5 are shown as "trace."
- Good and excellent sources of vitamins (A, C, E, B_6, B_{12}, thiamine, niacin, riboflavin, folacin) and minerals (calcium and iron) have been identified according to the criteria established for nutrition labelling (Guide for Food Manufacturers and Advertisers, 1988).

  A serving which supplies 15% of the Recommended Daily Intake (RDI) for a vitamin or mineral (30% for vitamin C) is a good source of that nutrient. An excellent source must supply 25% of the RDI (50% for vitamin C).
- A serving providing at least 2 grams of dietary fibre is considered a moderate source. Servings providing 4 grams and 6 grams are high and very high sources, respectively (Guide for Food Manufacturers and Advertisers, 1988).

POTASSIUM

Potassium is thought to have a positive effect on hypertension and strokes. A diet promoting foods high in potassium, emphasizing fruit and vegetables, is recommended.

DAILY TOTAL PROTEIN, FAT AND CARBOHYDRATE INTAKE

Based on 15% of calories from protein, 30% of calories from fat and 55% of calories from carbohydrate. According to Nutrition Recommendations for Canadians, Health and Welfare Canada, 1990.

calorie intake	grams protein per day	grams fat per day	grams carbohydrate per day
1200	45	40	165
1500	56	50	206
1800	68	60	248
2100	79	70	289
2300	86	77	316
2600	98	87	357
2900	109	97	399
3200	120	107	440

HEALTHFUL MENU PLANNING

HEALTHFUL EATING

Today, healthful eating means that a moderately active woman should eat between 1800 and 2100 calories a day; a man should consume between 2300 and 3000 calories. At the same time, a woman should eat no more than 65 grams of fat per day; a man should consume a maximum of 90 grams (see table on page 24 for recommended daily protein, fat and carbohydrate intake).

If you want to find the percentage of fat in a serving, remember that there are 9 calories in every gram of fat. Therefore, multiply the grams of fat per serving by 9 and divide by the number of calories per serving and multiply by 100. Simply put, if a recipe has 3 grams of fat or less per 100 calories per serving, you know it's a good choice.

In 1978, I first started offering low-fat cooking classes because I firmly believed this was the future of good food. Not very many people came to those classes then, because delicious food was associated with rich ingredients. I persevered because I knew there were just as many delicious natural low-fat ingredients as there were rich ones.

Over the years, people have come to appreciate both the health benefits and the taste benefits of cooking with low-fat ingredients. Instead of covering up food with rich sauces, we are now more concerned with buying the best-quality ingredients and cooking them properly to bring out the most flavour. And cooks have replaced the flavour of fat and salt by using fresh herbs, fragrant spices, pungent peppers, acidic liquids and cooling citrus tastes.

I don't think eating should be a math test, and rather than counting calories or grams of fat, I prefer to exercise and eat healthfully by avoiding processed foods, eating less sodium and fat, more fruits and vegetables and more whole grains.

The overall guideline is that only 30 percent of your calories should come from fat. You can achieve this easily with careful menu planning. For example, a small plain steak may contain more than 30 percent fat, but if it is served with a low-fat grain and vegetables, the total fat percentage of the meal comes down.

You can also consider the day's or week's menus this way. If you know you are going out to dinner and may be eating more than usual, simply cut back at lunch that day or the following day. Because fat has more than twice the calories of protein or carbo-hydrate, if you keep your fat calories down, you can actually eat much more food and stay within the recommended calorie range. Not only that, but because it takes more energy to metabolize protein and carbohydrate, if you are on a lower-fat diet (even if you are eating the same number of calories as someone on a high-fat diet), it should be much easier to manage your weight.

To make healthful menu planning a little easier, I have tried to make sure that most of the recipes in this book are under or very close to the 30 percent mark. This way you can put together meals without worrying too much about counting grams of fat.

MENU PLANNING PRINCIPLES

Many people know that it is important to plan a meal when they entertain. They set aside the time and enjoy the process. But these same people often find it tedious planning everyday meals. However, if you apply the same principles and give yourself even a short amount of time to organize, soon it will become second nature.

TASTES AND INGREDIENTS

Try not to repeat ingredients. You obviously wouldn't serve a shepherd's pie topped with mashed potatoes with potatoes as a side dish, but it would also be repetitive to serve a potato soup right before the shepherd's pie. A more interesting first course might be a light vegetable soup or salad that doesn't repeat a major ingredient in the main course and balances the heaviness of the main dish.

If you use herbs or spices, they should not be too repetitive, either. Each dish should have its own distinct taste.

EYE APPEAL

Picture the finished recipes in your mind. If you consider the colour, shapes and texture of each dish, you won't need to garnish your food and you won't need fancy serving platters. For example, imagine a chicken breast with mashed potatoes and cauliflower served on a plain white plate; then imagine the same chicken breast on a bed of corn ragout, accompanied by broccoli with pine nuts and raisins. A colourful combination of food also usually means you are getting a variety of vitamins and minerals.

Try to vary the textures on the plate as well. When the food processor first became popular, people used to joke that entire meals were being pureed! In general, if one dish is pureed, nothing else should be. You can also increase the interest of the meal by varying the shapes as well as textures of foods; you wouldn't, for example, want to serve potato cakes and salmon patties together.

COOKING METHODS

As a cooking teacher, one of the questions I am asked the most is "How can I get all the dishes ready at the same time?" This is one example of why menu planning, not just good cooking, is so important. If you serve three stir-fried dishes that all have to be made at the last minute, it will be difficult to have everything ready at the same time. But if you serve something baked, something made ahead and something stir-fried, you'll have a much better chance of achieving your goal.

Varying your cooking methods also adds interest to your menus. Baking, broiling and pot-roasting are oven methods; braising, stewing, sautéeing, steaming, grilling and boiling are stove-top methods. By varying cooking methods, chances are you won't run out of pots or be short a burner or oven when you are cooking up a storm. You can also plan make-ahead dishes, so you are not doing too many things at the last minute. Also, it's important to write out a work plan, however brief, to help you know when to cook what and what order to cook it in. This way you won't be waiting around before starting something else.

GARNISHING

If you do want to garnish your food, your garnishes should be edible, and they should relate to the dish. Sprinkling a leek and potato soup with chopped chives or green onions, for example, will give the diner some idea of what is in the dish, as well as bringing out the flavour of the soup.

HOW TO FOLLOW A RECIPE

If you are just starting to cook, here are a few basic points about how to use recipes:

- Read the recipe completely and note any cross references before starting to cook.

- Look up any cooking terms or ingredients that are unfamiliar.

- Make a shopping list of ingredients you do not have or decide if you are going to substitute an ingredient for something you have on hand.

- If you are cooking more than one recipe, organize a work plan so that you will not have to wait until one recipe is finished before starting another.

- Be sure to keep your work area clean as you cook.

- Assemble all the ingredients and equipment you will need – this is called a "mise en place" in a professional kitchen. It means that everything is in place ready to go.

- Smile, relax and start cooking!

FOOD TEMPERATURE AND HOW TO SERVE FOOD HOT

Varying the temperatures of the food can make a meal more interesting, too. Try serving a cold appetizer before a hot soup. Warm salads, cold soups, hot desserts, etc., can all make a menu more appealing.

Many students ask me how to serve food as hot as restaurants do. I say you should never try to be a restaurant, where there may be eight people working on your dinner, when at home there is usually one person working on eight dinners. Besides, not everyone likes their food served extremely hot — food actually has the most flavour at more gentle temperatures. (Really, it's only partners who complain that food isn't hot enough; guests are always just happy that they're not cooking their own dinner!)

I feel the whole appeal of eating at someone's home is that it isn't a restaurant, and I prefer to serve family style from large platters so that I can just sit back and enjoy the company of family and friends. However, if you want your food piping hot at the table, here are some tips that may help:

- heat individual plates

- heat your serving bowl (a pasta dish can be placed over the pot of boiling pasta to heat)

- when making a pasta dish, use an extra-large pan to prepare the sauce; when the pasta is ready, toss it with the sauce right in the pan over low heat

- rush food to the table as soon as it is on the plates, with help from your partner or an accommodating guest

- tell everyone to start eating as soon as their food arrives.

SEASONAL FOODS AND ECONOMY IN THE KITCHEN

Eating foods in season can help you stay in tune with your environment, as well as keeping costs down. Deep in our Canadian winter, eating seasonally is not always practical, but it's still a good idea to be flexible enough in your menu planning to take advantage of market specials. On the other hand, be careful about stockpiling ingredients just because they are available at a good price. Spices and herbs, for example, lose their potency quickly and should be bought in small quantities. Oil can also deteriorate once opened, and should not be kept indefinitely — there are times when you should let your supermarket be your pantry.

COOKING WITH LEFTOVERS

Using leftovers can save you time and money as well as adding variety to your meals. Good cooks never waste food; instead they transform leftovers into new dishes. Remember that a roast turkey is only a roast turkey once. You'll have much better success using the leftovers in a casserole or salad than trying to pass it off as roast turkey a second time.

Here are a few ideas for using leftovers:

- leftover bread can become the base for bruschetta (page 42), croutons (page 60), bread salad (page 81) or ribollita (page 134)
- leftover soup can sometimes become a pasta sauce or salad dressing with a little vinegar added
- leftover pasta can be used in a salad or frittata
- leftover mashed potatoes can be used on a pot pie or casserole
- leftover frittata can be cut into small squares and served as an appetizer or as croutons in salads
- leftover salad can be pureed into a soup or chopped up and used as a sandwich spread
- leftover rice and grains can be used in salads, soups, frittatas, breads and pancake batters
- leftover vegetables can be pureed and turned into soups or sauces; they can be used in casseroles, sandwiches or salads
- leftover meat, fish or poultry can be used in salads, sandwiches, casseroles, fajitas, quesadillas, soups, pasta sauces or stir-fries
- leftover hamburgers, meatloaf or stew can be used in a pot pie or ground into a shepherd's pie
- leftover cake and cookies can be added to trifles; they can be crumbled and used as a topping for a fruit crisp
- leftover cooked fruit desserts can be pureed and made into sorbets or dessert sauces
- leftover fresh fruit desserts can be baked in crisps and cobblers

ENTERTAINING

When you are deciding how many courses to serve or how complicated the recipes should be, consider how much time you have, your own cooking expertise and how much you can do ahead. You may want to impress someone, but if you are running around like a chicken with its head cut off when your company arrives and are too nervous to enjoy yourself, no one will be impressed!

For a special occasion, you may want to serve many courses. If you have time to cook it all, it can be fun to serve small portions of lots of different foods. But keep things simple if you don't have a lot of time.

Good menu planning involves many common-sense principles. If you consider flavours, colour, temperature and cooking methods as well as reducing the amount of fat and sodium in your meals, you'll find yourself serving dishes that are beautiful to look at, efficient to prepare and delicious and nutritious to eat.

Here are some examples to start you on your way to easy and healthful menu planning:

ENTERTAINING TIPS

- Set the table ahead of time. A set table is a welcoming sight (and if your guests arrive ahead of time or before you've finished cooking, at least they will know they've come to the right place!).
- Check to see whether your guests are allergic to anything when you invite them, not after they arrive at your house.
- Serve food that's fit for the occasion. Although you may like a certain dish and want to showcase it, it may not be appropriate for your company. Remember that your goal in entertaining is making people comfortable when they're in your home. Consider the tastes of small children, parents, people with allergies and picky eaters!

MENUS

SPRING BRUNCH

I love to entertain at breakfast or brunch. People are more awake and vibrant, it is a very casual and relatively inexpensive way to entertain, wine is optional, and you don't have to spend the whole day cooking or worrying about entertaining.

This menu is perfect for a spring brunch. Set the table and plan your cooking schedule the night before.

Caponata (page 40) served with pita chips (page 37)

Chèvre and Fresh Herb Soufflé with Roasted Red Pepper Sauce (page 236)

Steamed Asparagus

Multigrain Yogurt Bread (page 250)

Strawberry Meringue Shortcakes (page 280)

Calories 565; total fat 12 g; % calories from fat 18; dietary fibre 9 g

PICNIC LUNCH

Be sure to make things that do not spoil quickly, salads that do not wilt easily and food that can be eaten without a lot of cutlery (forks only).

Grilled Bread and Cherry Tomato Salad (page 81) [half serving]

Moroccan Chicken (page 162), pre-sliced

Tabbouleh Salad (page 72) [half serving]

Cranberry Streusel Muffins (page 240)

Fresh Fruit

Calories 636; total fat 14 g; % calories from fat 19; dietary fibre 8 g

COTTAGE DINNER

The weekend you open and close the cottage is always the fussiest weekend to cook. I like to use things that are already in the cupboards.

Spaghettini with Clam Sauce (page 109)

Oatmeal and Raisin Spice Cookie Squares (page 284) [2 cookies per serving]

Fresh Fruit

Calories 614; total fat 12 g; % calories from fat 17; dietary fibre 8 g

BARBECUE DINNER

Barbecues are the most popular way to entertain in summer. If you are not sure that everyone likes beef, add Barbecued Chicken Fingers to the menu (page 170). Some points to remember when you are barbecuing:
- *marinate foods in the refrigerator*
- *preheat the barbecue*
- *always take a clean plate to the barbecue so you can put the cooked food on a surface that has not been contaminated with raw meat, fish or poultry juices; you should also use one set of utensils for the raw food and a separate set of utensils for the cooked food*
- *never serve the marinade as a sauce without bringing it to a boil and cooking it for several minutes, to cook any raw meat juices*
- *use long-handled brushes, tongs, spatulas, etc.*
- *allow meat to rest for a few minutes before carving*

Ricotta Bruschetta (page 42)

Potato Salad (page 80) [half serving]

Asian Coleslaw (page 77) [half serving]

Sirloin Steak with Mustard Pepper Crust (page 195)

Herb Barbecued Corn on the Cob (page 210)

Rhubarb and Strawberry Cobbler (page 271)

Calories 767; total fat 20 g; % calories from fat 23; dietary fibre 11 g

COSY WINTER MENU

There are so many delicious soups, stews and casseroles that are perfect for a winter menu. Hearty fare feeds the body and warms the soul. Other good dishes would be Southern Barbecued Pork Roast (page 201), Chicken with Forty Cloves of Garlic (page 177), Chicken Pot Pie (page 164) and Beef Sukiyaki (page 193).

Lentil Vegetable Soup (page 64)

Meatloaf with Irish Mashed Potatoes (page 186)

Spicy Corn Ragout (page 211)

Creamy Rice Pudding (page 265)

Calories 910; total fat 20 g; % calories from fat 20; dietary fibre 15 g

DINNER FOR TWO

When you are cooking for two, find recipes that can be halved easily or use ones that keep well as leftovers. (The leftover hummos in this menu can be used in sandwiches or as a spread; half the tomato sauce for the pasta can be frozen or kept in the refrigerator for a few days.) Bake as many apples as you need; extra cookies freeze well.

Hummos with Sesame (page 37) and pita chips
(page 37) [¼ cup/50 mL dip
and ½ cup/125 mL pita chips per serving]

Linguine with Tomatoes and Scallops (page 108)

Baked Apples Amaretti (page 261)

Mocha Meringue Kisses (page 281)
[2 cookies per serving]

....

Calories 764; total fat 12 g; % calories from fat 14; dietary fibre 11 g

KIDS' SLEEPOVER BREAKFAST

When your children have their friends sleep over, they always seem to want to impress them with a special breakfast. They love to make the shakes themselves, and you can prepare the French toast the night before. Other good breakfast dishes for children are Lemon Ricotta Pancakes (page 232), Buttermilk Oatmeal Pancakes (page 233) and Caramelized Pear Puff Pancake (page 235).

Breakfast Shake (page 227)

Baked French Toast (page 231)

Oatmeal and Raisin Spice Cookie Squares
(page 284)

....

Calories 524; total fat 12 g; % calories from fat 21; dietary fibre 5 g

TEEN MENU

Every August we give cooking courses to students who are going away to university. Parents (my regular students) send their children as they are terrified that their kids will eat nothing once they leave home! Teenagers love chicken dishes, pasta dishes and stir-fries, so if your kids are having friends over to dinner, those items are usually safe bets.

Pesto Pizza (page 45)

Stir-fried Chicken and Vegetables (page 174)

Steamed Rice (page 50)

Quick Apple Cake (page 273)

....

Calories 616; total fat 17 g; % calories from fat 24; dietary fibre 6 g

TEENAGERS' VEGETARIAN DINNER

Many young people are becoming vegetarians for ecological, moral and diet reasons, but it is a great idea for the whole family to have a vegetarian meal once in a while. Try this menu, and you'll never miss meat. Other meatless dishes that everyone will love are Pasta with Tomato Sauce and Ricotta (page 106), Springtime Stir-fried Rice and Vegetables (page 128), Falafel Vegetable Burgers (page 130) and Quickbread Pizza (page 129).

Green Minestrone with Cheese Croutons
(page 56)

Noodles with Vegetables and Peanut Sauce
(page 107)

Oatmeal Honey Rolls (page 244)

Plum Crisp (page 270)

....

Calories 851; total fat 24 g; % calories from fat 25; dietary fibre 15 g

CHILDREN'S DINNER

When my kids have friends over, everyone seems to eat so well. They are all happy and distracted, and the food just seems to disappear. There are lots of great child-friendly recipes in this book, like Barbecued Chicken Fingers (page 170), Korean Flank Steak (page 194), pasta dishes, stir-fries and most of the desserts. Kids love to dip vegetables and pita chips into plain yogurt, but if you use a little less garlic in the tzatziki, that is popular, too.

Tzatziki (page 39) with pita chips (page 37)

Chicken Burgers Teriyaki (page 166)

Roasted Rosemary French Fries (page 216)

Corn on the cob [½ cob]

Chocolate Angel Food Cake
with Chocolate Sauce (page 276)

....

Calories 801; total fat 15 g; % calories from fat 17; dietary fibre 8 g

ATLANTIC DINNER

Some of my most wonderful memories are from the times I spent at summer camp in Nova Scotia. Too bad I didn't love fish then as much as I do now. Any of the salmon dishes would work well in this menu, too, served with a pilaf.

Mussels with Black Bean Sauce (page 156)

Oven-baked Fish and Chips (page 149)

Steamed Fiddleheads

Blueberry Grunt (page 269) [half serving]

....

Calories 741; total fat 16 g; % calories from fat 19; dietary fibre 7 g

WEST COAST DINNER

I love travelling to British Columbia because I admire the laid-back, calm attitude towards life there. Many food trends start on the west coast due to the variety and abundance of fresh fruits and vegetables, the longer growing season, Asian influence, and a willingness to experiment with new ideas.

Chèvre Dip with Potatoes (page 41)

Pasta with Grilled Salmon
and Stir-fried Vegetables (page 110)

Baked Apples Amaretti (page 261)

••••••••••••••••••••••••••••••••••••••

Calories 762; total fat 17 g; % calories from fat 20; dietary fibre 12 g

NEW YEAR'S EVE DINNER

It is getting more and more difficult to go out for dinner on New Year's Eve. Restaurants are expensive, cabs can be tricky to find, it is hard to book a babysitter and it's getting harder to stay up until midnight! All in all, I find it easier to have friends over for dinner. New Year's Eve is usually a time when you don't mind spending a little more money for ingredients and spending a little more time preparing food.

Polenta Bites (page 47)

Louisiana Barbecued Shrimp
with Steamed Rice (page 50)

Steamed Salmon with Korean Dressing
(page 140)

Glazed Cumin Carrots (page 205)

Dessert Fruit Curry (page 264)
with Vanilla Frozen Yogurt

••••••••••••••••••••••••••••••••••••••

Calories 983; total fat 22 g; % calories from fat 20; dietary fibre 12 g

EASTER DINNER

Although Easter dinners are usually big celebration-style meals, they seem to have a light and spring-like tone to them. It's a great time to serve a variety of foods, but keep portions small and flavours fresh.

Grilled Bread with Tomato, Pepper
and Basil Salsa (page 43)

Seafood Soup with Ginger Broth (page 52)

Roast Lamb with Rosemary and Potatoes
(page 199)

Asparagus with Ginger (page 206)

Braised White Beans (page 218) [half serving]

Upside-down Lemon Meringues (page 268)

••••••••••••••••••••••••••••••••••••••

Calories 844; total fat 16 g; % calories from fat 17; dietary fibre 16 g

THANKSGIVING

Many of the vegetable recipes in this book combine several vegetables and grains, so if you decide to make only one side dish, you are still getting a nice variety of textures, flavours and nutrients. At Thanksgiving, though, I set aside more time to cook and like to make lots of side dishes; when you do this, of course, serve much smaller portions of each.

Apple and Squash Soup (page 54)

Roast Chicken with Bulgur Stuffing (page 179)

Maple Mashed Sweet Potatoes (page 214)
[half serving]

Corn with Garlic and Chives (page 209)
[half serving]

Red River Cereal Bread (page 254)

Apple Strudel Pie (page 272)

••••••••••••••••••••••••••••••••••••••

Calories 960; total fat 21 g; % calories from fat 20; dietary fibre 19 g

PASSOVER SEDER

A Seder is when Jewish families come together at Passover to celebrate freedom. The Passover story is told during a ritual meal. The meal always includes a hard-cooked egg served with salt water to remind people how their ancestors shed tears in their suffering (you can serve a hard-cooked egg white instead), and matzo (unleavened bread) is always eaten because when the Jewish people fled Egypt, they didn't have time to wait for their bread to rise.

Here's a great Passover menu that combines traditional and new-style dishes. Remember when you are having a multicourse meal to keep portions small. This menu is based on sixteen people.

Gefilte Fish with Beet Horseradish Salad
(page 152)

"Cream" of Fennel, Leek and Carrot Soup
with Spicy Salsa (page 60)
[made without croutons]

Roast Turkey Breast with Rosemary and Garlic
(page 182) [recipe doubled]

Aunt Pearl's Tzimmes (page 191)

Steamed Broccoli

Pears Poached in Spiced Red Wine (page 259)
[half serving]

Mocha Meringue Kisses (page 281)
[2 cookies per serving]
[made without cornstarch]

••••••••••••••••••••••••••••••••••••••

Calories 733; total fat 16 g; % calories from fat 20; dietary fibre 9 g

WORLD SERIES PARTY

This menu would be perfect for any sports event. Be sure to make things that can be made ahead and that taste great cold or can be reheated easily (in case the game goes into overtime just as you are ready to serve). Other good dishes for games would be Asian Chicken Chili (page 163), Vegetarian Muffuletta (page 117) and Mixed Bean Chili (page 121). This is plenty for eight to ten guests.

Guacamole (page 38)

Black Bean Chèvre Quesadillas (page 120)
[half serving]

Refried Black Bean Dip (page 35) with corn chips (page 87) [½ cup/125 mL chips]

Chicken Fajitas (page 171)

Mixed Grain Salad (page 73) [half serving]

Fruit Yogurt Dip and Peach Salsa (page 263)
with Fresh Fruit Slices

Nick Malgieri's Biscotti (page 282)
[2 cookies per serving]

Calories 967; total fat 23 g; % calories from fat 21; dietary fibre 14 g

BRIDAL SHOWER BUFFET

For a party like this, I usually like to make a variety of dishes in case guests do not like something or are allergic to something. With this menu, if you make a single recipe of each dish, you will have enough food for at least twelve to sixteen guests. (The more guests you have, the more make-ahead dishes you should serve, since there are more things that may need your attention once the guests arrive.)

Smoked Salmon Tortilla Spirals (page 46)
[2 pieces per serving]

Hummos with Sesame (page 37),
served in mini pitas [2 per serving]

Ginger Eggplant Salad (page 198),
served with pita chips (page 37)
[½ cup/125 mL chips per serving]

Spaghetti Salad with Tuna (page 83)
[half serving]

Chopped Grilled Chicken Salad (page 88)
[half serving]

Anna's Angel Food Cake with
Berry Berry Sauce (page 274)

Matrimonial Squares (page 283)

Calories 880; total fat 17 g; % calories from fat 17; dietary fibre 12 g

QUICK WORKDAY MEALS

There are many quick recipes in this book. Try to plan your menu ahead and organize a rough work plan — even if you do this on your way home from work!

Chicken and Seafood Gumbo (page 59)

Double Cornbread with Mild Green Chiles
(page 246)

Raspberry Sorbet

Calories 406; total fat 7 g; % calories from fat 16; dietary fibre 6 g

Stir-fried Pork (page 202)

Rice with Pasta and Chickpeas (page 223)

Fresh Fruit

Calories 642; total fat 14 g; % calories from fat 19; dietary fibre 10 g

Chicken Breasts with Black Bean Sauce
(page 172)

Steamed Rice (page 50)

Strawberries with Balsamic Vinegar (page 258)

Calories 330; total fat 2 g; % calories from fat 7; dietary fibre 3 g

Grilled Tofu Kebabs (page 136)

Navajo Rice Pilaf (page 222)

Mocha Meringue Kisses (page 281)
[2 cookies per serving]

Calories 461; total fat 7 g; % calories from fat 14; dietary fibre 12 g

Spaghetti Salad with Tuna (page 83)

Plum Crisp (page 270)

Calories 514; total fat 13 g; % calories from fat 22; dietary fibre 6 g

Pasta with Red Peppers and Eggplant (page 98)

Green Salad with Mustard Pepper Dressing
(page 92)
[1½ tbsp/20 mL dressing per serving]

Lemon Sorbet

Calories 609; total fat 11 g; % calories from fat 17; dietary fibre 11 g

Oven-poached Halibut with Herb Vinaigrette
(page 220)

Middle Eastern Couscous (page 220)

Fruit Salad

Calories 417; total fat 8 g; % calories from fat 16; dietary fibre 5 g

White Bean Soup with Salad Salsa *(page 62)*
Rosemary Monkey Bread *(page 255)*

Black Bean, Corn and Rice Salad *(page 74)*
Spaghettini with Salad Greens *(page 82)*
Salad Niçoise *(page 78)*

APPETIZERS

Eggplant Spread with Tahini

Refried Black Bean Dip

White Bean Spread with Greens

Hummos with Sesame

Guacamole

Tzatziki

Caponata

Chèvre Dip with Potatoes

Ricotta Bruschetta

Grilled Bread with Tomato, Pepper and Basil Salsa

Provence-style Herb Onion Toasts

Pesto Pizza

Smoked Salmon Tortilla Spirals

Polenta Bites

Chicken Dumplings with Sweet and Sour Sauce

Louisiana Barbecued Shrimp

EGGPLANT SPREAD WITH TAHINI

I firmly believe that people who do not like eggplant simply have not had it cooked properly for them! This creamy version makes a great spread or dip with pita or vegetables. Serve it as a starter or as a relish with roast beef. Use it in place of mayonnaise in sandwiches or as a dressing on marinated grilled vegetables. For other eggplant dishes, try the caponata (page 40) and ginger eggplant salad (page 198).

You can leave this spread chunky or puree it. If you can, barbecue the eggplant for a wonderful smoky flavour.

Makes about 2 cups / 500 mL

2 lb	eggplant	1 kg
1½ tbsp	tahini paste, stirred before measuring	20 mL
¼ cup	lemon juice	50 mL
2 tbsp	hot water	25 mL
½ tsp	pepper	2 mL
¼ tsp	hot red pepper sauce	1 mL
2	cloves garlic, minced	2
	Salt to taste	
2 tbsp	chopped fresh cilantro or parsley	25 mL

1. Cook eggplant whole on barbecue for about 40 minutes, turning often, until charred and tender. (Alternatively, place eggplant in baking dish and bake in preheated 375°F/190°C oven for 45 to 50 minutes, until very tender. Or place eggplant in glass dish, pierce in a few places and microwave on High for 8 to 10 minutes, until tender.) Allow eggplant to cool.

2. Peel eggplant and cut into chunks. Drain if necessary. Dice or puree in food processor.

3. Combine tahini, lemon juice, hot water, pepper, hot pepper sauce, garlic and salt. Whisk until smooth. Stir or blend into eggplant. Taste and adjust seasonings if necessary. Sprinkle with cilantro.

TAHINI PASTE AND SESAME SEEDS

Tahini paste is a sesame seed puree that has tremendous flavour but a high fat content. You can buy it prepared or dry (reconstitute it according to the package directions) in health food stores and Middle Eastern markets. Use it in small quantities. Store in the refrigerator.

When I use sesame seeds, I toast them first, unless they are going to be browned in some way in the recipe. Place them in a heavy skillet and cook, shaking the pan, until they are almost golden and start to pop. Or spread in a single layer on a baking sheet and place in a preheated 350°F/180°C oven for a few minutes, watching closely. You can also toast the seeds in a microwave; place on a glass pie plate and cook on High for 30 to 60 seconds. Keep toasted and untoasted sesame seeds in the freezer.

PER TBSP (15 mL)

Calories	11
g carbohydrate	2
g fibre	1
g total fat	trace
g saturated fat	trace
g protein	trace
mg cholesterol	0
mg sodium	1
mg potassium	61

REFRIED BLACK BEAN DIP

This dip is traditionally made with red pinto beans, but I like using black beans. (Either will work, and so will white beans.) For a quick version, use canned beans. If you have chipotle chiles (page 149) on hand, mince one and add it to the recipe for a great hot, smoky flavour.

This dip can be made ahead and reheated just before serving. Serve it with corn chips (page 87) or pita chips (page 37).

TORTILLA STACKS

Lay out two flour tortillas and spread each one with ¼ cup/50 mL refried black bean dip and ⅓ cup/75 mL grated light Monterey Jack or Cheddar cheese. Stack the tortillas and cover with a third tortilla. Place on a baking sheet and bake in a preheated 400°F/200°C oven for 10 minutes, or until the cheese melts. Cut into wedges and serve with corn salsa (page 43).

Makes 6 pieces.

Makes about 3 cups/750 mL

2 tsp	olive oil	10 mL
1	small onion, finely chopped	1
3	cloves garlic, finely chopped	3
1 tbsp	chili powder	15 mL
1 tsp	cumin	5 mL
½ tsp	cayenne, optional	2 mL
3 cups	cooked black beans (page 68)	750 mL
1 cup	water or cooking liquid from beans	250 mL
¼ tsp	pepper	1 mL
	Salt to taste	
1	tomato, seeded and diced	1
2 tbsp	chopped fresh cilantro or parsley	25 mL

1. Heat oil in large non-stick skillet. Add onion and garlic. Cook gently for a few minutes until fragrant and tender. Add chili powder, cumin and cayenne. Cook for about 30 seconds.

2. Add beans to skillet and combine well. Heat thoroughly. With potato masher or large fork, partially mash beans (the beans can also be mashed in a food processor). Stir in enough water to make mixture "dippable." Add pepper and salt. Taste and adjust seasonings if necessary. Keep warm until ready to serve (if dip thickens, add water).

3. Transfer bean mixture to shallow bowl and sprinkle with tomato and cilantro.

PER TBSP (15 mL)

Calories	18
g carbohydrate	3
g fibre	1
g total fat	trace
g saturated fat	0
g protein	1
mg cholesterol	0
mg sodium	2
mg potassium	51

WHITE BEAN SPREAD WITH GREENS

Some restaurants are now putting bean spread or hummos on their tables instead of butter; this recipe shows how delicious a white bean spread can be. You can make it with or without the greens.

Serve this spread with grilled bread (page 43), pita chips (page 37) or polenta bites (page 47).

Makes about 1½ cups/375 mL

1	19-oz/540 mL tin white kidney beans, rinsed and drained, or 2 cups/500 mL cooked beans	1
2 tbsp	lemon juice	25 mL
½ tsp	pepper	2 mL
dash	hot red pepper sauce	dash
1	clove garlic, minced	1
	Salt to taste	
1½ tbsp	olive oil	20 mL
2	cloves garlic, finely chopped	2
2 cups	diced rapini or broccoli	500 mL
½ cup	water	125 mL

1. In food processor or blender, puree beans with lemon juice, pepper, hot pepper sauce, minced garlic and salt.

2. Heat olive oil in large non-stick skillet. Cook chopped garlic until fragrant, about 1 minute. Add rapini and water and cook, stirring, for about 5 minutes, until water evaporates and rapini is tender. Cool.

3. Stir rapini into bean spread or use it as garnish on top of spread. Taste and adjust seasonings if necessary.

QUICK DIPS

- salsa (see index)
- yogurt cheese (page 228) mixed with salsa
- yogurt cheese mixed with pesto (page 45)
- roasted garlic dressing (page 93)
- roasted red pepper dressing (page 96)
- leftover pureed soups
- peanut sauce (page 86)
- Niçoise dressing (page 78)
- Middle Eastern dressing (page 130)
- plum dipping sauce (page 167)
- honey garlic sauce (page 167)
- warm tomato sauce (e.g., page 186 or 196)

PER TBSP (15 mL)

Calories	15
g carbohydrate	2
g fibre	1
g total fat	1
g saturated fat	trace
g protein	1
mg cholesterol	0
mg sodium	27
mg potassium	32

HUMMOS WITH SESAME

I love this dip because it can be made in a minute with ingredients that are always in the cupboard. Serve it as a dip with pita bread or crackers or use it instead of mayonnaise in sandwiches.

Makes about 1½ cups / 375 mL

1	19-oz/540 mL tin chickpeas, rinsed and drained, or 2 cups/500 mL cooked chickpeas	1
2	cloves garlic, minced	2
3 tbsp	lemon juice	45 mL
1 tbsp	olive oil, optional	15 mL
½ tsp	hot red pepper sauce	2 mL
1 tbsp	sesame oil	15 mL
½ tsp	ground cumin	2 mL
	Lemon slices	
2 tbsp	chopped fresh cilantro or parsley	25 mL

1. In food processor or blender, puree chickpeas coarsely (if you are using blender, add ¼ cup/50 mL water and puree in two batches).

2. Add garlic, lemon juice, olive oil, hot pepper sauce, sesame oil and cumin. Puree until mixture is as smooth as you wish. Taste and adjust seasonings if necessary.

3. Transfer to serving bowl and garnish with lemon slices and cilantro.

PITA CHIPS

Make your own low-fat chips for dips and spreads.

To make pita chips, separate four 8-inch/20 cm pita breads and cut into wedges. Spread in a single layer on a baking sheet and bake in a preheated 400°F/200°C oven for 8 to 10 minutes, or until crisp. (To season chips, brush with lightly beaten egg white and sprinkle with chopped fresh or dried herbs, sesame seeds or poppy seeds before cutting into wedges.)

Makes about 6 cups/1.5 L.

BAGEL CHIPS

Slice leftover bagels as thinly as possible. Place in a single layer on a baking sheet and bake for 45 to 50 minutes in a preheated 300°F/150°C oven or until dry and crisp.

PER TBSP (15 mL)

Calories	27
g carbohydrate	4
g fibre	1
g total fat	1
g saturated fat	trace
g protein	1
mg cholesterol	0
mg sodium	35
mg potassium	25

GUACAMOLE

Although avocados are high in fat, you can use them in a lower-fat way by combining the avocado with cooked and pureed peas, or asparagus or light ricotta cheese, as in this recipe.

Use this mixture as a sandwich spread, as a dip or as a sauce with fajitas (page 171), chili (page 121) or grilled fish, chicken and meat.

Makes about 2 cups / 500 mL

1	tomato, seeded and diced	1
2	cloves garlic, minced	2
¼ cup	finely chopped green onions	50 mL
1	jalapeño, seeded and diced	1
2 tbsp	lime juice	25 mL
⅓ cup	chopped fresh cilantro or parsley	75 mL
	Salt to taste	
1 cup	light ricotta cheese or soft yogurt cheese (page 228)	250 mL
1	small ripe avocado	1

1. Combine tomato, garlic, green onions, jalapeño, lime juice, cilantro and salt.

2. Mash in ricotta cheese.

3. Cut avocado in half. Remove pit, scoop out flesh and mash into cheese mixture (I prefer a chunky texture rather than pureed). Taste and adjust seasonings if necessary.

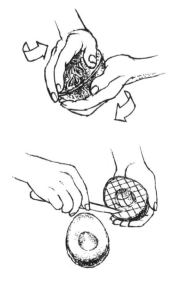

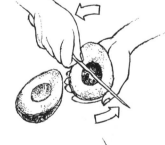

CUTTING AN AVOCADO

Cut the avocado in half lengthwise. Gently rotate the two sections back and forth until you can separate them. To remove the pit, stick a knife blade into the pit and gently wiggle the pit until it loosens.

Hold the avocado half in the palm of your hand and dice it without cutting through the skin. Then scoop out the diced flesh.

PER TBSP (15 mL)

Calories	15
g carbohydrate	1
g fibre	trace
g total fat	1
g saturated fat	trace
g protein	1
mg cholesterol	2
mg sodium	11
mg potassium	44

AVOCADOS

I try to buy the ugly Haas avocados that are small and dark green with a wrinkled skin. They are more dense and "buttery" than the other varieties.

It is hard to find ripe avocados the day you need them, so buy them a few days ahead of time. Keep perfectly ripe avocados in the refrigerator. Unripe ones can be left on the counter out of direct sunlight; they should ripen in two to three days. If you are in a hurry, place them in a perforated paper bag.

To prevent a cut avocado from darkening, sprinkle the cut side with lemon or lime juice and cover tightly with plastic wrap. If the surface of your guacamole discolours, scrape off the very top layer rather than mixing it in.

TZATZIKI

This is a popular concoction that can be used as a dip, a spread or a sauce for grilled chicken, lamb or fish. Use less garlic if you are faint of heart. Salting the cucumber draws out excess liquid and prevents the dip from being watery.

If you like extra-thick tzatziki, use firm yogurt cheese (page 228).

Makes 2 cups / 500 mL

1	**English cucumber**	1
1 tsp	salt	5 mL
1½ cups	**soft or firm yogurt cheese (page 228) or thick yogurt**	375 mL
4	**cloves garlic, minced**	4
2 tbsp	**chopped fresh dill**	25 mL
¼ tsp	**hot red pepper sauce, optional**	1 mL

1. Grate cucumber and combine with salt. Place in sieve set over bowl and allow to rest for 15 minutes. Press out excess liquid.

2. Combine yogurt cheese, garlic, dill and hot pepper sauce.

3. Stir in cucumber. Taste and adjust seasonings if necessary.

PER TBSP (15 mL)

Calories	13
g carbohydrate	2
g fibre	trace
g total fat	trace
g saturated fat	trace
g protein	1
mg cholesterol	1
mg sodium	82
mg potassium	54

CAPONATA

This mixture will keep for about two weeks in the refrigerator, or it can be frozen. If it is a bit watery when you defrost it, simply bring it to a boil and cook until it thickens.

Makes about 8 cups / 2 L

2 lb	eggplant	1 kg
1 tbsp	olive oil	15 mL
2	onions, chopped	2
3	cloves garlic, finely chopped	3
pinch	hot red pepper flakes, optional	pinch
2	stalks celery, chopped	2
1	sweet red pepper, diced	1
1	sweet yellow pepper, diced	1
1	28-oz/796 mL tin plum tomatoes, with juices	1
2 tbsp	granulated sugar	25 mL
¼ cup	red wine vinegar or balsamic vinegar	50 mL
½ tsp	pepper	2 mL
¼ cup	chopped fresh parsley	50 mL
¼ cup	chopped fresh chives or green onions	50 mL
¼ cup	chopped fresh basil	50 mL
2 tbsp	pine nuts, toasted (page 245), optional	25 mL

1. Cut eggplant into 1–inch/2.5 cm slices. Broil or barbecue until lightly browned. Turn and grill other side. Cut into cubes.

2. Heat oil in large, deep non-stick skillet or Dutch oven. Add onions, garlic and hot pepper flakes and cook gently until wilted.

3. Add eggplant, celery, peppers and tomatoes. Cook, uncovered, for about 15 minutes.

4. Stir sugar and vinegar into vegetable mixture. Add pepper and cook, uncovered, until mixture is thick – about 20 minutes.

5. Taste and adjust seasonings if necessary. Stir in parsley, chives, basil and pine nuts.

CAPONATA
This mixed vegetable melange can be used in many ways. It can be served as a spread with bread or crackers or as a dip with bread sticks or vegetables. It can be used on top of greens or grilled bread (page 43). It can also be served as a vegetable side dish or relish on roast meats, and it can be tossed with pasta. You can use it hot or cold, although cold is more traditional.

PER TBSP (15 mL)

Calories	6
g carbohydrate	1
g fibre	trace
g total fat	trace
g saturated fat	0
g protein	trace
mg cholesterol	0
mg sodium	11
mg potassium	39

Chèvre Dip with Potatoes

When creamy, unripened goat cheese is used in a dip or spread, the flavour becomes milder, often appealing to people who may not like goat cheese.

Belgian endive, carrot sticks, cucumber rounds, green and yellow beans, broccoli and cauliflower florets can be used with or instead of the potatoes. To use the chèvre mixture to stuff mushrooms or as a spread, use about 2 tbsp/25 mL soft yogurt cheese instead of 1 cup/250 mL. For a great potato salad, combine everything together.

Makes about 2 cups/500 mL dip

2 lb	baby new potatoes (about 32)	1 kg
4 oz	chèvre (goat cheese)	125 g
4 oz	low-fat pressed cottage cheese	125 g
1 cup	soft yogurt cheese (page 228) or thick yogurt	250 mL
1	clove garlic, minced	1
2 tbsp	chopped fresh parsley	25 mL
2 tbsp	chopped fresh basil or dill	25 mL
2 tbsp	chopped fresh chives or green onions	25 mL
1 tsp	chopped fresh thyme or rosemary, or pinch dried	5 mL
½ tsp	hot red pepper sauce	2 mL
¼ tsp	pepper	1 mL
	Salt to taste	

1. Boil potatoes in large pot of water until tender. Drain and halve.

2. Meanwhile, cream or puree chèvre with cottage cheese. Blend in yogurt cheese. Mixture should be smooth.

3. Blend in garlic, parsley, basil, chives, thyme, hot pepper sauce, pepper and salt. Taste and adjust seasonings if necessary. Place dip in bowl and arrange potatoes around it.

Blue Cheese Dip: Use mild Gorgonzola or Roquefort instead of chèvre; use 1 tbsp/15 mL chopped fresh tarragon (or 1 tsp/5 mL dried) instead of basil. Omit thyme.

Tuna Dip: Omit chèvre and cottage cheese. Puree yogurt cheese with 1 7-oz/284 mL tin white tuna (water-packed), drained and flaked.

PER TBSP (15 mL) + potato

Calories	41
g carbohydrate	6
g fibre	trace
g total fat	1
g saturated fat	1
g protein	2
mg cholesterol	4
mg sodium	50
mg potassium	120

RICOTTA BRUSCHETTA

A great deal of fuss is being made these days about bruschetta and crostini — Italian toasts that are used as a base for toppings. They seem to be everywhere, and they are absolutely delicious.

You can also use the spread on crackers, as a sandwich filling or stuffed into vegetables or small pita breads. For a smoky flavour, barbecue the toasts instead of broiling them.

I always try to buy the driest ricotta cheese available, but if your brand is very wet, drain the cheese first as described below.

Makes about 24 appetizers

1 lb	light ricotta cheese	500 g
1	thin French stick (about 16 inches/40 cm)	1
½ tsp	pepper	2 mL
2 tbsp	chopped fresh parsley	25 mL
2 tbsp	chopped fresh chives or green onions	25 mL
2 tbsp	chopped fresh basil or dill	25 mL
1 tbsp	chopped fresh mint, or ¼ tsp/1 mL dried	15 mL
2 tbsp	olive oil, optional	25 mL
¼ tsp	hot red pepper flakes	1 mL
2	cloves garlic, minced	2
	Salt to taste	

1. If ricotta is watery, cut in quarters, place in strainer and allow to drain for a few hours or overnight in refrigerator.

2. Slice bread on diagonal into ½-inch/1 cm slices. Arrange in single layer on baking sheets. Preheat broiler and broil until slightly crusty on each side but still a little soft in centre.

3. Place ricotta in bowl and beat in pepper, parsley, chives, basil and mint. Add olive oil, hot pepper flakes, garlic and salt. Taste and adjust seasonings if necessary.

4. Spread each piece of bread with about 4 tsp/20 mL ricotta mixture.

SALSAS

Salsas are usually made with fresh vegetables and/or fruits, fresh herbs and seasonings. They are served raw or very lightly cooked, so the flavours are bright and cheerful. Although you can buy commercial salsas, nothing beats the fresh ones you make yourself.

Serve salsa on top of grilled bread or as a dip, alone or combined with yogurt or yogurt cheese (page 228). Use it as a sauce with plain grilled fish or meat, as a topping for baked potatoes or as a condiment in sandwiches.

PER PIECE

Calories	59
g carbohydrate	8
g fibre	trace
g total fat	1
g saturated fat	1
g protein	3
mg cholesterol	6
mg sodium	96
mg potassium	40

SPICY CORN SALSA

Use this as a dip, garnish for soups, topping for bruschetta (page 42) or pizza (page 45), or as a sauce with plain grilled lamb, fish or chicken. If you don't want the sauce to be spicy, leave out the hot pepper, or remove the ribs and seeds. You can also add 1 cup/250 mL cooked black turtle beans.

In food processor, place 2 cups/500 mL cooked corn niblets, 1 roasted, seeded and peeled sweet red pepper (page 154), 1½ tsp/7 mL minced chipotle or jalapeño and 1 minced clove garlic. Process on/off until mixture is slightly pasty and sticks together. Add 1 tbsp/15 mL balsamic vinegar or rice vinegar, ¼ cup/50 mL chopped fresh cilantro or parsley, 2 tbsp/25 mL chopped fresh chives or green onions and ¼ tsp/ 1 mL salt. Process just until mixed in.

Makes about 2 cups/500 mL.

PER SERVING

Calories	59
g carbohydrate	9
g fibre	1
g total fat	2
g saturated fat	trace
g protein	2
mg cholesterol	0
mg sodium	92
mg potassium	47

GRILLED BREAD WITH TOMATO, PEPPER AND BASIL SALSA

Although there are many commercial salsas on the market now, I prefer them made with fresh, unprocessed ingredients. This homemade version is easy to make and a clear example of what a salsa should be.

Makes 16 servings

Salsa:

1	sweet red pepper, roasted (page 154), peeled and diced	1
1	tomato, seeded and diced	1
½ cup	chopped fresh basil	125 mL
2 tbsp	chopped black olives	25 mL
1 tbsp	olive oil	15 mL
1 tbsp	balsamic vinegar	15 mL
1	clove garlic, minced	1
¼ tsp	pepper	1 mL
	Salt to taste	

Grilled Bread:

1 tbsp	olive oil	15 mL
1 tsp	chopped fresh rosemary or ¼ tsp/1 mL dried	5 mL
¼ tsp	pepper	1 mL
pinch	salt	pinch
8	large slices Italian bread, ½ inch/1 cm thick	8

1. To make salsa, combine red pepper and tomato. Stir in basil, olives, oil, vinegar, garlic, pepper and salt. Allow to marinate for at least 10 minutes while preparing grilled bread. Taste and adjust seasonings if necessary.

2. To prepare bread, in small bowl, combine olive oil, rosemary, pepper and salt. Brush one side of bread with this mixture.

3. Preheat barbecue or broiler. Grill oiled side of bread slices until lightly browned. Turn and lightly brown second side.

4. Cut each slice of bread in half. Serve herb side up in a basket with salsa on the side.

PROVENCE-STYLE HERB ONION TOASTS

This is a take-off on the provençal specialty, pissaladière. I've used bread instead of pizza dough to make it quick, and red peppers instead of anchovies to cut back on the salt. But the traditional onion/garlic topping is as delicious as ever. Serve these as an appetizer or light meal.

Makes 8 servings

1 tbsp	olive oil	15 mL
2	cloves garlic, minced	2
3	onions, chopped or thinly sliced	3
¼ tsp	pepper	1 mL
1 tsp	chopped fresh thyme (or ¼ tsp/1 mL dried)	5 mL
	Salt to taste	
1	thin French stick (about 16 inches/40 cm)	1
2	sweet red peppers, preferably roasted (page 154), peeled and cut in strips	2
¼ cup	halved black olives	50 mL

1. Heat olive oil in large non-stick skillet. Add garlic and onions and cook gently for about 10 minutes, until very tender and golden. Add pepper, thyme and salt.

2. Trim ends off bread. Cut bread in half lengthwise. Spread with onion mixture. Arrange red pepper strips in crisscross pattern on top. Arrange olives in crosshatches.

3. Place bread on baking sheet and bake in preheated 400°F/200°C oven for 15 to 20 minutes, or until hot and crisp. To serve, cut into 2-inch/5 cm pieces.

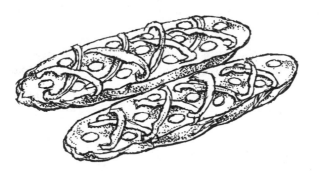

PER SERVING

Calories	152
g carbohydrate	27
g fibre	2
g total fat	3
g saturated fat	1
g protein	4

Excellent: vitamin C

mg cholesterol	0
mg sodium	257
mg potassium	144

PESTO PIZZA

Traditional pesto sauces contain lots of olive oil, pine nuts and cheese — all ingredients that are relatively high in fat. When I make my own pesto, I usually use half the traditional amount of oil, only one or two tablespoons of pine nuts (I toast them to increase their flavour), and I add cheese as I use the pesto, if the dish needs it. But if you want a really low-fat version of pesto sauce, here is a great one. In place of the V-8 juice, you could use balsamic vinegar, lemon juice or a pureed roasted red pepper (page 154). Add 1 tbsp/15 mL olive oil to make the sauce smoother, and 2 tbsp/25 mL Parmesan cheese if you wish.

Pesto is a celebration of fresh herbs. If you do not have fresh basil, use fresh parsley, dill, cilantro, spinach or a combination. But do not use dried basil or other dried herbs.

This pizza makes a great vegetarian main course as well as an appetizer.

Makes 32 wedges

Pesto Sauce:

2	cloves garlic, peeled	2
2 cups	fresh basil leaves	500 mL
1 tbsp	pine nuts, toasted (page 245)	15 mL
¼ cup	V-8 juice or tomato juice	50 mL
½ tsp	pepper	2 mL

Pizza:

4	10-inch/25 cm flour tortillas	4
1 cup	grated part-skim mozzarella cheese	250 mL
4	sweet red peppers, roasted (page 154), peeled and cut in strips	4
	Sprigs fresh basil	

1. To make pesto, chop garlic in food processor until minced. Add basil and pine nuts and chop. Add V-8 juice and pepper and puree until smooth.

2. Prick tortillas with fork. Bake in preheated 425°F/220°C oven, directly on oven racks, for 3 to 5 minutes, until lightly browned and crisp. Place on baking sheets in single layer.

3. Spread each tortilla with 2 tbsp/25 mL pesto sauce. Sprinkle with cheese and top with red pepper strips. Bake for 8 minutes, or until cheese is bubbly. Garnish with sprigs of fresh basil. Cut into wedges.

PER WEDGE

Calories	39
g carbohydrate	5
g fibre	1
g total fat	1
g saturated fat	1
g protein	2

Good: vitamin C

mg cholesterol	2
mg sodium	53
mg potassium	47

SMOKED SALMON TORTILLA SPIRALS

This is the lightened version of one of the most popular recipes in my Appetizers cookbook. Anyone who makes these spirals can feel like a culinary hero, and you will probably be able to concoct many variations of your own using different spreads and cold cuts or cooked vegetables.

Serve the rolls, spiral side up, on a bed of shredded lettuce.

Makes about 32 to 40 pieces

1 cup	low-fat pressed cottage cheese or firm yogurt cheese (page 228)	250 mL
2 tbsp	honey-style mustard	25 mL
4	10-inch/25 cm flour tortillas	4
½ lb	smoked salmon, thinly sliced	250 g
2 tbsp	chopped fresh dill	25 mL
2 tbsp	chopped fresh chives or green onions	25 mL
4	leaves lettuce, shredded	4

1. In small bowl, combine cottage cheese and mustard. (If cheese is a little lumpy, puree in blender or food processor.)

2. Arrange tortillas on counter and spread evenly with cheese spread.

3. Arrange smoked salmon on top of cheese. (Leave about 1 inch/2.5 cm border at top of each tortilla just covered with cheese so rolls will stick together.) Sprinkle with dill, chives and lettuce.

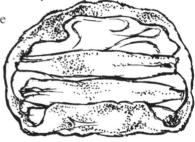

4. Roll tortillas up tightly, pressing firmly to seal. Wrap well and refrigerate for 2 hours, or until ready to serve. Trim off ends of rolls (eat them) and cut each roll slightly on the diagonal into 8 to 10 slices.

PER PIECE	
Calories	40
g carbohydrate	5
g fibre	trace
g total fat	1
g saturated fat	trace
g protein	3
mg cholesterol	2
mg sodium	84
mg potassium	26

POLENTA BITES

Polenta can be made from regular cornmeal or instant cornmeal, and it can be served creamy or firm, as in this recipe. Although this is great on its own, it also makes a great base for spreads such as white bean spread (page 36) or salsa (page 43). You can also use polenta rounds as a base for pizza toppings.

The warm polenta can also be piped into oiled mini muffin pans for little polenta muffins.

Makes about 32 bites

4 cups	water	1 L
¾ tsp	salt	4 mL
½ tsp	pepper	2 mL
1 cup	cornmeal (regular or instant)	250 mL
½ tsp	ground cumin	2 mL
1 tbsp	olive oil	15 mL
½ cup	milk	125 mL
2 tbsp	chopped fresh parsley	25 mL
2 tbsp	grated Parmesan cheese	25 mL

1. In large saucepan, bring water to boil. Add salt and pepper. Add cornmeal in thin stream, whisking constantly. Add cumin.

2. Cook polenta for 15 to 20 minutes on low heat, stirring occasionally with wooden spoon (instant polenta takes 5 minutes).

3. Stir in oil, milk, parsley and cheese. Taste and adjust seasonings if necessary.

4. Pour polenta into 13 x 9-inch/3.5 L oiled pan and refrigerate for a few hours. Unmould and cut into squares, diamonds or rounds.

5. Just before serving, preheat broiler and place bites on baking sheet. Broil for 2 minutes until heated through.

PER BITE

Calories	23
g carbohydrate	4
g fibre	trace
g total fat	1
g saturated fat	trace
g protein	1
mg cholesterol	1
mg sodium	64
mg potassium	15

CHICKEN DUMPLINGS WITH SWEET AND SOUR SAUCE

Oriental style dumplings are usually wrapped in thin wheat or rice flour wrappers but it is much faster to make dumplings without the wrappers (I call them "naked" dumplings). These can be served with toothpicks or cocktail forks as an appetizer, or you can serve them over noodles or rice as a main course. For a great variation, use half chicken and half shrimp.

Sweet and sour sauce has a reputation for being sugary and sticky, but this recipe is based on an authentic version I learned at the Wei-Chuan School of Cooking in Taiwan. You can toss the sauce with pieces of grilled or broiled chicken or cooked shrimp, or you can use the sauce in meat and vegetable stir-fries.

Makes about 32 dumplings

½ lb	fresh spinach, or 1 10-oz/300 g package frozen spinach	250 g
1 lb	boneless, skinless chicken breasts, ground	500 g
1	egg white	1
1 tbsp	cornstarch	15 mL
½ tsp	salt	2 mL
¼ tsp	hot chili paste	1 mL
1	carrot, finely chopped	1
1 tsp	minced fresh ginger root	5 mL

Sweet and Sour Sauce:

⅓ cup	ketchup	75 mL
3 tbsp	rice vinegar or cider vinegar	45 mL
3 tbsp	granulated sugar	45 mL
½ cup	water	125 mL
1 tbsp	soy sauce	15 mL
1 tsp	sesame oil	5 mL
2 tsp	cornstarch	10 mL
2 tsp	vegetable oil	10 mL
1½ tbsp	sesame seeds, toasted (page 34)	20 mL
¼ cup	chopped fresh cilantro or parsley	50 mL

1. Wash spinach. Place in saucepan, cover and cook until spinach just wilts. Rinse with cold water. Squeeze out excess moisture and chop. Reserve. (If you are using frozen spinach, simply defrost, squeeze dry and chop.) Squeeze again if necessary to extract any remaining moisture.

2. In large bowl, combine ground chicken, egg white, 1 tbsp/ 15 mL cornstarch and salt. Stir in chili paste, carrot, ginger and reserved spinach.

3. Line baking sheet with waxed paper. Shape mixture into 1-inch/2.5 cm balls and flatten slightly. Place on baking sheet. Refrigerate or freeze until ready to cook.

4. In small bowl, combine all ingredients for sauce. Reserve.

5. Heat vegetable oil in large non-stick skillet. Add chicken in single layer. Cook until lightly browned on bottom. Loosen dumplings and turn over. Add sauce and cover pan. Cook gently for 3 to 5 minutes, or until chicken feels firm. Stir to combine well. Sauce should thicken.

6. Turn chicken balls out onto serving platter and sprinkle with sesame seeds and cilantro.

PER DUMPLING

Calories	35
g carbohydrate	3
g fibre	trace
g total fat	1
g saturated fat	trace
g protein	4
mg cholesterol	8
mg sodium	113
mg potassium	96

LOUISIANA BARBECUED SHRIMP

This is an extremely flavourful appetizer, so even a small serving feels like a special treat. Serve it with steamed rice (see sidebar), couscous (page 184) or mashed sweet potatoes (page 214).

The barbecue name comes from the sauce, but you could also barbecue or broil the shrimp for a minute on each side before adding it to the sauce. This dish can be prepared ahead, but reheat it quickly so as not to overcook the shrimp.

Makes 8 appetizer servings

1 tsp	paprika	5 mL
½ tsp	pepper	2 mL
¼ tsp	cayenne	1 mL
¼ tsp	dried oregano	1 mL
¼ tsp	dried thyme	1 mL
1 lb	cleaned shrimp	500 g
2 tsp	olive oil	10 mL
1	small onion, finely chopped	1
3	cloves garlic, finely chopped	3
¼ cup	Worcestershire sauce	50 mL
⅓ cup	beer	75 mL
1 tbsp	lemon juice	15 mL
½ cup	water	125 mL
2 tbsp	chopped fresh parsley	25 mL

1. In small bowl, combine paprika, pepper, cayenne, oregano and thyme.

2. Pat shrimp very dry and toss with half of spice mixture. Reserve.

3. Heat olive oil in large non-stick skillet. Add onion and garlic and cook gently for about 5 minutes, or until very fragrant and tender. Do not brown.

4. Add remaining spice mixture and cook for 1 minute. Add Worcestershire, beer, lemon juice and water. Bring to boil and cook, uncovered, until about ⅓ cup/75 mL remains.

5. Add shrimp to sauce and combine well. Cook for 3 to 4 minutes, or until shrimp is just cooked. Taste and adjust seasonings if necessary. Serve sprinkled with parsley.

STEAMED RICE

I use this method to cook all kinds of long-grain rice — basmati, Thai-scented and regular.

Wash 1½ cups/375 mL long-grain white rice well. Place in a medium saucepan and add 2¼ cups/550 mL cold water. Bring to a boil. Reduce heat to medium and continue to cook, uncovered, until water disappears and holes appear on surface of rice, about 5 to 8 minutes. Cover and cook on very low heat for 15 minutes. Turn off heat and allow to rest for up to 30 minutes before serving. (To make steamed brown rice, use ¼ cup/50 mL additional water and allow rice to cook on low heat for 30 minutes instead of 15.)

Makes about 4 cups/1 L.

PER SERVING

Calories	71
g carbohydrate	3
g fibre	trace
g total fat	2
g saturated fat	trace
g protein	10

Good: vitamin B₁₂

mg cholesterol	65
mg sodium	156
mg potassium	115

SOUPS

Seafood Soup with Ginger Broth

Hot and Sour Soup

Apple and Squash Soup

Cabbage Borscht

Green Minestrone with Cheese Croutons

Potato and Garlic Soup with Pesto Swirls

Leek and Potato Soup

Chicken and Seafood Gumbo

"Cream" of Fennel, Leek and Carrot Soup

Chickpea and Spinach Soup

White Bean Soup with Salad Salsa

Lentil Vegetable Soup

Mushroom, Bean and Barley Soup

Moroccan Lentil Soup with Pasta

Black Bean Soup with Yogurt and Spicy Salsa

Split Pea Soup with Dill

Seafood Soup with Ginger Broth

This fresh, light-tasting soup is low in fat. Diced chicken breasts can be used instead of the seafood.

Makes 8 servings

1 tsp	vegetable oil	5 mL
2	cloves garlic, finely chopped	2
1 tbsp	finely chopped fresh ginger root	15 mL
1 tsp	grated lemon peel	5 mL
¼ tsp	hot red pepper flakes	1 mL
4 cups	homemade chicken stock (page 59), or 1 10-oz/284 mL tin chicken broth plus water, or homemade fish stock (page 53)	1 L
2 tbsp	Thai fish sauce (nam pla) or soy sauce	25 mL
1 tbsp	lemon juice	15 mL
3	carrots, sliced	3
¼ lb	scallops, diced	125 g
¼ lb	cleaned shrimp, diced	125 g
1 tsp	sesame oil	5 mL
4	green onions, finely chopped	4
2 tbsp	chopped fresh cilantro or parsley	25 mL

1. Heat oil in large saucepan or Dutch oven. Add garlic, ginger, lemon peel and hot pepper flakes. Cook gently until very fragrant.

2. Add stock, fish sauce and lemon juice and bring to boil.

3. Add carrots. Reduce heat and simmer gently for 15 minutes.

4. Add scallops, shrimp, sesame oil and green onions. Cook for just a few minutes, or until seafood is barely cooked. Serve sprinkled with cilantro.

CARROT FLOWERS
To cut carrots into flowers to use in soups, pastas or stir-fries, peel the carrot and then make V-shaped indentations along its length in three or four places. When you slice the carrot into coins, the slices will look like flowers.

PER SERVING

Calories	73
g carbohydrate	5
g fibre	1
g total fat	2
g saturated fat	trace
g protein	8

Excellent: vitamin A
Good: niacin; vitamin B_{12}

mg cholesterol	21
mg sodium	282
mg potassium	267

HOT AND SOUR SOUP

Hot and sour soup is full of flavour, easy to make and low in fat, so when Lin Eleoff, the host of CFTO's Eye on Toronto, asked if I would make a hot and sour soup on the show, I thought it was a great idea. Here it is.

Makes 6 to 8 servings

10	dried shiitake mushrooms or fresh mushrooms	10
½ lb	extra-firm tofu	250 g
2 tbsp	cornstarch	25 mL
¼ cup	water	50 mL
6 cups	homemade chicken stock (page 59), or 1 10-oz/284 mL tin chicken broth plus water	1.5 L
3	leeks, trimmed and shredded, or 1 onion, very thinly sliced	3
1 cup	thinly sliced bamboo shoots	250 mL
3 tbsp	black Chinese vinegar or Worcestershire sauce	45 mL
2 tbsp	soy sauce	25 mL
2 tbsp	minced fresh ginger root	25 mL
½ tsp	pepper	2 mL
1 tsp	sesame oil	5 mL
½ tsp	hot chili paste	2 mL
2	egg whites, or 1 egg, beaten	2
3	green onions, thinly sliced	3

1. If you are using dried mushrooms, cover with hot water and let soften for 20 minutes. Drain, rinse, discard stems and slice caps.

2. Cut tofu into thin strips. (If you are using regular tofu, wrap in tea towel and place heavy weight on top. Allow to rest for 30 minutes.) Blend together cornstarch and water. Reserve.

3. In large saucepan, combine stock, mushrooms, leeks, bamboo shoots and tofu. Bring to boil. Skim if necessary and cook for about 3 minutes. Add vinegar, soy sauce, ginger, pepper, sesame oil and chili paste to soup. Taste and adjust seasonings.

4. Stir cornstarch mixture and add to soup. Cook until slightly thickened, stirring to prevent lumps.

5. Remove soup from heat and slowly add beaten egg whites, stirring all the while to make sure egg forms strands and cooks thoroughly. Add green onions. Serve hot.

HOMEMADE FISH STOCK

Good fish stock is hard to find, so it is worth making your own. Use only lean, white-fleshed fish. Freeze any leftover stock (page 69).

Place 3 lb/1.5 kg fish bones, tails and heads in a large pot with 2 onions, 2 carrots, 2 stalks celery and 1 leek (all cut in chunks). Add a small handful of fresh parsley, 1 bay leaf, ½ tsp/2 mL dried thyme, 6 peppercorns and 1 cup/ 250 mL dry white wine (optional) or water. Cover with approximately 3 qt/3 L cold water, bring to a boil and skim off any scum. Reduce heat and cook gently for 30 minutes. Strain.

Makes about 3 qt/3 L.

PER SERVING

Calories	155
g carbohydrate	19
g fibre	3
g total fat	3
g saturated fat	1
g protein	15

Excellent: niacin

mg cholesterol	1
mg sodium	428
mg potassium	594

APPLE AND SQUASH SOUP

The rich colour and flavour of this soup make you think of autumn, but it is delicious any time of year. Although any winter squash will work in this recipe, I like the texture and colour of butternut the best. The apple adds a wonderful tart sweetness, but you can also use a pear.

Makes 6 to 8 servings

2 tsp	vegetable oil	10 mL
2	leeks, trimmed and sliced	2
1	apple, peeled, cored and diced	1
2 lb	butternut squash, peeled and diced	1 kg
1	potato, peeled and diced	1
4 cups	homemade chicken stock (page 59), or 1 10-oz/284 mL tin chicken broth plus water	1 L
1 tsp	chopped fresh thyme, or ¼ tsp/1 mL dried	5 mL
1 tsp	chopped fresh rosemary, or ¼ tsp/1 mL dried	5 mL
¼ tsp	pepper	1 mL
	Salt to taste	
½ cup	grated light Cheddar cheese, optional	125 mL

1. Heat oil in large saucepan or Dutch oven. Add leeks and cook gently until tender and fragrant.

2. Add apple, squash and potato. Combine well. Add stock, thyme, rosemary, pepper and salt. Bring to boil. Reduce heat, cover and simmer gently for 30 minutes, or until squash is very tender.

3. Puree soup. If soup is too thick, add more stock or water. Taste and adjust seasonings if necessary. Sprinkle each serving with grated cheese.

PER SERVING

Calories	129
g carbohydrate	23
g fibre	4
g total fat	3
g saturated fat	trace
g protein	5

Good: niacin; vitamin B$_6$

mg cholesterol	1
mg sodium	30
mg potassium	615

CABBAGE BORSCHT

For a quicker version, you can make this with chicken instead of beef. Remove the skin first and add the cabbage as soon as you have skimmed the froth from the stock. Or, for a vegetarian version, leave out the meat or chicken entirely.

For a hearty main course, add boiled potatoes.

Makes 12 servings

1 lb	brisket or short ribs, trimmed of all visible fat and cut in 1-inch/2.5 cm pieces	500 g
4 qt	cold water	4 L
1	small cabbage, cut in 1-inch/2.5 cm chunks	1
2	onions, coarsely chopped	2
2	carrots, sliced	2
1	28-oz/796 mL tin plum tomatoes, with juices, coarsely chopped	1
½ tsp	pepper	2 mL
	Salt to taste	
3 tbsp	granulated sugar	45 mL
3 tbsp	lemon juice or vinegar	45 mL

1. Place beef in Dutch oven with water. Bring to boil. Skim off froth that rises to surface and discard. Reduce heat, cover and cook gently for 1 hour.

2. Add cabbage, onions, carrots, tomatoes, pepper and salt. Cover and cook gently for 1 hour.

3. Add sugar and lemon juice and simmer gently for 30 minutes, uncovered. Taste and adjust seasonings with salt, pepper, sugar or lemon juice if necessary.

PER SERVING

Calories	97
g carbohydrate	12
g fibre	2
g total fat	3
g saturated fat	1
g protein	7

Excellent: vitamin A; vitamin B_{12}
Good: vitamin C

mg cholesterol	15
mg sodium	152
mg potassium	374

GREEN MINESTRONE WITH CHEESE CROUTONS

This is a tomato-free minestrone that is bright in colour and fresh in flavour. The cheese croutons can be made ahead; they are an amazing garnish for many soups and salads. For a tomato-based minestrone, see the ribollita (page 134).

Makes 8 to 10 servings

2 tsp	olive oil	10 mL
1	onion, chopped	1
2	leeks, trimmed and chopped	2
3	cloves garlic, finely chopped	3
1	bunch Swiss chard, rapini or broccoli, chopped	1
2	zucchini, sliced	2
8 cups	homemade chicken stock (page 59), or 1 10-oz/284 mL tin chicken broth plus water	2 L
½ cup	small soup pasta	125 mL
½ lb	green beans, cut in ½-inch/1 cm pieces	250 g
2 cups	fresh or frozen peas	500 mL
¼ cup	chopped fresh parsley	50 mL
2 tbsp	chopped fresh basil	25 mL
¼ tsp	pepper	1 mL
	Salt to taste	
¾ cup	grated Parmesan cheese	175 mL
¼ cup	pesto (page 45), optional	50 mL

1. Heat oil in large saucepan or Dutch oven. Add onion, leeks and garlic. Cook gently for 5 minutes without browning.

2. Add Swiss chard, zucchini and stock. Bring to boil. Add pasta and cook for 5 minutes. Add beans and peas and cook for 3 minutes longer. Add parsley, basil, pepper and salt. Taste and adjust seasonings if necessary.

3. To make cheese croutons, spread Parmesan in thin layer on non-stick baking sheet. Bake in preheated 350°F/180°C oven for 2 to 5 minutes, or until cheese is melted and browned. Cool until crisp. Remove from baking sheet and break into chunks.

4. Stir in pesto and top with croutons.

SOUP STOCKS

Salt-free, fat-free homemade stocks are the best, but if you do not have any homemade stock, there are substitutes:

- Frozen stock is usually salt free, with fat removed. It is expensive, so I always dilute it with water.

- Canned broth usually contains much more salt than is necessary and can also contain MSG, fat and colouring. If you refrigerate the can before opening, the fat will solidify on the surface so you can remove it before using. I always dilute canned broth more than the package recommends; freeze any extra. Buy lower-salt, lower-fat broths if possible.

- Bouillon cubes and powdered soup bases are generally very concentrated and salty. I dilute them even more than canned broth. Look for lower-salt, lower-fat brands.

- Water can be a good substitute for stock when there are many other flavourful ingredients in the recipe.

PER SERVING

Calories	184
g carbohydrate	21
g fibre	5
g total fat	6
g saturated fat	2
g protein	14

Excellent: niacin; folacin
Good: vitamin A, vitamin C; riboflavin; calcium; iron; vitamin B$_{12}$

mg cholesterol	9
mg sodium	325
mg potassium	778

POTATO AND GARLIC SOUP WITH PESTO SWIRLS

When whole garlic cloves are cooked gently for a long time, they become unbelievably sweet. Raw garlic, on the other hand, is very assertive-tasting. If a long-simmering soup or stew calls for forty cloves of garlic, don't worry; but do worry if an uncooked salad dressing calls for a lot of raw garlic.

If you can't find fresh basil for the pesto swirls, use fresh parsley, dill, green onions or cilantro, but don't substitute dried herbs.

Makes 8 servings

2 tsp	olive oil	10 mL
24	cloves garlic, peeled	24
2 lb	potatoes, peeled and cut in 2-inch/5 cm pieces	1 kg
5 cups	homemade chicken stock (page 59), or 1 10-oz/284 mL tin chicken broth plus water	1.25 L
½ tsp	pepper	2 mL
	Salt to taste	

Pesto Swirls:

1 cup	fresh basil leaves	250 mL
1	clove garlic, minced	1
¼ tsp	salt	1 mL
¼ tsp	pepper	1 mL
1 tbsp	olive oil	15 mL
3 tbsp	boiling water	45 mL

1. Heat oil in large saucepan or Dutch oven. Add whole garlic cloves and cook gently for about 5 minutes, until very fragrant. Do not brown.

2. Add potatoes, stock, pepper and salt. Bring to boil. Reduce heat, cover and simmer gently for 30 minutes, or until potatoes and garlic are very tender.

3. Puree soup through food mill (or in blender or food processor with some stock). Heat thoroughly. Taste and adjust seasonings if necessary.

4. To make pesto mixture, in food processor or blender, puree basil with garlic, salt, pepper and oil. Blend in boiling water.

5. Serve soup in shallow bowls and swirl in some pesto.

PER SERVING

Calories	137
g carbohydrate	21
g fibre	1
g total fat	4
g saturated fat	1
g protein	5

Good: niacin; vitamin B$_6$

mg cholesterol	1
mg sodium	98
mg potassium	461

LEEK AND POTATO SOUP

When I first started my cooking school, this soup was "hot," and twenty years later, it is hot again. (Actually, when it is served cold, it becomes the classic Vichyssoise.)

The soup can be served pureed or chunky style, and sometimes it is cooked with half milk, half stock.

Makes 8 servings

1 tbsp	olive oil	15 mL
3	large leeks, trimmed and chopped	3
1	clove garlic, finely chopped	1
3	large potatoes, peeled and diced	3
5 cups	homemade chicken stock (page 59), or 1 10-oz/284 mL tin chicken broth plus water	1.25 L
1 tsp	chopped fresh thyme, or pinch dried	5 mL
½ tsp	pepper	2 mL
	Salt to taste	
¼ cup	chopped fresh chives or green onions	50 mL

1. Heat oil in large saucepan or Dutch oven. Add leeks and garlic. Cook gently for 5 to 7 minutes, or until leeks wilt. Add potatoes and combine well.

2. Add stock and bring to boil. Add thyme, pepper and salt. Reduce heat and simmer gently for 20 minutes, or until potatoes are tender.

3. Puree soup through food mill or in food processor or blender.

4. Return soup to heat and heat thoroughly. Taste and adjust seasonings if necessary. Sprinkle with chives before serving.

Clam Chowder: Drain and reserve liquid from two 5-oz/142 g tins clams. Add water to reserved liquid to make 4 cups/1 L. Use this clam broth instead of chicken stock and make soup up to Step 3. Puree half of soup, leaving some potatoes in chunks. Add drained clams and heat thoroughly. Sprinkle with chives.

PER SERVING

Calories	111
g carbohydrate	17
g fibre	1
g total fat	3
g saturated fat	1
g protein	5

Good: niacin

mg cholesterol	1
mg sodium	28
mg potassium	384

HOMEMADE CHICKEN STOCK

I always remove any visible fat from the chicken before making stock, but I do use the skin, because it has a lot of flavour. (Even though the skin contains fat, when the stock cools, any fat will rise to the surface and can be skimmed off and discarded.) Place 4 lb/2 kg chicken pieces in a large pot. Add enough cold water to cover by about 2 inches/5 cm. Bring to a boil and skim off any scum.

Add 2 onions, 2 carrots, 2 stalks celery and 2 leeks (all cut in chunks). Bring to a boil and skim again if necessary. Add 1 bay leaf, ½ tsp/2 mL dried thyme, 6 peppercorns and a small handful of fresh parsley. Reduce heat and cook gently, uncovered, for 1½ hours. If necessary, add water to keep chicken covered. Strain. To freeze, see (page 69).

Makes about 3 qt/3 L.

PER SERVING

Calories	175
g carbohydrate	26
g fibre	4
g total fat	3
g saturated fat	1
g protein	11

Excellent: vitamin C; niacin; vitamin B$_{12}$
Good: vitamin B$_6$; folacin

mg cholesterol	18
mg sodium	357
mg potassium	606

CHICKEN AND SEAFOOD GUMBO

This is a thick stew-like mixture with Louisiana flavours. Okra is a traditional ingredient, but if you can't find it, omit it.

Makes 8 to 10 servings

1 tbsp	vegetable oil	15 mL
2 tbsp	all-purpose flour	25 mL
¼ tsp	cayenne	1 mL
2	onions, chopped	2
3	stalks celery, sliced	3
1	sweet green pepper, diced	1
1	sweet red pepper, diced	1
3	cloves garlic, chopped	3
3 cups	homemade chicken stock (see sidebar), or 1 10-oz/284 mL tin chicken broth plus water	750 mL
1	28-oz/796 mL tin plum tomatoes, with juices	1
¼ lb	uncooked chicken, diced	125 g
¼ lb	okra, sliced	125 g
½ cup	long-grain rice	125 mL
½ tsp	hot red pepper sauce	2 mL
	Salt and pepper to taste	
1 cup	fresh or frozen corn niblets	250 mL
¼ lb	canned crabmeat, picked over and squeezed dry	125 g
3	green onions, sliced	3

1. Heat oil in large saucepan or Dutch oven.

2. In small bowl, combine flour and cayenne. Whisk into oil and cook carefully over medium-high heat until mixture is dark brown. Be careful not to burn it.

3. Add onions, celery, peppers and garlic. Reduce heat and cook for 5 to 10 minutes, until vegetables are slightly wilted. Add stock and tomatoes and heat, breaking up tomatoes with spoon.

4. Add chicken, okra, rice, hot pepper sauce, pepper and salt. Cover and cook gently for about 20 minutes. Add corn and crabmeat. Cook for 5 minutes. Add green onions and cook for 5 minutes longer. Taste and adjust seasonings if necessary.

"CREAM" OF FENNEL, LEEK AND CARROT SOUP

Although I am a big fan of the food processor and have dedicated two cookbooks to the subject, I have to say that soups pureed in a blender are unbelievably smooth. Pureeing in the food processor results in a slightly coarser consistency that I usually prefer, but when you want a really creamy soup without cream, get your old blender out of the attic and use it! You'll be amazed.

Makes 8 servings

1 tbsp	olive oil	15 mL
2	leeks, trimmed and chopped	2
2	cloves garlic, finely chopped	2
2	bulbs fennel or 3 stalks celery, trimmed and chopped	2
2	carrots, chopped	2
1	potato, peeled and chopped	1
5 cups	homemade chicken stock (page 59), or 1 10-oz/284 mL tin chicken broth plus water	1.25 L
¼ tsp	pepper	1 mL
½ tsp	chopped fresh thyme, or pinch dried	2 mL
	Salt to taste	
1 cup	*homemade croutons (see sidebar)	250 mL
2 tbsp	chopped fresh parsley	25 mL

1. Heat oil in large saucepan or Dutch oven. Add leeks, garlic, fennel and carrots and cook gently for about 5 minutes, or until vegetables are beginning to soften.

2. Add potato, stock, pepper, thyme and salt. Bring to boil. Reduce heat, cover and simmer gently for 20 to 25 minutes, until vegetables are very tender.

3. Puree in blender, food processor or food mill until very smooth (puree in batches if necessary). Taste and adjust seasonings if necessary. Serve sprinkled with croutons and parsley.

★ *If this soup is included in the Passover menu (page 31), omit croutons.*

HOMEMADE CROUTONS

Use leftover French or Italian bread as well as rye, pumpernickel, cornbread (page 246), sourdough or multigrain bread (page 250).

Cut 5 slices of bread into cubes and spread out on a baking sheet. Bake in a preheated 400°F/200°C oven for 15 minutes, or until crisp and light-brown.

For garlic croutons, toast the bread slices, rub each slice with a cut garlic clove and then cut into cubes. For flavored croutons, sprinkle bread cubes with chopped herbs or spices before baking.

Makes about 2 cups/500 mL.

PER SERVING

Calories	119
g carbohydrate	18
g fibre	1
g total fat	3
g saturated fat	1
g protein	6

Excellent: vitamin A
Good: niacin

mg cholesterol	1
mg sodium	114
mg potassium	517

CHICKPEA AND SPINACH SOUP

This high-fibre soup is a favourite in our course on the role of nutrition in the kitchen. For a thicker version, puree half the soup before adding the pasta.

Makes 6 servings

2 tsp	olive oil	10 mL
1	onion, chopped	1
2	cloves garlic, finely chopped	2
½ tsp	ground cumin or curry powder	2 mL
pinch	hot red pepper flakes	pinch
1	19-oz/540 mL tin chickpeas, rinsed and drained, or 2 cups/ 500 mL cooked chickpeas	1
4 cups	homemade chicken stock (page 59), or 1 10-oz/284 mL tin chicken broth plus water	1 L
½ cup	small soup pasta	125 mL
10 oz	fresh spinach, chopped, or 1 10-oz/300 g package frozen spinach, defrosted, squeezed dry and chopped	300 g
¼ tsp	pepper	1 mL
	Salt to taste	
2 tbsp	chopped fresh parsley	25 mL

1. Heat oil in large saucepan or Dutch oven. Add onion, garlic, cumin and hot pepper flakes. Cook gently until tender.

2. Add chickpeas and stock and bring to boil. Reduce heat and simmer gently for 10 minutes.

3. Add pasta and cook for 5 minutes, or until almost tender.

4. Add spinach, pepper and salt and cook for about 3 minutes. Taste and adjust seasonings if necessary. Sprinkle with parsley.

PER SERVING

Calories	230
g carbohydrate	37
g fibre	5
g total fat	4
g saturated fat	1
g protein	12

Excellent: vitamin A; folacin
Good: niacin; iron; vitamin B$_6$

mg cholesterol	1
mg sodium	191
mg potassium	483

WHITE BEAN SOUP WITH SALAD SALSA

See photo opposite page 32.

For a quick version of this soup, use two 19-oz/540 mL tins of rinsed and drained white kidney beans. Cook the canned beans with the potatoes until the potatoes are tender, about 15 to 20 minutes.

Makes 8 to 10 servings

1½ cups	dried white kidney beans or navy beans	375 mL
2 tsp	olive oil	10 mL
3	cloves garlic, finely chopped	3
1	onion, finely chopped	1
¼ tsp	hot red pepper flakes	1 mL
8 cups	homemade vegetable stock (see sidebar) or water	2 L
1	large potato, peeled and diced	1
½ cup	small soup pasta	125 mL
½ tsp	pepper	2 mL
	Salt to taste	

Salad Salsa:

2	large tomatoes, chopped and drained	2
½ cup	chopped fresh arugula or watercress	125 mL
2 tbsp	chopped fresh chives or green onions	25 mL
2 tbsp	chopped fresh basil	25 mL
2 tbsp	chopped fresh parsley	25 mL
1	small clove garlic, minced	1
½ tsp	pepper	2 mL
	Salt to taste	

HOMEMADE VEGETABLE STOCK

Use this all-purpose vegetable stock in vegetarian recipes (season it with salt as you use it) or as an alternative to chicken stock.

In a large pot, combine 1 onion, 2 carrots, 2 stalks celery, 1 leek, 1 potato, 2 tomatoes and ¼ lb/125 g mushrooms (all cut in chunks). Add 3 qt/3 L cold water, 1 bay leaf, ½ tsp/2 mL dried thyme, a handful of fresh parsley, 4 peeled cloves garlic and 6 peppercorns. Bring to a boil and remove any scum. Cover and simmer gently for 1 hour. Strain. This stock freezes well.

Makes about 3 qt/3 L.

1. Cover beans with plenty of water and soak for 3 hours at room temperature or overnight in refrigerator. Rinse and drain well.

2. Heat oil in large saucepan or Dutch oven. Add garlic, onion and hot pepper flakes and cook gently for a few minutes without browning.

3. Add beans and stock. Bring to boil, lower heat and simmer gently, covered, for 1 hour, or until beans are tender.

4. Add potato and cook for 10 minutes longer, or until tender.

5. Puree all or half of soup. Return to saucepan and thin with additional stock or water until soup reaches desired consistency.

6. Add pasta and cook for 10 minutes. Add pepper and salt. Pasta will thicken soup slightly, so thin soup again if you wish. Taste and adjust seasonings if necessary.

7. Meanwhile, combine all salsa ingredients. Taste and adjust seasonings if necessary.

8. Serve soup in flat bowls with large spoonful of salsa in centre of each serving.

PER SERVING

Calories	204
g carbohydrate	36
g fibre	10
g total fat	3
g saturated fat	trace
g protein	11

Excellent: folacin
Good: thiamine; iron

mg cholesterol	0
mg sodium	47
mg potassium	639

LENTIL VEGETABLE SOUP

Lentil soup is quick and easy to prepare. You can use either green or red lentils, but I prefer red lentils for soups as they cook more quickly and reduce to a softer consistency.

Makes 6 servings

1 tbsp	olive oil	15 mL
1	large onion, diced	1
2	cloves garlic, finely chopped	2
1 tsp	curry powder or ground cumin	5 mL
1	carrot, diced	1
1	stalk celery, diced	1
1	potato, peeled and diced	1
1 cup	dried red lentils, rinsed	250 mL
4 cups	homemade chicken stock (page 59), or 1 10-oz/284 mL tin chicken broth plus water	1 L
¼ tsp	pepper	1 mL
	Salt to taste	
1 tbsp	lemon juice	15 mL
dash	hot red pepper sauce, optional	dash
2 tbsp	chopped fresh cilantro or parsley	25 mL

1. Heat oil in large saucepan or Dutch oven. Add onion and garlic and cook until tender and fragrant, about 5 minutes. Add curry powder and cook for 30 seconds.

2. Add carrot, celery and potato and combine well. Stir in lentils and stock. Bring to boil. Add pepper and salt. Cook gently, covered, for 30 minutes.

3. Serve as is or puree soup for a smoother texture. Add lemon juice and hot pepper sauce. Taste and adjust seasonings if necessary. Serve sprinkled with cilantro.

PER SERVING

Calories	192
g carbohydrate	28
g fibre	5
g total fat	4
g saturated fat	1
g protein	13

Excellent: vitamin A; niacin; iron; folacin
Good: thiamine; vitamin B$_6$

mg cholesterol	1
mg sodium	40
mg potassium	649

Vegetable Paella
(page 116)

Vegetarian Muffuletta
(page 117)

MUSHROOM, BEAN AND BARLEY SOUP

WILD MUSHROOMS

Wild mushrooms can be quite expensive, but they add a lot of flavour to a dish. Fresh wild mushrooms include portobello (cultivated porcini mushrooms) shiitake, oyster, trumpets, morels and enoki. They can be stored for a few days in a single layer on a plate covered with a damp tea towel.

Dried wild mushrooms are more easily available than fresh, and while a half ounce can cost a few dollars, they often have more flavour than a pound of fresh mushrooms. To reconstitute, soak dried mushrooms in 1 cup/250 mL warm water for 30 minutes. Strain liquid through cheesecloth, a paper towel or coffee filter set in a strainer. Reserve the strained liquid and rinse each mushroom before chopping. The liquid is very flavourful and should be used as part of the liquid in the dish, or it can be frozen for future use.

PER SERVING

Calories	154
g carbohydrate	26
g fibre	8
g total fat	2
g saturated fat	trace
g protein	10

Excellent: vitamin A; niacin; folacin
Good: iron

mg cholesterol	1
mg sodium	43
mg potassium	522

A chapter on soups would not be complete without a version of this hearty classic. I always make lots so that I have it for a few days. Thin the soup with water, as it thickens as it sits in the refrigerator. One 19-oz/540 mL tin white kidney beans, rinsed and drained, can be used instead of the dried beans; add them in Step 4 after the soup has cooked for 30 minutes.

Makes 12 to 14 servings

½ lb	dried white kidney beans or navy beans (about 1 cup/250 mL)	250 g
1	½-oz/15 g package dried wild mushrooms	1
⅔ cup	pearl barley, rinsed	150 mL
10 cups	homemade chicken stock (page 59), or 1 10-oz/284 mL tin chicken broth plus water	2.5 L
1	onion, chopped	1
2	carrots, diced	2
2	stalks celery, diced	2
3	cloves garlic, minced	3
½ lb	fresh mushrooms, sliced	250 g
½ tsp	pepper	2 mL
	Salt to taste	
¼ cup	chopped fresh parsley	50 mL

1. Cover beans generously with water and soak for few hours at room temperature or overnight in refrigerator. Rinse and drain.

2. Cover dried wild mushrooms with 1 cup/250 mL warm water and allow to rest for 30 minutes. Strain liquid through sieve lined with paper towel and reserve. Rinse each mushroom, as they can be very sandy. Chop dried mushrooms and reserve.

3. Place barley, beans, reserved mushroom juice and stock in large saucepan or Dutch oven. Bring to boil. Remove any scum that rises to surface.

4. Add onion, carrots, celery, garlic, fresh mushrooms and dried mushrooms. Cook for 1 hour, until beans are tender and soup thickens. Stir occasionally. Add pepper and salt. If soup is too thick, add water. Taste and adjust seasonings if necessary. Serve sprinkled with parsley.

MOROCCAN LENTIL SOUP WITH PASTA

This soup has an exotic flavour, but it is easy to make. Garam masala is a blend of spices. It is commercially available at specialty stores or East Indian markets, but if you cannot find it, use ¼ tsp / 1 mL each of cinnamon, ground cloves or allspice, ground coriander, cardamom and a pinch of nutmeg.

Makes 8 to 10 servings

1 tbsp	olive oil	15 mL
2	onions, chopped	2
2	cloves garlic, finely chopped	2
1 tbsp	finely chopped fresh ginger root	15 mL
1 tsp	garam masala	5 mL
½ tsp	turmeric	2 mL
¼ tsp	cayenne	1 mL
¾ cup	dried red lentils, rinsed	175 mL
1	28-oz/796 mL tin plum tomatoes, with juices	1
8 cups	homemade chicken stock (page 59), or 1 10-oz/284 mL tin chicken broth plus water	2 L
1	19-oz/540 mL tin chickpeas, rinsed and drained, or 2 cups/ 500 mL cooked chickpeas	1
1	19-oz/540 mL tin white kidney beans, rinsed and drained, or 2 cups/500 mL cooked kidney beans	1
½ cup	vermicelli noodles, broken up	125 mL
3 tbsp	lemon juice	45 mL
¼ tsp	pepper	1 mL
	Salt to taste	
⅓ cup	chopped fresh cilantro or parsley	75 mL

SOUP GARNISHES
- chopped fresh herbs
- swirl of plain or seasoned soft yogurt cheese (page 228)
- crushed baked corn chips
- croutons
- dusting of spices (paprika, freshly ground pepper, curry, cumin)
- sprinkling of seeds (sesame, poppy, cumin, caraway)
- light sprinkling of lower-fat grated cheese
- light dusting of finely chopped toasted nuts
- finely chopped salad or salsa
- cooked rice
- diced cooked potatoes or other vegetables
- small cooked soup pasta
- edible flowers (page 72)
- baked potato skins (page 214)
- chopped cooked chickpeas

1. Heat oil in large saucepan or Dutch oven. Add onions, garlic and ginger. Cook gently for a few minutes until onions wilt.

2. Add garam masala, turmeric and cayenne. Cook for 2 to 3 minutes; if mixture begins to stick or burn, add ½ cup/125 mL water.

3. Stir in lentils, tomatoes and stock. Bring to boil, reduce heat and simmer gently for 20 minutes.

4. Add chickpeas and beans and simmer for 20 minutes. Puree about one-third of soup mixture and return to pot. If soup is too thick, add some water.

5. Add vermicelli and cook for 15 minutes, until very tender. Stir in lemon juice, pepper and salt. Taste and adjust seasonings if necessary. Serve sprinkled with cilantro.

PER SERVING

Calories	302
g carbohydrate	47
g fibre	10
g total fat	5
g saturated fat	1
g protein	19

Excellent: niacin; iron; vitamin B$_6$; folacin
Good: thiamine

mg cholesterol	1
mg sodium	407
mg potassium	935

BLACK BEAN SOUP WITH YOGURT AND SPICY SALSA

Black bean soup can be served as a starter or main course. Be sure to use dried black turtle beans and not the fermented black beans used in Asian cooking. You could also use canned black beans in this soup; use two 19-oz/540 mL tins, rinsed and drained, and cook the soup for only 30 minutes after you have added them.

Makes 8 to 10 servings

1 lb	dried black beans (about 2 cups/500 mL)	500 g
2 tsp	olive oil	10 mL
1	onion, chopped	1
6	cloves garlic, finely chopped	6
1 tbsp	ground cumin	15 mL
1 tbsp	paprika	15 mL
½ tsp	cayenne	2 mL
8 cups	homemade chicken stock (page 59), or 1 10-oz/284 mL tin chicken broth plus water	2 L
1	chipotle or jalapeño, chopped, optional	1
	Salt to taste	

Spicy Salsa:

2 tbsp	chopped onion, preferably red	25 mL
1	tomato, seeded and diced	1
1	jalapeño, chopped	1
1	small clove garlic, minced	1
¼ cup	chopped fresh cilantro or parsley	50 mL
½ cup	low-fat yogurt	125 mL

BLACK BEANS
Do not confuse dried or canned black turtle beans (usually used in large quantities in Southwestern and Mexican dishes, soups and salads) with the fermented black beans used in small amounts as a seasoning in Asian dishes (page 156).

To cook dried black turtle beans, soak 1 lb/500g (2 cups/500 mL) dried beans in cold water for a few hours at room temperature or overnight in the refrigerator. Drain, rinse and place in a saucepan with enough cold water to cover generously. Add 1 peeled and quartered onion. Bring to a boil, skim off scum and cook gently, covered, for 1 to 1½ hours, or until tender. Remove onion. Rinse beans and drain well. These freeze well. For instructions on cooking other types of dried beans see pages 126–27.

Makes about 4 cups/1 L cooked beans.

1. Cover beans with water and soak for a few hours at room temperature or overnight in refrigerator. Rinse and drain. Reserve.

2. Heat oil in large saucepan or Dutch oven. Add onion and garlic and cook gently until fragrant. Add cumin, paprika and cayenne. Cook for about 30 seconds.

3. Add stock, chipotle and beans. Bring to boil. Cover, reduce heat and simmer until beans are very tender, $1\frac{1}{2}$ hours or longer.

4. Puree soup until smooth. Add salt. Taste and adjust seasonings if necessary.

5. To make salsa, combine onion, tomato, jalapeño, garlic and cilantro.

6. To serve, ladle soup into shallow bowls. Spoon yogurt on each serving and top with salsa. (For a fancier presentation, thin yogurt with a little milk if necessary and drizzle design on soup. Place spoonful of salsa in centre of each serving.)

FREEZING STOCK
If you don't have a lot of freezer space, make your own condensed frozen homemade bouillon cubes. Boil down stock to one-eighth of the original amount. Freeze in ice cube trays and pack in bags (label them clearly). To use, dilute each cube with 1 cup/ 250 mL water.

PER SERVING

Calories	273
g carbohydrate	41
g fibre	10
g total fat	4
g saturated fat	1
g protein	20

Excellent: thiamine; niacin; iron; folacin
Good: vitamin B$_{12}$

mg cholesterol	2
mg sodium	48
mg potassium	875

SPLIT PEA SOUP WITH DILL

This is one of our favourite family soups. Split peas do not need soaking, so this soup can be prepared more quickly than most soups based on dried legumes.

If you make the soup a day ahead, it will thicken even more. Simply thin it with water if necessary when you reheat it.

Makes 8 to 10 servings

1 tbsp	vegetable oil	15 mL
2	onions, diced	2
2	cloves garlic, finely chopped	2
2	carrots, diced	2
2	parsnips, peeled and diced	2
1	large potato, peeled and diced	1
1 cup	dried split green peas, rinsed	250 mL
8 cups	homemade chicken stock (page 59), or 1 10-oz/284 mL tin chicken broth plus water	2 L
1 cup	broken spaghetti	250 mL
2 tbsp	chopped fresh dill	25 mL
¼ tsp	pepper	1 mL
	Salt to taste	

1. Heat oil in large saucepan or Dutch oven. Add onions and garlic and cook for 5 minutes, or until fragrant and tender. Do not brown.

2. Add carrots, parsnips and potatoes and combine well. Cook for another 5 minutes.

3. Add peas and stock. Bring to boil, reduce heat and simmer gently, covered, for 1 hour, or until peas are tender and soup is very thick. (Soup will probably not need pureeing.) Thin with water if necessary.

4. Add spaghetti and cook for 10 to 15 minutes, until very tender. Thin soup again if necessary.

5. Stir in dill, pepper and salt. Taste and adjust seasonings if necessary.

SPLIT PEAS
I often use split peas in soups and do not presoak them. I usually buy green split peas, but the yellow ones are also delicious and are traditionally used in French Canadian pea soup and in East Indian and Scandinavian recipes.

PER SERVING

Calories	273
g carbohydrate	45
g fibre	7
g total fat	4
g saturated fat	1
g protein	15

Excellent: vitamin A; niacin; folacin
Good: thiamine; iron

mg cholesterol	1
mg sodium	51
mg potassium	764

SALADS AND SALAD DRESSINGS

Tabbouleh Salad

Mixed Grain Salad

Black Bean, Corn and Rice Salad

Sushi Salad

Tomato and Cucumber Salad

Asian Coleslaw

Salad Niçoise

Beet Salad

Potato Salad

Grilled Bread and Cherry Tomato Salad

Spaghettini with Salad Greens

Spaghetti Salad with Tuna

Thai Chicken and Noodle Salad

Grilled Chicken Salad with Peanut Sauce

Chopped Grilled Chicken Salad

Letty's Noodle Salad

Balsamic Spa Dressing

Mustard Pepper Dressing

Roasted Garlic Dressing

Citrus Vinaigrette

Sesame Ginger Dressing

Roasted Red Pepper Dressing

TABBOULEH SALAD

This wonderful Middle Eastern salad can be served as an appetizer, side dish or main course. Sometimes I add chickpeas or leftover cooked chicken to it. I even stuff it into pita bread for a vegetarian sandwich.

This salad keeps well in the refrigerator for a few days.

Makes 8 servings

1½ cups	bulgur	375 mL
1 cup	chopped fresh parsley	250 mL
½ cup	chopped fresh chives or green onions	125 mL
¼ cup	chopped fresh mint	50 mL
3	tomatoes, seeded and chopped	3
3 oz	feta cheese, rinsed, drained and crumbled	90 g
⅓ cup	lemon juice	75 mL
1 tbsp	olive oil	15 mL
1	clove garlic, minced	1
½ tsp	pepper	2 mL
	Salt to taste	
1	English cucumber, thinly sliced	1
1	lemon, thinly sliced	1
2 tbsp	chopped black olives	25 mL

1. Place bulgur in large bowl and cover generously with boiling water. Allow to rest until cool (about 45 minutes). Drain well and squeeze out excess moisture. Fluff.

2. Add parsley, chives, mint, tomatoes and feta.

3. To make dressing, whisk together lemon juice, oil, garlic, pepper and salt. Toss dressing with salad. Taste and adjust seasonings if necessary.

4. Mound salad on platter and surround with cucumber and lemon slices. Dot with olives.

SALAD GARNISHES

- croutons (page 60)
- corn chips or flour tortilla chips (page 87)
- herbs
- edible flowers (chive flowers, daisies, dandelions, marigolds, nasturtiums, pansies, roses, impatiens, squash blossoms and violets. There are other edible flowers, but be sure to check before using.)
- cheese croutons (page 56)
- dusting of finely chopped toasted nuts
- crunchy cereals
- dried cherries or cranberries
- sprinkling of grated or crumbled lower-fat cheese
- cornbread croutons
- diced cold frittata, omelettes or soufflés
- baked potato skins (page 214)
- chickpeas

PER SERVING

Calories	159
g carbohydrate	26
g fibre	6
g total fat	5
g saturated fat	2
g protein	6

Good: vitamin C; iron; folacin

mg cholesterol	10
mg sodium	155
mg potassium	305

MIXED GRAIN SALAD

You'll find these grains in health food stores and many bulk food stores, but the salad is so good that you shouldn't wait until you have all the different grains before you make it. Use all of one type of rice or whatever grains you have on hand. Cooked chickpeas or cooked black beans can also be added (about 1 cup/250 mL).

Makes 8 servings

½ cup	long-grain brown rice, preferably basmati	125 mL
½ cup	wehani rice	125 mL
½ cup	pearl barley	125 mL
½ cup	quinoa, well rinsed	125 mL
1 cup	cooked corn niblets	250 mL
1	sweet red pepper, roasted (page 154), peeled and diced	1
1	4-oz/114 mL tin mild green chiles, rinsed, drained and chopped	1
1	small jalapeño, finely chopped	1
2 tbsp	pine nuts, toasted (page 245)	25 mL
¼ cup	chopped fresh cilantro or parsley	50 mL
¼ cup	chopped fresh chives or green onions	50 mL
¼ cup	chopped fresh parsley	50 mL
¼ cup	rice vinegar	50 mL
2 tbsp	olive oil	25 mL
1	clove garlic, minced	1
½ tsp	ground cumin	2 mL
¼ tsp	pepper	1 mL
	Salt to taste	

1. Bring large pot of water to boil. Add brown rice, wehani rice and barley. Cook for 25 minutes, or until tender.

2. Meanwhile, cook quinoa in another pot of boiling water for about 10 minutes, or until just tender.

3. Drain grains and combine with corn, red pepper, green chiles, jalapeño, pine nuts, cilantro, chives and parsley.

4. Prepare dressing by whisking together vinegar, oil, garlic, cumin, pepper and salt. Combine with grains. Taste and adjust seasonings if necessary.

HANDLING CHILE PEPPERS

With all chiles, most of the heat is in the ribs (the seeds are also hot because they touch the ribs), so if you prefer milder chiles, remove the ribs and seeds. Many books recommend that you wear plastic gloves if you have sensitive skin. And never touch your eyes, mouth or nose during or after handling chiles. If you do feel a burning sensation, try washing the affected area with milk to soothe it.

PER SERVING

Calories	241
g carbohydrate	43
g fibre	5
g total fat	6
g saturated fat	1
g protein	6

Excellent: vitamin C
Good: niacin; iron; vitamin B$_6$

mg cholesterol	0
mg sodium	147
mg potassium	275

Black Bean, Corn and Rice Salad

Each bite of this beautiful salad contains a burst of herbal flavours and a wonderful blend of textures. If you can't find fresh cilantro, basil or mint, just use more parsley and green onions.

See photo opposite page 33.

Makes 8 servings

1 cup	dried black beans	250 mL
1 cup	long-grain rice, preferably basmati	250 mL
2 cups	cooked corn niblets	500 mL
2	sweet red peppers, roasted (page 154), peeled and diced	2
1	jalapeño, diced	1
1	bunch arugula or watercress, trimmed and chopped	1
⅓ cup	chopped fresh cilantro or parsley	75 mL
⅓ cup	chopped fresh basil	75 mL
2 tbsp	chopped fresh mint	25 mL
2 tbsp	chopped fresh chives or green onions	25 mL
3 tbsp	red wine vinegar	45 mL
½ tsp	pepper	2 mL
1	clove garlic, minced	1
	Salt to taste	
3 tbsp	olive oil	45 mL

1. Soak beans in cold water for few hours at room temperature or overnight in refrigerator. Rinse and drain well.

2. In large pot, cover beans generously with water. Bring to boil, reduce heat and cook gently for 1 to 1½ hours, or until tender. Drain well. Reserve in large bowl.

3. Meanwhile, wash rice well. Bring large pot of water to boil. Add rice and cook for 12 minutes, or until just tender. Drain well. Combine with beans.

4. Add corn, peppers, jalapeño, arugula, cilantro, basil, mint and chives to salad.

5. To make dressing, whisk together vinegar, pepper, garlic and salt. Whisk in olive oil.

6. Toss dressing with salad. Taste and adjust seasonings if necessary.

SALAD DRESSINGS

Any salad dressing that contains oil will likely have a high percentage of calories from fat, because most of the calories are in the oil. But when the dressing hits the salad, the total fat percentage usually comes down, depending on the salad ingredients.

The dressings in this book are very delicious, natural and low in fat when combined with an actual salad.

PER SERVING

Calories	265
g carbohydrate	45
g fibre	6
g total fat	6
g saturated fat	1
g protein	10

Excellent: vitamin C; folacin
Good: vitamin A; thiamine; vitamin B₆

mg cholesterol	0
mg sodium	10
mg potassium	485

SUSHI SALAD

This is a homestyle version of the sushi served in Japanese restaurants. There is absolutely no fat in the dressing, and the recipe can be varied in many ways. The rice and vinegar are the only essential items; you can add leftover chicken or shrimp, corn, zucchini, green beans, green onions, etc.

Makes 6 to 8 servings

1½ cups	short-grain rice, preferably Japanese	375 mL
1¾ cups	cold water	425 mL
¼ lb	snow peas, trimmed	125 g
¼ cup	rice vinegar	50 mL
2	sheets nori, preferably toasted, broken up	2
2 tbsp	diced pink pickled ginger root	25 mL
1	carrot, grated	1
½ cup	cooked peas	125 mL
2 tbsp	sesame seeds, toasted (page 34)	25 mL
2 tbsp	chopped fresh dill	25 mL
2 tbsp	chopped fresh chives or green onions	25 mL
2 tbsp	chopped fresh cilantro or parsley	25 mL

1. Place rice in sieve and rinse until water runs clear. Place rice in a medium saucepan and add cold water. Cover. Bring to vigorous boil and cook for 5 minutes. Reduce heat and cook for 5 to 8 minutes longer, until water has been absorbed. Turn off heat and allow rice to rest for 10 minutes.

2. Blanch snow peas by immersing them in boiling water for 30 seconds. Drain and rinse with cold water. Slice peas on diagonal.

3. Transfer rice to large bowl. Toss rice gently while fanning it, to prevent it from being too sticky. As you are fanning, gradually add vinegar, tossing gently, until all vinegar has been absorbed.

4. Add snow peas, nori, ginger, carrot, peas, sesame seeds, dill, chives and cilantro. Toss and serve at room temperature.

RICE VINEGAR

Rice vinegar is very mild. I often use it sprinkled on salads without any oil at all. If you do not have rice vinegar, substitute cider vinegar (although the taste will be a little more acidic).

You can also buy seasoned rice vinegar, which contains salt and sugar (sushi su). This is used to flavour sushi rice, but it is also delicious on salads. If you can't find sushi su, use regular rice vinegar with or without a little salt and sugar added.

PER SERVING

Calories	226
g carbohydrate	46
g fibre	2
g total fat	2
g saturated fat	trace
g protein	6

Excellent: vitamin A

mg cholesterol	0
mg sodium	20
mg potassium	189

TOMATO AND CUCUMBER SALAD

This is a light and refreshing salad that my mom makes. The salad can be made a day ahead and left to marinate in the refrigerator overnight.

Makes 6 to 8 servings

3	large tomatoes, thinly sliced	3
1	English cucumber, thinly sliced	1
1	large sweet onion, thinly sliced	1
½ cup	chopped fresh parsley	125 mL
3 tbsp	rice vinegar or cider vinegar	45 mL
2 tbsp	granulated sugar	25 mL
	Salt to taste	

1. Layer tomatoes, cucumber and onion in salad bowl. Sprinkle parsley over top.

2. Combine vinegar, sugar and salt. Whisk until sugar has dissolved.

3. Pour dressing over salad and allow to marinate for at least 30 minutes at room temperature before serving. Taste and adjust seasonings if necessary.

CUCUMBERS
English cucumbers have unwaxed skins and fewer seeds than regular cucumbers. If I am using cucumbers in a salad, I usually slice them, sprinkle them with some salt and allow them to drain in a colander or sieve to remove excess liquid. Rinse and pat dry. This way the cucumbers will not ooze too much liquid when combined with yogurt in a tzatziki (page 39) or other dressing (taste before adding any extra salt).

PER SERVING

Calories	55
g carbohydrate	13
g fibre	2
g total fat	trace
g saturated fat	trace
g protein	2

Good: vitamin C; folacin

mg cholesterol	0
mg sodium	12
mg potassium	368

See photo opposite page 97.

ASIAN COLESLAW

Coleslaws made with all kinds of international ingredients are becoming very common in upscale restaurants, but they are easy to make at home — inexpensive and low in fat! This salad can be prepared in advance and keeps well in the refrigerator for four days. If you prefer, you can use the cabbage and carrots raw instead of wilting them in boiling water. You can also use just one type of cabbage.

Makes 6 to 8 servings

½	head Chinese (Napa) cabbage or green cabbage, shredded	½
½	small red cabbage, shredded	½
4	carrots, grated	4
3	green onions, chopped	3
½ cup	chopped fresh cilantro or parsley	125 mL

Dressing:

3 tbsp	lemon juice	45 mL
3 tbsp	rice vinegar	45 mL
3 tbsp	honey	45 mL
1 tbsp	soy sauce	15 mL
½ tsp	hot chili paste, optional	2 mL
2	cloves garlic, minced	2
1 tsp	minced fresh ginger root	5 mL
1 tbsp	sesame oil	15 mL

1. Place green and red cabbage and carrots in large bowl. Pour boiling water over. Drain well. Rinse with cold water and drain well again.

2. Toss green onions and cilantro with cabbage.

3. To make dressing, combine lemon juice, rice vinegar, honey, soy sauce, chili paste, garlic, ginger and sesame oil. Toss dressing with cabbage mixture. Taste and adjust seasonings if necessary.

Country-style Coleslaw: Omit Chinese cabbage, red cabbage and cilantro. Shred 1 green cabbage and 1 carrot. Combine with dressing made of ½ cup/125 mL rice vinegar, 2 tbsp/ 25 mL granulated sugar, 1 minced clove garlic, 5 chopped green onions and salt to taste. Taste and adjust seasonings if necessary.

PER SERVING

Calories	109
g carbohydrate	22
g fibre	4
g total fat	3
g saturated fat	trace
g protein	3

Excellent: vitamin A; vitamin C; folacin
Good: vitamin B$_6$

mg cholesterol	0
mg sodium	174
mg potassium	528

SALAD NIÇOISE

If you can find fresh tuna, use it in this recipe. Cook it according to instructions found on page 146. Slice the tuna on the diagonal and arrange it on top of the potatoes.

Makes 6 to 8 servings

Niçoise Dressing:

2 tbsp	red wine vinegar	25 mL
1 tsp	Dijon mustard	5 mL
1	clove garlic, minced	1
2	anchovies, mashed	2
¼ tsp	pepper	1 mL
¼ cup	tomato juice or V-8 juice	50 mL
2 tbsp	olive oil	25 mL
2 tbsp	chopped pitted black olives	25 mL

Salad:

2 lb	red potatoes, cut in 2-inch/5 cm chunks	1 kg
1 lb	green beans, trimmed	500 g
1	small head Romaine or leaf lettuce	1
1 cup	cherry tomatoes	250 mL
2	7-oz/198 g tins white tuna (water-packed), drained and flaked	2
2 tbsp	chopped fresh parsley	25 mL
2 tbsp	chopped fresh chives or green onions	25 mL
1 tbsp	chopped fresh tarragon, or ½ tsp/2 mL dried	15 mL

1. To make dressing, whisk together vinegar, mustard, garlic, anchovies, pepper and tomato juice. Whisk in oil and olives. Taste and adjust seasonings if necessary.

2. Place potatoes in large pot of water. Cook potatoes in boiling water for 20 minutes or until tender. While potatoes are cooking, add beans to boiling water and cook for 5 minutes. Remove with tongs and rinse with cold water to stop cooking. Pat dry and reserve. When potatoes are cooked, drain and cut into 1-inch/2.5 cm cubes.

3. Line large salad bowl with lettuce and arrange potatoes in middle. Surround potatoes with green beans and cherry tomatoes. Pour dressing over vegetables. Spoon tuna on top of potatoes. Sprinkle parsley, chives and tarragon over salad.

See photo opposite page 33.

OLIVES

Although olives are high in fat and sodium, they are also high in flavour, so a little goes a long way. Rather than putting out bowls of olives for nibbling, use small quantities as a seasoning in salads and pasta sauces. Black olives are ripe olives; green olives are unripe.

Generally, the best olives have pits. Cut the meat off the pit with a sharp knife or whack the olives on a cutting board with the side of a knife or meat pounder; in most cases the pits will pop out.

PER SERVING

Calories	265
g carbohydrate	34
g fibre	5
g total fat	7
g saturated fat	1
g protein	19

Excellent: vitamin C; niacin; vitamin B$_6$; folacin; vitamin B$_{12}$
Good: vitamin A; thiamine; iron

mg cholesterol	23
mg sodium	339
mg potassium	1079

BEET SALAD

It is a shame that beets are often overlooked, because they are so delicious. Buy beets that are approximately the same size so that they will cook evenly. Although you can cut them up and boil them, they "bleed" less when you bake them whole as suggested below. Baking also gives them a far more intense flavour.

You can also cook the beets in the microwave. Pierce them in several places and place in a microwave-safe dish with ¼ cup/50 mL water. Cover and microwave at High (100%) for 10 to 14 minutes, or until tender.

Makes 4 to 6 servings

2 lb	beets	1 kg
2 tbsp	lemon juice	25 mL
¼ cup	chopped fresh cilantro or parsley	50 mL
1 tsp	honey	5 mL
½ tsp	ground cumin	2 mL
¼ tsp	pepper	1 mL
	Salt to taste	

1. Trim beets but do not peel. Wrap in foil packages in single layer. Place beets of a similar size together. Bake in preheated 400°F/200°C oven for 1 hour, or until tender when pierced with a knife. Cool, peel, dice and place in large bowl.

2. Whisk together lemon juice, cilantro, honey, cumin, pepper and salt.

3. Toss dressing with beets. Taste and adjust seasonings if necessary. Serve at room temperature.

CILANTRO

Cilantro is also called fresh coriander or Chinese parsley. Aficionados love its fresh, clean taste, and people who hate it say it reminds them of soap! If you cannot find it, use parsley instead, but there is really no substitute.

PER SERVING

Calories	63
g carbohydrate	14
g fibre	4
g total fat	trace
g saturated fat	0
g protein	2

Excellent: folacin

mg cholesterol	0
mg sodium	88
mg potassium	572

POTATO SALAD

I learned the trick of cooking potatoes in vinegared water from Italian cooking master Giuliano Bugialli. The vinegar gives the potatoes a mild but delicious flavour, and a skin forms on the outside that helps prevent them from falling apart in salads.

Instead of the dressing in this recipe, I sometimes use roasted garlic dressing (page 93) or roasted red repper dressing (page 96). Be sure to try the mashed potato salad variation, too.

Makes 6 servings

⅓ cup	red wine vinegar	75 mL
2 lb	small red potatoes, scrubbed	1 kg
2	sweet red peppers, preferably roasted (page 154), peeled and diced	2

Dressing:

2 tbsp	red wine vinegar	25 mL
2	cloves garlic, minced	2
½ tsp	pepper	2 mL
	Salt to taste	
2 tbsp	olive oil	25 mL
¼ cup	chopped fresh chives or green onions	50 mL

1. Bring large pot of water to boil. Add ⅓ cup/75 mL vinegar. Cut potatoes into 2-inch/5 cm pieces if they are large. Cook for 15 to 20 minutes, or until tender. Drain well.

2. Combine potatoes and red peppers in large bowl.

3. To make dressing, whisk together 2 tbsp/25 mL vinegar, garlic, pepper, salt and olive oil. Toss dressing with potatoes and stir in chives. Taste and adjust seasonings if necessary. Serve warm or at room temperature.

Mashed Potato Salad: Peel 2 lb/1 kg baking potatoes and cook in large pot of boiling water (omit vinegar). When potatoes are tender, drain well, reserving cooking liquid, and mash. Beat in dressing and about ½ cup/125 mL potato cooking liquid. Serve warm or at room temperature.

Creamy Potato Salad: Add ½ cup/125 mL soft yogurt cheese (page 228) or thick yogurt to dressing.

PER SERVING

Calories	164
g carbohydrate	29
g fibre	3
g total fat	5
g saturated fat	1
g protein	3

Excellent: vitamin C; vitamin B$_6$
Good: vitamin A

mg cholesterol	0
mg sodium	7
mg potassium	571

GRILLED BREAD AND CHERRY TOMATO SALAD

Everyone seems to have leftover bread, and it's a shame to waste it. Tuscan cooks use up leftover bread in salads, and as unusual as it sounds, it is really delicious. (Think of it as a salad that has more croutons than lettuce!) Use red or yellow cherry tomatoes, or a combination, in this recipe.

Makes 6 servings

1	small clove garlic, minced	1
$\frac{1}{3}$ cup	balsamic vinegar	75 mL
$1\frac{1}{2}$ tbsp	olive oil	20 mL
$\frac{1}{4}$ tsp	pepper	1 mL
	Salt to taste	
2 tbsp	chopped fresh chives or green onions	25 mL
$\frac{1}{3}$ cup	chopped fresh basil or parsley	75 mL
6	slices French or Italian bread, about $\frac{3}{4}$ inch/4 cm thick	6
4 cups	cherry tomatoes, halved	1 L

1. In small bowl, whisk together garlic, vinegar, oil, pepper and salt. Stir in chives and basil. Reserve.

2. Barbecue or toast bread. Cut each slice into $1\frac{1}{2}$-inch/4 cm pieces.

3. Toss bread with cherry tomatoes and dressing. Taste and adjust seasonings if necessary.

OLIVE OIL

I like to use olive oil, partly because it is a monounsaturated fat, but also because it is delicious, with a strong taste of olives. Extra-virgin olive oil has a lower acidity than regular olive oil; it is made with ripe olives without the use of heat or chemicals.

Olive oil doesn't last forever, so buy it in small quantities. Once opened, use it quickly or keep it in the refrigerator (the oil may firm up and become cloudy, but it will be fine when it returns to room temperature).

When I don't want the taste of olives in a dish, I usually use safflower, corn or canola oil.

LIGHT OLIVE OILS

The so-called "light" olive oils are deceptive. Most consumers believe, falsely, that these light oils have fewer calories, when all they really have (to date, anyway) is less taste.

PER SERVING

Calories	134
g carbohydrate	22
g fibre	2
g total fat	4
g saturated fat	1
g protein	4
mg cholesterol	0
mg sodium	183
mg potassium	232

SPAGHETTINI WITH SALAD GREENS

This refreshing salad-style pasta dish can be served warm or at room temperature. If you cannot find arugula and radicchio, use any greens you like; you'll need about 4 cups / 1 L chopped greens.

Makes 8 servings

1 lb	spaghettini	500 g
5	tomatoes, seeded and diced	5
1	bunch arugula or watercress, coarsely chopped	1
1	head radicchio or leaf lettuce, coarsely chopped	1
2	cloves garlic, minced	2
¼ tsp	hot red pepper flakes	1 mL
½ tsp	pepper	2 mL
	Salt to taste	
2 tbsp	olive oil	25 mL
2 tbsp	balsamic vinegar	25 mL
¼ cup	chopped black olives	50 mL

1. Bring large pot of water to boil. Add spaghettini and cook until tender but firm.

2. Meanwhile, in large shallow dish, combine tomatoes, arugula and radicchio. Stir in garlic, hot pepper flakes, pepper and salt. Stir in oil, vinegar and olives.

3. Drain pasta well and combine immediately with sauce. Taste and adjust seasonings if necessary.

See photo opposite page 33.

SALAD GREENS

You can buy all kinds of different salad greens. Bitter greens like arugula, radicchio, endive and frisee are especially popular, either on their own or combined with sweeter greens like Romaine or curly lettuce. (I find that if I use interesting tasting greens, I need less dressing on the salad.) Spinach is also great in salads, as long as it is well washed (page 207).

Wash salad greens well and pat dry. Wrap them in tea towels and store in airtight bags or containers. The tea towels absorb excess moisture so the greens don't spoil as quickly.

PER SERVING

Calories	271
g carbohydrate	48
g fibre	4
g total fat	5
g saturated fat	1
g protein	9

Good: vitamin A; vitamin C; folacin

mg cholesterol	0
mg sodium	49
mg potassium	365

PEELING AND
SEEDING TOMATOES

You do not have to peel tomatoes if you are using them raw, but in cooked dishes the peel will come off and look unattractive as well as adding a strange texture to your finished dish. To peel tomatoes easily, cut a small cross in the bottom end and submerge the tomato in boiling water for 10 to 15 seconds. When the tomatoes are cool enough to handle, the skins should slip off easily. Seed raw tomatoes if you don't want a mixture to become too wet. Cut the tomato in half horizontally and squeeze the seeds out gently.

PER SERVING

Calories	347
g carbohydrate	48
g fibre	4
g total fat	7
g saturated fat	1
g protein	22

Excellent: vitamin C; niacin; vitamin B$_{12}$
Good: vitamin A; vitamin B$_6$; folacin

mg cholesterol	22
mg sodium	235
mg potassium	382

SPAGHETTI SALAD WITH TUNA

You can buy roasted peppers in jars to make this delicious salad even easier to make. If you cannot find fresh basil, just use more parsley or green onions.

If you want to prepare this recipe ahead of time, refrigerate it and bring to room temperature before serving.

Makes 6 servings

¾ lb	spaghetti	375 g
2 tbsp	olive oil	25 mL
2	cloves garlic, minced	2
¼ tsp	hot red pepper flakes, optional	1 mL
½ tsp	pepper	2 mL
	Salt to taste	
2	tomatoes, seeded and diced	2
2	sweet red or yellow peppers, preferably roasted (page 154), peeled and diced	2
2	7-oz/198-mL tins white tuna (water-packed), drained and flaked	2
2 tbsp	chopped black olives	25 mL
¼ cup	chopped fresh parsley	50 mL
¼ cup	chopped fresh basil	50 mL
2	green onions, chopped	2

1. Cook spaghetti in large pot of boiling water until just tender.

2. Meanwhile, in large bowl, combine olive oil, garlic, hot pepper flakes, pepper and salt. Stir in tomatoes, peppers, tuna and olives. Add parsley, basil and green onions.

3. When spaghetti is ready, drain well and toss with sauce. Taste and adjust seasonings if necessary. Serve warm or at room temperature.

THAI CHICKEN AND NOODLE SALAD

I make this salad with either rice noodles or regular spaghettini. If you use rice noodles, try to find the ones made in China; oddly enough, they have a nicer texture than the ones made in Thailand. If you can't find all the fresh herbs, just use more parsley and green onions.

Makes 8 to 10 servings

1 lb	boneless, skinless chicken breasts	500 g
3 tbsp	hoisin sauce	45 mL
1 tbsp	lime juice	15 mL
1 tsp	pepper	5 mL
¾ lb	rice vermicelli or spaghettini	375 g
¼ cup	vegetable oil	50 mL
6	cloves garlic, finely chopped	6
1	English cucumber	1
½ cup	chopped fresh cilantro or parsley	125 mL
½ cup	chopped fresh mint	125 mL
½ cup	chopped fresh basil	125 mL
6	green onions, chopped	6
1	sweet red pepper, preferably roasted (page 154), peeled and diced	1

Thai Dressing:

¼ cup	lemon juice	50 mL
¼ cup	lime juice	50 mL
¼ cup	water	50 mL
2 tbsp	Thai fish sauce (nam pla) or soy sauce	25 mL
¼ tsp	hot red pepper flakes	1 mL
2 tbsp	granulated sugar	25 mL
	Salt to taste	
	Lettuce leaves	

THAI FISH SAUCE
Thai fish sauce is the fermented Thai and Vietnamese equivalent of soy sauce. It is made by layering fish (usually anchovies, but sometimes crab or shrimp) and salt. The Thai version is called nam pla and the Vietnamese nuoc nam. The sauce is inexpensive and keeps for a long time but, like soy sauce, it is high in sodium, so use it sparingly.

1. Combine chicken with hoisin sauce, lime juice and pepper. Refrigerate for 6 hours or overnight.

2. Preheat broiler or barbecue and grill chicken until just cooked through, about 4 to 6 minutes per side, depending on thickness. Cool and slice thinly on diagonal.

3. If you are using rice noodles, pour boiling water over them and soak for 5 to 7 minutes, or until tender. Drain well (they do not need further cooking). If you are using spaghettini, cook noodles in large pot of boiling water until tender but firm. Drain and cool under cold running water.

4. Meanwhile, heat oil in small skillet over low heat. Add garlic and cook gently until tender and fragrant, but do not brown. Toss garlic/oil mixture with noodles.

5. Cut cucumber into four lengthwise pieces and slice thinly.

6. Add chicken, cucumber, cilantro, mint, basil, green onions and red pepper to noodles and toss well.

7. To make dressing, whisk together lemon juice, lime juice, water, fish sauce, hot pepper flakes, sugar and salt. Toss dressing with salad. Taste and adjust seasonings if necessary. Serve on bed of lettuce.

PER SERVING

Calories	348
g carbohydrate	45
g fibre	2
g total fat	9
g saturated fat	1
g protein	22

Excellent: vitamin C; niacin; vitamin B$_6$

mg cholesterol	48
mg sodium	345
mg potassium	382

GRILLED CHICKEN SALAD WITH PEANUT SAUCE

This is my version of a salad that I tasted in Florida, and it has become one of my favourites. It is very easy to make, and the chicken can be baked instead of grilled. You can also use sliced leftover chicken or smoked chicken (use 3 to 4 cups / 750 mL to 1 L). The servings look very generous because of all the lettuce, but don't worry — you'll get through it!

This salad can be served fresh and crisp, but it is also great when it gets a bit soggy. If you don't have corn tortillas, substitute commercial baked corn chips that have been broken up coarsely — use about 1 cup / 250 mL.

Makes 6 to 8 servings

1½ lb	boneless, skinless chicken breasts	750 g
1 tbsp	honey-style mustard	15 mL
1 tsp	sesame oil	5 mL
1	clove garlic, minced	1

Lime Honey Dressing:

¼ cup	lime juice	50 mL
2 tsp	honey-style mustard	10 mL
2 tbsp	honey	25 mL
2 tbsp	olive oil	25 mL
½ tsp	pepper	2 mL
1	small clove garlic, minced	1
	Salt to taste	

Peanut Sauce:

2 tbsp	peanut butter	25 mL
2 tbsp	honey	25 mL
2 tbsp	soy sauce	25 mL
2 tbsp	hot water	25 mL

HOMEMADE "LIGHT" PRODUCTS

"Light" products are not necessarily low in fat. Some are light in taste (light olive oil) or light in salt (soy sauce), so be sure to read the labels carefully. Only buy light products if you like the taste of them. If not, make your own light versions at home:

• Make lower-sodium soy sauce by blending your favourite regular soy sauce with the same amount of water.

• Make a lighter-tasting olive oil by blending good extra-virgin olive oil with an unflavoured oil like canola or safflower.

• Make lower-fat soft cheese by blending your favourite regular-fat cheese with low-fat cottage cheese or firm yogurt cheese (page 228).

• Make lower-fat mayonnaise by combining regular mayonnaise with soft yogurt cheese.

1	large head Romaine lettuce	1
1	head radicchio or ½ small red cabbage	1
2	carrots, grated	2
1	sweet red pepper, preferably roasted (page 154), peeled, and cut in thin strips	1
4	corn tortillas	4
1	bunch fresh cilantro or parsley, chopped	1

1. Pat chicken breasts dry. In small bowl, combine mustard, sesame oil and garlic. Rub into chicken. Preheat broiler or barbecue and grill chicken until just cooked through. Cool and slice very thinly on diagonal. Reserve.

2. To make lime honey dressing, blend together lime juice, mustard, honey, olive oil, pepper, garlic and salt. Reserve.

3. To make peanut sauce, blend together peanut butter, honey, soy sauce and hot water. Reserve.

4. Shred lettuce and radicchio and toss together in large bowl. Add carrots and red pepper.

5. Cut tortillas into thin strips (scissors work well). Place on baking sheet in single layer. Bake in preheated 400°F/200°C oven for about 8 minutes, or until crisp. Add tortilla strips, chicken and cilantro to salad.

6. Toss salad with lime honey dressing. Drizzle peanut sauce over all.

CORN CHIPS

Cut four 8-inch/20 cm corn tortillas into wedges (scissors work well for this) and arrange in a single layer on a baking sheet. Bake in a preheated 400°F/200°C oven for about 8 minutes, or until lightly browned and crisp. You can also make flour tortilla chips using this method.

Makes about 3 cups/750 mL.

PER SERVING

Calories	328
g carbohydrate	29
g fibre	4
g total fat	11
g saturated fat	2
g protein	31

Excellent: vitamin A; vitamin C; niacin; vitamin B$_6$; folacin
Good: thiamine; riboflavin; iron; vitamin E

mg cholesterol	70
mg sodium	411
mg potassium	865

CHOPPED GRILLED CHICKEN SALAD

In this salad many ingredients are chopped, so every bite is full of tastes and textures. You can also use 1 lb/500 g shrimp or ¾ lb/375 g beef instead of the chicken, and you can roast the chicken and vegetables instead of barbecuing them.

This salad is also great with a sesame ginger dressing (page 95).

Makes 6 to 8 servings

1 tbsp	Dijon mustard	15 mL
1 tbsp	soy sauce	15 mL
¼ tsp	pepper	1 mL
1 lb	boneless, skinless chicken breasts	500 g
2	sweet yellow peppers	2
2	sweet red peppers	2
1 lb	eggplant, cut in ¼-inch/5 mm slices	500 g
2	small zucchini, halved lengthwise	2
1	large red onion, cut in 1-inch/ 2.5 cm slices	1
2	ears corn, husked	2
½ lb	asparagus, trimmed	250 g
2	tomatoes, seeded and chopped	2
¼ cup	chopped black olives	50 mL
¼ cup	chopped fresh basil or parsley	50 mL
¼ cup	chopped fresh chives or green onions	50 mL

BUYING TOMATOES

If you cannot find nice ripe round tomatoes, try using fresh plum (Roma) tomatoes, or use canned Italian plum tomatoes.

To ripen tomatoes, place in a perforated paper bag and leave on the counter for a few days. Never store tomatoes in the refrigerator, as their texture will become mealy.

SUN-DRIED TOMATOES

To make your own "sun"-dried tomatoes, halve or slice fresh Italian plum tomatoes and place in a single layer on a rack over a baking sheet. Bake in a 200°F/100°C oven for 6 to 24 hours, or until dried. Freeze.

Dressing:

3 tbsp	red wine vinegar	45 mL
3 tbsp	balsamic vinegar	45 mL
1	clove garlic, minced	1
½ tsp	pepper	2 mL
	Salt to taste	
3 tbsp	olive oil	45 mL
6 cups	chopped mixed salad greens (arugula, radicchio, red oak leaf, frisee, etc.)	1.5 L

1. In shallow dish, combine mustard, soy sauce and pepper. Coat chicken with mixture and marinate overnight in refrigerator.

2. Preheat broiler or barbecue. Grill peppers until blackened (page 154). Cool, peel and cut into 1-inch/2.5 cm pieces.

3. Grill chicken for 6 to 8 minutes per side, or until cooked through. Cut into 1-inch/2.5 cm pieces.

4. Grill eggplant, zucchini, onion, corn and asparagus until just cooked. Chop eggplant, zucchini, onion and asparagus into 1-inch/2.5 cm pieces. Cut corn from cob.

5. In large bowl, combine chicken, grilled vegetables, tomatoes, olives, basil and chives.

6. To make dressing, whisk together wine vinegar, balsamic vinegar, garlic, pepper and salt. Whisk in oil. Taste and adjust seasonings if necessary.

7. Toss dressing with chicken and vegetable mixture. Just before serving, add greens and toss again.

EGGPLANT

I usually prefer to use the thin, zucchini-shaped Japanese eggplants, but if you can only find large eggplants, choose longer, thinner ones, because they contain fewer seeds, which can be bitter.

Some people like to salt large eggplants (the smaller Japanese eggplants do not need salting) to remove bitterness and excess water. Sprinkle slices with salt and allow to drain in colander for about 30 minutes. Rinse and pat dry.

Traditionally, eggplant is fried in lots of oil, but if you broil or barbecue it, you do not need any oil or only a light brushing to flavour the food and prevent sticking.

PER SERVING

Calories	295
g carbohydrate	34
g fibre	8
g total fat	10
g saturated fat	1
g protein	23

Excellent: vitamin A; vitamin C; thiamine; niacin; vitamin B$_6$; folacin
Good: riboflavin; iron

mg cholesterol	47
mg sodium	232
mg potassium	1099

LETTY'S NOODLE SALAD

Letty Lastima, who works at the cooking school with me, is our resident rice and noodle expert. When we asked Letty where she had learned this great recipe, she just said that she ate it all the time in the Philippines, and that it was nothing special. Now we eat it all the time, too, but we think it's very special.

Makes 6 servings

1 lb	rice vermicelli or regular vermicelli	500 g
1 tbsp	vegetable oil	15 mL
3	cloves garlic, finely chopped	3
1 tbsp	finely chopped fresh ginger root	15 mL
¼ tsp	hot red pepper flakes	1 mL
1	onion, thinly sliced	1
1	carrot, cut in matchstick pieces	1
2 cups	diced cooked chicken or pork	500 mL
2	stalks celery, sliced	2
¼ lb	snow peas, trimmed	125 g
2 cups	diced Chinese (Napa) cabbage	500 mL
1½ cups	homemade chicken stock (page 59), or water	375 mL
3 tbsp	oyster sauce	45 mL
1 tbsp	sesame oil	15 mL
3	green onions, chopped	3
¼ cup	chopped fresh cilantro or parsley	50 mL

1. If you are using rice vermicelli, soak noodles in boiling water for 5 minutes. Drain and rinse with cold water. If you are using regular vermicelli, bring large pot of water to boil. Add noodles and cook until barely tender. Rinse and drain well. Reserve.

2. Meanwhile, heat vegetable oil in large, deep skillet or wok. Add garlic, ginger, hot pepper flakes and onion. Cook gently until very fragrant. Add carrot and chicken to skillet. Cook for a few minutes.

3. Add noodles, celery, snow peas, cabbage and stock to skillet and combine well. Cook for 10 minutes.

4. Stir in oyster sauce and sesame oil. Cook for another minute. Taste and adjust seasonings if necessary. Sprinkle with green onions and cilantro. Serve warm, at room temperature or cold.

CABBAGE

Cabbage is low in calories as well as being a good source of vitamin C. Savoy cabbage looks similar to the common white/green cabbage, but it has a deeper colour and crinkly leaves. Napa cabbage (sometimes called Chinese cabbage) has an elongated shape and delicate flavour. (When buying Napa cabbage, make sure the leaves do not have any black spotted mould on them.) Bok choy, another Chinese green, is also a cabbage but is usually served cooked.

When making coleslaw, you can reduce any harsh taste by covering the shredded cabbage with boiling water for a minute or two and then draining well. Or you can increase the crunchiness by soaking the shredded cabbage in ice water for 30 minutes and then draining well.

PER SERVING

Calories	448
g carbohydrate	67
g fibre	3
g total fat	9
g saturated fat	2
g protein	22

Excellent: vitamin A; niacin; vitamin B$_6$
Good: vitamin C; iron; folacin

mg cholesterol	42
mg sodium	492
mg potassium	498

BALSAMIC SPA DRESSING

This dressing can also be made with other mild vinegars such as raspberry, sherry, Champagne or good red wine vinegar.

BALSAMIC VINEGAR

Balsamic vinegar is the ultimate sweet-tasting vinegar. It is made from the juice of Trebbiano grapes, which has been aged in different kinds of woods. The woods (and how long and in which order the vinegar is kept in them) account for part of the reason why various balsamic vinegars taste so different.

Balsamic vinegars can actually range in price from $3 to $250 a bottle. Usually, the older the vinegar, the less acidic it is. A good balsamic vinegar (even some in the ten-dollar range) can be used straight on a salad without any oil. If you have a harsh-tasting balsamic vinegar, combine 2 cups/ 500 mL in a saucepan with 2 tbsp/25 mL brown sugar. Cook, uncovered, until cooked down to 1 cup/ 250 mL.

Makes about 1³⁄₄ cups/425 mL

½ cup	balsamic vinegar	125 mL
2 tbsp	lemon juice	25 mL
1 tbsp	Dijon mustard	15 mL
2 tbsp	olive oil	25 mL
2 tsp	Worcestershire sauce	10 mL
1	clove garlic, minced	1
¼ tsp	pepper	1 mL
1 cup	water	250 mL
1 tsp	honey, optional	5 mL
¼ tsp	salt, optional	1 mL

1. Whisk together vinegar, lemon juice, mustard, oil, Worcestershire, garlic and pepper. Whisk in water.

2. Taste and add honey and salt only if necessary.

PER TBSP (15 mL)

Calories	10
g carbohydrate	trace
g fibre	0
g total fat	1
g saturated fat	trace
g protein	trace
mg cholesterol	0
mg sodium	12
mg potassium	8

MUSTARD PEPPER DRESSING

This is a terrific all-purpose creamy dressing for salads or roasted meats. Try it on potato salad (page 80).

Makes about ³/₄ cup / 175 mL

2 tbsp	red wine vinegar	25 mL
1	clove garlic, minced	1
1 tbsp	Dijon mustard	15 mL
1 tsp	pepper	5 mL
	Salt to taste	
2 tsp	honey	10 mL
½ cup	soft yogurt cheese (page 228), thick yogurt, chicken stock or tomato juice	125 mL
2 tbsp	olive oil	25 mL

1. Whisk together vinegar, garlic, mustard, pepper and salt.

2. Stir in honey, yogurt cheese and olive oil. Taste and adjust seasonings if necessary.

LOWER-FAT SALAD "DRESSINGS"

- rice vinegar (page 75)
- balsamic vinegar, used as is or reduced (page 91)
- drizzle of lemon juice
- orange or pineapple juice
- yogurt or yogurt cheese (page 228)
- salsas (see index)
- pureed roasted tomatoes
- pureed roasted red peppers (page 154)
- leftover soup, at room temperature
- tomato sauce (page 102)
- ponzu sauce (page 96)
- Thai dressing (page 96)

PER TBSP (15 mL)

Calories	36
g carbohydrate	2
g fibre	0
g total fat	3
g saturated fat	1
g protein	1
mg cholesterol	1
mg sodium	26
mg potassium	39

ROASTED GARLIC DRESSING

This unusual dressing is sweet and delicious, although most people would be shocked to know how much garlic is in it. Use it as a dressing on salads or potato salad (page 80), as a topping for baked potatoes, as a dip for vegetables or as a sauce with roast meats, poultry or fish. You can also use the garlic puree (with or without the yogurt cheese) on bruschetta or pita with a little salsa on top. For a great pasta dish, toss the dressing with 3 oz (90 g) crumbled goat cheese, ½ lb (250 g) pasta, cooked, and ¼ cup (50 mL) chopped fresh basil or parsley. Season with salt and pepper to taste.

Makes about ½ cup / 125 mL

1	head garlic (about 12 cloves), peeled	1
1 cup	homemade chicken stock (page 59) or water	250 mL
1 tsp	honey	5 mL
pinch	chopped fresh or dried rosemary	pinch
pinch	chopped fresh or dried thyme	pinch
2 tbsp	balsamic vinegar	25 mL
1 tbsp	olive oil	15 mL
¼ tsp	pepper	1 mL
	Salt to taste	
¼ cup	soft yogurt cheese (page 228), thick yogurt, chicken stock or tomato juice	50 mL

1. Place peeled garlic in small saucepan with stock, honey, rosemary and thyme. Bring to boil.

2. Reduce heat and cook gently for about 30 minutes, or until garlic is very tender and liquid has almost disappeared.

3. In food processor or blender, puree garlic with any juices. Blend in vinegar, oil, pepper, salt and yogurt cheese. Taste and adjust seasonings if necessary.

MAYONNAISE SAUCES

Mayonnaise sauces are very popular and delicious. Although you can use commercial, low-fat mayonnaise as a base, I prefer to substitute low-fat, soft yogurt cheese and use a little, regular mayonnaise to flavour it.

Mayonnaise can be flavoured with garlic puree (see recipe), roasted red peppers (page 154), pesto (page 45), mustards and salsas (see index).

PER TBSP (15 mL)

Calories	37
g carbohydrate	3
g fibre	trace
g total fat	2
g saturated fat	trace
g protein	2
mg cholesterol	1
mg sodium	11
mg potassium	71

CITRUS VINAIGRETTE

Not only is this good on salad greens, it adds glamour to poached or baked salmon or chicken.

Makes about 1 cup/250 mL

1	small clove garlic, minced	1
1 tsp	minced fresh ginger root	5 mL
1 tbsp	honey	15 mL
2 tbsp	lemon juice	25 mL
2 tbsp	grapefruit juice	25 mL
¼ cup	orange juice	50 mL
2 tbsp	rice vinegar	25 mL
	Salt to taste	
2 tbsp	olive oil	25 mL
1 tsp	sesame oil	5 mL
2 tbsp	chopped fresh cilantro or parsley	25 mL
2 tbsp	chopped fresh basil or parsley	25 mL
2 tbsp	chopped fresh chives or green onions	25 mL
dash	hot red pepper sauce, optional	dash

1. Whisk together garlic, ginger, honey, lemon juice, grapefruit juice, orange juice, rice vinegar and salt.

2. Whisk in olive oil and sesame oil. Add cilantro, basil, chives and hot pepper sauce. Taste and adjust seasonings if necessary.

VINAIGRETTES

Vinaigrettes are sauces based on vinegar-and-oil combinations. They used to be reserved for salads but are now often used on fish or meat. The proportion of oil to vinegar in traditional salad dressings used to be extremely high, but now we know that if a good-quality, sweet-tasting vinegar is used, you can actually use much less oil. Therefore the oil and vinegar that you choose are equally important.

PER TBSP (15 mL)

Calories	25
g carbohydrate	2
g fibre	trace
g total fat	2
g saturated fat	trace
g protein	trace
mg cholesterol	0
mg sodium	1
mg potassium	21

SESAME GINGER DRESSING

This dressing explodes with the taste of fresh herbs. The small amount of sesame oil adds an exotic, mysterious flavour but only a minimal amount of fat. Buy it at Asian markets and keep refrigerated after opening.

This dressing is good on mixed lettuces, grains and chicken or salmon salads. Or try it with the Chopped Grilled Chicken Salad (page 88) instead of the dressing suggested there.

Makes about ²/₃ cup/150 mL

2	cloves garlic, minced	2
1 tbsp	minced fresh ginger root	15 mL
¼ tsp	hot red pepper sauce, optional	1 mL
2 tsp	honey-style mustard	10 mL
2 tsp	honey	10 mL
2 tbsp	lemon juice	25 mL
2 tbsp	balsamic vinegar	25 mL
1 tbsp	soy sauce	15 mL
¼ cup	orange juice	50 mL
1 tsp	sesame oil	5 mL
1 tbsp	olive oil	15 mL
¼ cup	chopped fresh cilantro or parsley	50 mL
¼ cup	chopped fresh chives or green onions	50 mL

1. Whisk together garlic, ginger, hot pepper sauce, mustard, honey, lemon juice, vinegar, soy sauce, orange juice, sesame oil and olive oil.

2. Stir in cilantro and chives. Taste and adjust seasonings if necessary.

REDUCING OIL IN SALAD DRESSINGS

There are many ways to reduce the harsh taste of vinegar so that you can cut back on the oil in a dressing:

- Use mild vinegars like balsamic, raspberry, rice and sherry.
- Use olive oil (other salad oils are unflavoured; a small amount of flavourful olive oil goes a long way).
- Use a puree of vegetables, orange juice, buttermilk, yogurt or soft yogurt cheese (page 228) instead of some of the oil.
- Use fresh herbs and spices.

PER TBSP (15 mL)

Calories	29
g carbohydrate	3
g fibre	trace
g total fat	2
g saturated fat	trace
g protein	trace
mg cholesterol	0
mg sodium	79
mg potassium	37

ROASTED RED PEPPER DRESSING

The pureed red pepper gives a thick texture to the dressing, roasting the pepper adds a special earthy taste, and the balsamic vinegar adds a tart sweetness. This dressing is particularly good on pasta salads, grain salads and chunky vegetable salads. You can also use it as a sauce on plain grilled fish, chicken, lamb or steak.

When the dressing is refrigerated it gels slightly; add a little more water before serving, if necessary.

Makes about ³/₄ cup / 175 mL

1	sweet red pepper	1
1	clove garlic, minced	1
¼ cup	balsamic vinegar	50 mL
½ tsp	pepper	2 mL
	Salt to taste	
2 tbsp	chopped fresh basil or fresh parsley	25 mL
1 tbsp	olive oil	15 mL
2 tbsp	water	25 mL

1. Cut red pepper in half and discard core and seeds. Arrange halves on baking sheet, cut sides down. Grill under preheated broiler until blackened and blistered. Cool completely. Remove skin and brush off any charred bits.

2. In food processor or blender, puree red pepper with garlic.

3. Blend in vinegar, pepper, salt, basil and oil. Whisk in water. Taste and adjust seasonings if necessary.

THAI DIP OR DRESSING

Combine 2 tbsp/25 mL Thai fish sauce, 1 tbsp/15 mL granulated sugar, 1 tbsp/15 mL lemon juice, 1 tbsp/15 mL rice vinegar, 1 tbsp/15 mL water, 1 small minced clove garlic and ½ tsp/2 mL hot chili paste.

Makes about ¹/₃ cup/75 mL.

PONZU DIP OR DRESSING

Combine 2 tbsp/25 mL soy sauce, 2 tbsp/25 mL rice wine and 2 tbsp/25 mL lime juice.

Makes about ¹/₃ cup/75 mL.

PER TBSP (15 mL)

Calories	14
g carbohydrate	1
g fibre	trace
g total fat	1
g saturated fat	trace
g protein	trace
mg cholesterol	0
mg sodium	0
mg potassium	25

Black Bean Chèvre Quesadillas
(page 120)

Asian Tuna Burgers *(page 145)*
Herb Barbecued Corn on the Cob *(page 210)*
Asian Coleslaw *(page 77)*

PASTAS

Pasta with Red Peppers and Eggplant

Penne Arrabbiata

Penne with Potatoes and Rapini

Spaghetti Puttanesca

Mark's Spaghetti with Tomato Sauce

Spaghettini with Corn

Pasta with Tomatoes and Beans

Curried Tofu and Noodles

Pasta with Tomato Sauce and Ricotta

Noodles with Vegetables and Peanut Sauce

Linguine with Tomatoes and Scallops

Spaghettini with Clam Sauce

Pasta with Grilled Salmon and Stir-fried Vegetables

Linguine with Grilled Seafood and Pesto Tomato Sauce

Rigatoni with Tuna, Peppers and Tomato Sauce

Spaghetti with Meatballs

PASTA WITH RED PEPPERS AND EGGPLANT

Eggplant has a very "meaty" texture when it is used in this dish, and it gives the sauce body. The sauce can be made ahead of time and reheated, but cook the pasta just before serving.

Makes 6 servings

1 lb	eggplant	500 g
1 tbsp	olive oil	15 mL
1	red onion, chopped	1
3	cloves garlic, finely chopped	3
¼ tsp	hot red pepper flakes	1 mL
3	sweet red peppers, cut in 1½-inch/4 cm chunks	3
1	28-oz/796 mL tin plum tomatoes, with juices	1
	Salt to taste	
1 lb	rigatoni or other tube pasta	500 g
½ cup	grated Parmesan cheese	125 mL
¼ cup	chopped fresh basil or parsley	50 mL

1. Trim ends off eggplant and cut into ¼-inch/5 mm slices. Cut each slice into 1-inch/2.5 cm pieces.

2. Heat oil in large, deep non-stick skillet. Add onion, garlic and hot pepper flakes and cook gently until very tender and fragrant. Do not brown.

3. Add sweet red peppers and eggplant. Cook for 5 to 10 minutes, until wilted slightly.

4. Add tomatoes and break up with spoon. Cook for 10 to 15 minutes, until sauce reduces and thickens slightly. Add salt.

5. Bring large pot of water to boil. Add pasta and cook until tender but firm. Drain well and toss with sauce. Taste and adjust seasonings if necessary. Sprinkle with cheese and parsley. Toss well and serve immediately.

PER SERVING

Calories	429
g carbohydrate	77
g fibre	9
g total fat	7
g saturated fat	2
g protein	16

Excellent: vitamin A; vitamin C; niacin; vitamin B$_6$
Good: thiamine; calcium; iron; folacin

mg cholesterol	7
mg sodium	381
mg potassium	749

PENNE ARRABBIATA

This spicy pasta sauce (arrabbiata means angry) is easy and very quick to make. Use more or less of the hot pepper flakes, depending on how feisty you and your guests like your food.

Makes 6 servings

1 tbsp	olive oil	15 mL
4	cloves garlic, finely chopped	4
½ tsp	hot red pepper flakes (more or less to taste)	2 mL
1	28-oz/796 mL tin plum tomatoes, pureed with juices	1
½ tsp	pepper	2 mL
	Salt to taste	
⅓ cup	chopped fresh basil or parsley	75 mL
1 lb	penne or other tube pasta	500 g
½ cup	grated Parmesan cheese	125 mL

1. Heat oil in large, deep non-stick skillet. Add garlic and hot pepper flakes. Cook gently until fragrant, but do not brown.

2. Add tomatoes, pepper and salt and cook for 10 to 15 minutes, or until sauce is medium thick. Add half of basil. (Sauce can be made ahead to this point and reheated just before pasta is ready.)

3. Bring large pot of water to boil. Add pasta and cook until tender but firm. Drain well and place in large bowl. Pour sauce over top and sprinkle with remaining basil and cheese. Toss well. Taste and adjust seasonings if necessary. Serve immediately.

PER SERVING

Calories	370
g carbohydrate	63
g fibre	5
g total fat	7
g saturated fat	2
g protein	14

Good: niacin; calcium

mg cholesterol	7
mg sodium	376
mg potassium	390

PENNE WITH POTATOES AND RAPINI

Some of the most satisfying pasta dishes I know are made with vegetables. I particularly love this one, as I adore the slightly bitter taste of rapini. If you are not used to rapini, this is a great way to introduce it, as its unique flavour is softened a bit by all the pasta. If you can't find it, use broccoli.

Even if (like me) you do not like anchovies on their own, try them in this recipe. They add a richness and body to the sauce but they don't dominate. (Any leftover anchovies can be frozen.)

Makes 6 servings

1	baking potato, peeled and diced	1
1 lb	penne	500 g
1	large bunch rapini or broccoli, trimmed and chopped	1
3 tbsp	olive oil	45 mL
4	cloves garlic, finely chopped	4
4	anchovies, minced	4
¼ tsp	hot red pepper flakes	1 mL
½ tsp	pepper	2 mL

1. Bring large pot of water to boil. Add potato and cook for 5 minutes.

2. Add pasta to same pot and cook for 3 minutes.

3. Add rapini to pot with pasta and potatoes and continue to cook until pasta is tender but firm, about 6 to 10 minutes.

4. Meanwhile, place oil, garlic, anchovies and hot pepper flakes in non-stick skillet and heat gently. Add ½ cup/125 mL boiling pasta water. Cook gently for 3 to 5 minutes, or until pasta is ready.

5. Drain pasta and vegetables well. Toss with sauce and add pepper. Taste and adjust seasonings if necessary.

ANCHOVIES
Anchovies can be bought canned and packed in oil or dried and packed in salt. Rinse them before using and chop them finely so they add flavour without making a dish too fishy or salty.

PER SERVING

Calories	393
g carbohydrate	66
g fibre	5
g total fat	9
g saturated fat	1
g protein	13

Excellent: vitamin C; folacin
Good: niacin; vitamin B$_6$

mg cholesterol	2
mg sodium	120
mg potassium	394

SPAGHETTI PUTTANESCA

This dish is so quick to make that one of the rumours of its origins is that the ladies of the night in Rome could whip it up for dinner between clients.

Makes 6 to 8 servings

1 tbsp	olive oil	15 mL
4	cloves garlic, finely chopped	4
¼ tsp	hot red pepper flakes	1 mL
2	anchovies, minced, optional	2
1	28-oz/796 mL tin plum tomatoes, drained and chopped	1
¼ cup	black olives, halved	50 mL
2 tbsp	capers	25 mL
1 lb	spaghetti	500 g
¼ cup	grated Parmesan cheese, optional	50 mL
2 tbsp	chopped fresh parsley	25 mL

1. Heat oil in large, deep non-stick skillet. Add garlic and hot pepper flakes. Cook gently until fragrant, but do not brown.

2. Stir in anchovies and tomatoes. Bring to boil and cook for 5 minutes. Add olives and capers. Cook for 3 minutes longer.

3. Meanwhile, bring large pot of water to boil. Add spaghetti and cook until tender but firm. Drain well and toss with sauce, cheese and parsley. Taste and adjust seasonings if necessary.

COOKING PASTA

• Use a large pot and lots of water (at least 5 qt/5 L for every pound of pasta), so the noodles won't stick to the pot or each other.

• Do not add oil to the cooking water. It adds unnecessary fat as well as preventing the pasta from absorbing the sauce properly. Although salt does season the pasta, you do not need to add it.

• Do not rinse pasta; rinsing removes the outside starch that helps the sauce cling to the noodles.

Any exceptions to these rules are specified within recipes.

PER SERVING

Calories	327
g carbohydrate	61
g fibre	4
g total fat	4
g saturated fat	1
g protein	11

Good: niacin

mg cholesterol	0
mg sodium	245
mg potassium	278

MARK'S SPAGHETTI WITH TOMATO SAUCE

My son, Mark, loves pasta, but only with an absolutely "basic" sauce. On the other hand, he does have a great palate, so this is the sauce I make for him.

When I serve this I let everyone add their own grated cheese, chopped parsley and a pinch of hot pepper flakes if they wish. The sauce can be made ahead and reheated; it can also be frozen. (I often freeze it in ice cube trays; two cubes make a perfect child-sized portion.)

You can also add leftover cooked chicken or vegetables to the sauce.

Makes 6 servings

1	28-oz/796 mL tin plum tomatoes, pureed with juices	1
1	small onion, peeled and halved	1
2	cloves garlic, smashed and peeled but left whole	2
1 tbsp	olive oil	15 mL
¼ tsp	pepper, optional	1 mL
	Salt to taste	
1 lb	spaghetti	500 g
¼ cup	grated Parmesan cheese	50 mL
2 tbsp	chopped fresh basil or parsley	25 mL
pinch	hot red pepper flakes, optional	pinch

1. Place tomatoes, onion halves, garlic cloves and oil in medium saucepan. Bring to boil, reduce heat and simmer gently for 10 to 20 minutes, uncovered, or until sauce has cooked down and is medium thick.

2. Remove and discard onion and garlic. Add pepper and salt.

3. Bring large pot of water to boil. Add spaghetti and cook until tender but firm. Drain well and toss with sauce. Taste and adjust seasonings if necessary. Serve and allow everyone to top pasta with cheese, basil and hot pepper flakes, if they wish.

CHEESE
You can buy some good-tasting lower-fat cheeses now, but some are quite rubbery, without much flavour. In this book I call for lower-fat cheese whenever possible, but taste the cheese first and decide whether you like it. If you cannot find a good-tasting lower-fat cheese, use half the amount of regular cheese.

PER SERVING

Calories	352
g carbohydrate	64
g fibre	5
g total fat	5
g saturated fat	1
g protein	13

Good: niacin

mg cholesterol	3
mg sodium	298
mg potassium	387

SPAGHETTINI WITH CORN

Pasta with corn and vegetables is a delicious idea from my cousin Barbara Glickman, who is always on the lookout for great low-fat, high-flavour recipes! You can sprinkle each serving with a little grated Parmesan cheese, although I prefer this dish without it.

Makes 6 to 8 servings

1 tbsp	olive oil	15 mL
3	cloves garlic, finely chopped	3
1	leek, trimmed and thinly sliced	1
1	small jalapeño, seeded and diced	1
1	sweet red pepper, diced	1
4 cups	fresh or frozen corn niblets	1 L
1 cup	fresh or frozen peas	250 mL
1/3 cup	homemade chicken stock (page 59) or water	75 mL
2 cups	chopped fresh spinach	500 mL
1/2 tsp	pepper	2 mL
	Salt to taste	
1 lb	spaghettini or spaghetti	500 g
1/4 cup	chopped fresh cilantro or parsley	50 mL
2 tbsp	chopped fresh chives or green onions	25 mL
2 tbsp	chopped fresh basil or parsley	25 mL

1. Heat olive oil in large, deep non-stick skillet. Add garlic and leek and cook gently for a few minutes, until tender and fragrant. Add jalapeño and red pepper and cook for 2 minutes.

2. Add corn and peas and combine well. Add stock, spinach, pepper and salt. Bring to boil and cook for 2 to 3 minutes, until corn is barely cooked and spinach wilts.

3. Meanwhile, bring large pot of water to boil. Add spaghettini and cook until tender but firm. Drain well and combine with sauce, cilantro, chives and basil. Taste and adjust seasonings if necessary.

PER SERVING

Calories	424
g carbohydrate	85
g fibre	8
g total fat	4
g saturated fat	1
g protein	15

Excellent: vitamin A; vitamin C; niacin; folacin
Good: thiamine; iron; vitamin B$_6$

mg cholesterol	0
mg sodium	44
mg potassium	421

PASTA WITH TOMATOES AND BEANS

I developed this recipe for a healthful, economical cooking class for Second Harvest (Toronto's food recovery program).

You can use dried beans instead of canned. Soak 1 cup/250 mL dried white kidney beans in lots of water for a few hours at room temperature or overnight in the refrigerator. Drain. Cover with water and cook for 1 hour, or until tender. Rinse and drain before using. This sauce can be frozen.

Makes 6 servings

1 tbsp	olive oil	15 mL
1	onion, chopped	1
3	cloves garlic, finely chopped	3
¼ tsp	hot red pepper flakes	1 mL
1	carrot, chopped	1
1	28-oz/796 mL tin plum tomatoes, broken up or pureed with juices	1
1	19-oz/540 mL tin white kidney beans, rinsed and drained, or 2 cups/500 mL cooked beans	1
½ tsp	pepper	2 mL
	Salt to taste	
1 lb	penne or other tube pasta	500 g
¼ cup	grated Parmesan cheese	50 mL
2 tbsp	chopped fresh parsley	25 mL

1. Heat oil in large, deep non-stick skillet. Add onion, garlic and hot pepper flakes. Cook gently until tender and fragrant, but do not brown.

2. Add carrot and cook for 5 minutes.

3. Add tomatoes and bring to boil. Lower heat and cook for 8 to 10 minutes, or until thickened, stirring occasionally to prevent burning and sticking.

4. Add beans and cook for 10 minutes longer. Add pepper and salt. (The sauce can be made ahead to this point.)

5. Bring large pot of water to boil. Add pasta and cook until tender but firm. Drain well and toss with sauce, cheese and parsley. Taste and adjust seasonings if necessary.

PASTA SHAPES

Different pasta shapes work better with different sauces. Chunky sauces are usually served with large macaroni-type pastas like penne or rigatoni, or with shells or bows, so that you get pasta and chunks of sauce with every forkful. Generally, if the sauce is pureed or has small bits in it, you can use long pasta because the sauce and small pieces will cling even when you twirl the noodles. Tiny pasta is used in soups so you can spoon it up easily.

PER SERVING

Calories	436
g carbohydrate	79
g fibre	11
g total fat	6
g saturated fat	1
g protein	18

Excellent: vitamin A; niacin; folacin
Good: iron; vitamin B$_6$

mg cholesterol	3
mg sodium	513
mg potassium	588

CURRIED TOFU AND NOODLES

This is my version of actress Judy McLane's recipe. She told me about it when I was doing a story on how the performers in the musical "Joseph and the Amazing Technicolor Dreamcoat" kept up their energy. The dish is wonderful, although I can't guarantee that you'll be able to dance in a musical after you've eaten it!

If you cannot find extra-firm tofu, use regular tofu and press for about 30 minutes before dicing (page 118).

Makes 6 servings

1 tbsp	olive oil	15 mL
3	cloves garlic, finely chopped	3
1	small onion, finely chopped	1
1 tbsp	finely chopped fresh ginger root	15 mL
½ tsp	ground cumin	2 mL
½ tsp	dry mustard	2 mL
½ tsp	pepper	2 mL
½ tsp	cayenne	2 mL
½ lb	extra-firm tofu, diced	250 g
2 cups	fresh or frozen peas	500 mL
1 cup	fresh or frozen corn niblets	250 mL
1	large carrot, grated	1
1 lb	medium pasta shells or spirals	500 g

1. Heat oil in large, deep non-stick skillet or wok. Add garlic, onion, ginger, cumin, mustard, pepper and cayenne. Cook gently for a few minutes, but do not brown.

2. Add tofu, peas, corn and carrot. Cook for a few minutes until thoroughly heated and vegetables are just cooked.

3. Meanwhile, bring large pot of water to boil. Add pasta and cook until tender but firm. Drain well and combine with tofu mixture. Taste and adjust seasonings if necessary.

PER SERVING

Calories	408
g carbohydrate	73
g fibre	8
g total fat	5
g saturated fat	1
g protein	19

Excellent: vitamin A
Good: thiamine; niacin; iron; folacin

mg cholesterol	0
mg sodium	50
mg potassium	312

PASTA WITH TOMATO SAUCE AND RICOTTA

The tomato sauce can be made ahead of time, but cook the pasta and toss with the sauce and ricotta just before serving. Although bacon and pancetta (unsmoked Italian bacon) are both high in fat, a small amount adds a unique flavour. You can find pancetta at Italian grocery stores (this dish is also delicious without it).

Makes 6 servings

1 tbsp	olive oil	15 mL
1 oz	pancetta or bacon, diced, optional	30 g
1	onion, chopped	1
2	cloves garlic, finely chopped	2
¼ tsp	hot red pepper flakes	1 mL
1	28-oz/796 mL tin plum tomatoes, pureed with juices	1
½ tsp	pepper	2 mL
	Salt to taste	
1 lb	pasta spirals or penne	500 g
½ lb	light ricotta or low-fat pressed cottage cheese, drained	250 g
¼ cup	grated Parmesan cheese	50 mL
¼ cup	chopped fresh basil or parsley	50 mL

1. Heat oil in large, deep non-stick skillet. Add pancetta and cook until crisp. Remove all but 2 tbsp/25 mL fat from pan.

2. Add onion, garlic and hot pepper flakes. Cook gently for about 5 minutes, but do not brown.

3. Add tomatoes and cook until sauce is reduced and thickened. Add pepper and salt.

4. Meanwhile, bring large pot of water to boil. Add pasta and cook until tender but firm. Drain well and toss with sauce. Top with ricotta, Parmesan and basil. Taste and adjust seasonings if necessary. Toss well before serving.

PER SERVING

Calories	398
g carbohydrate	66
g fibre	5
g total fat	7
g saturated fat	3
g protein	17

Good: niacin; calcium; iron

mg cholesterol	15
mg sodium	346
mg potassium	450

NOODLES WITH VEGETABLES AND PEANUT SAUCE

This unusual dish is always a big hit in my vegetarian classes.

Makes 8 servings

3 tbsp	peanut butter	45 mL
1 tbsp	hoisin sauce	15 mL
2 tbsp	soy sauce	25 mL
2 tbsp	lemon juice or rice vinegar	25 mL
1 tbsp	honey	15 mL
2 tsp	sesame oil	10 mL
1 tsp	hot chili paste	5 mL
¼ cup	warm water	50 mL
2 tsp	vegetable oil	10 mL
3	cloves garlic, finely chopped	3
1 tbsp	chopped fresh ginger root	15 mL
3	green onions, chopped	3
¼ lb	fresh shiitake mushrooms or button mushrooms, sliced	125 g
1	sweet red pepper, sliced	1
1 lb	spaghetti	500 g
1	bunch broccoli, trimmed and cut in florets	1
2	carrots, thinly sliced	2
⅓ cup	chopped fresh cilantro or parsley	75 mL
⅓ cup	chopped fresh basil	75 mL

1. Blend together peanut butter, hoisin sauce, soy sauce, lemon juice, honey, sesame oil, chili paste and water. Reserve.

2. Heat vegetable oil in wok or large skillet. Add garlic, ginger and green onions. Cook gently for 1 to 2 minutes, until very fragrant. Add mushrooms and red pepper and cook until tender. Add peanut butter mixture and heat for 1 minute. Reserve.

3. Meanwhile, bring large pot of water to boil. Add spaghetti and cook for 5 minutes. Add broccoli and carrots and cook for 5 minutes longer. Drain.

4. Combine sauce with spaghetti and vegetables. Toss with cilantro and basil. Taste and adjust seasonings if necessary.

SOY SAUCE

Soy sauce is made from fermented soy beans and wheat. I usually use Kikkoman or imported Chinese soy sauce. I don't really like low-sodium soy sauce and would rather dilute regular soy sauce with water. Chinese cooking expert Nina Simonds prefers to use less real soy sauce in a recipe and replace the lost flavour by increasing the amounts of other Asian seasonings like ginger, garlic and green onions.

PER SERVING

Calories	318
g carbohydrate	55
g fibre	5
g total fat	7
g saturated fat	1
g protein	12

Excellent: vitamin A; vitamin C; folacin
Good: niacin; vitamin B$_6$

mg cholesterol	0
mg sodium	311
mg potassium	422

LINGUINE WITH TOMATOES AND SCALLOPS

If you do not like things too spicy, reduce the pickled peppers in this recipe. It is hard to tell how hot the peppers are before you use them, so err on the side of caution, as you can always add more at the end. (If you puree the sauce, it will be hotter than if you leave it chunky.)

This sauce can be prepared ahead and reheated quickly just before serving.

Makes 6 servings

1 tbsp	olive oil	15 mL
1	large onion, chopped	1
3	cloves garlic, finely chopped	3
1	28-oz/796 mL tin plum tomatoes, with juices	1
2 tbsp	chopped pickled hot peppers (more or less to taste)	25 mL
1	sweet red pepper, cut in 1-inch/ 2.5 cm pieces	1
¼ tsp	pepper	1 mL
	Salt to taste	
¾ lb	scallops	375 g
1 lb	linguine	500 g
2 tbsp	chopped fresh basil or parsley	25 mL

1. Heat oil in large, deep non-stick skillet or Dutch oven. Add onion and garlic and cook gently until tender and fragrant, but do not brown.

2. Add tomatoes, breaking them up with spoon. Add pickled peppers, sweet red pepper, pepper and salt. Cook for 10 minutes, or until sauce is quite thick and any liquid has evaporated. Puree sauce if desired.

3. Add scallops to sauce and cook for 3 minutes. Remove from heat and reserve. Reheat when pasta is cooked.

4. Meanwhile, bring large pot of water to boil. Add linguine and cook until tender but firm. Drain well and toss with sauce and basil. Taste and adjust seasonings if necessary.

FRESH VERSUS DRIED PASTA

Basically there are three types of pasta. There is delicious, fresh homemade pasta that is cooked and eaten right after being made. There is the so-called "fresh" pasta from the pasta shops and supermarkets, but that is usually premade and often refrigerated or frozen. It is generally thick and/or coated with semolina flour. Finally, there is dry, commercial pasta which I think is great both in flavour and convenience. Although domestic-made dry pastas are fine when perfectly cooked, I actually prefer the dry pasta imported from Italy as it has a better texture and does not overcook as easily. All the recipes in this book use dry, commercial pasta.

PER SERVING

Calories	396
g carbohydrate	68
g fibre	5
g total fat	5
g saturated fat	1
g protein	21

Excellent: vitamin C; niacin; vitamin B$_{12}$
Good: vitamin A; iron; vitamin B$_6$; folacin

mg cholesterol	19
mg sodium	360
mg potassium	626

SPAGHETTINI WITH CLAM SAUCE

This is the perfect instant dinner dish. It is quick to cook, uses things you usually have on hand, and tastes so good that everyone thinks you have spent hours preparing it.

You can also use fresh clams in this recipe. Buy 1 pint/ 500 mL shucked clams and strain the juices (they are usually sandy) before adding them to the sauce.

You could also add one 28-oz/796 mL tin of pureed plum tomatoes to the sauce. Add the tomatoes with the stock and reduce until thick before adding the clams.

Makes 6 to 8 servings

1 tbsp	olive oil	15 mL
4	cloves garlic, finely chopped	4
¼ tsp	hot red pepper flakes	1 mL
2	5-oz/142 g tins baby clams, with juices	2
2 tbsp	chopped fresh parsley	25 mL
⅓ cup	dry white wine or chicken stock	75 mL
½ tsp	pepper	2 mL
1 lb	spaghettini	500 g
½ cup	fresh breadcrumbs, toasted	125 mL
¼ cup	chopped fresh basil or parsley	50 mL

1. Heat oil in large, deep non-stick skillet. Add garlic and hot pepper flakes. Cook gently for a few minutes, but do not brown.

2. Drain clams and reserve ⅓ cup/75 mL clam juice. Add parsley, wine and clam juice to skillet. Bring to boil and reduce slightly.

3. Add clams and pepper to skillet. Remove from heat and reserve.

4. Meanwhile, bring large pot of water to boil. Add spaghettini and cook until tender but firm.

5. Just before pasta is ready, reheat sauce. Drain pasta well and toss with sauce, breadcrumbs and basil. Taste and adjust seasonings if necessary.

PER SERVING

Calories	350
g carbohydrate	60
g fibre	3
g total fat	4
g saturated fat	1
g protein	16

Excellent: iron
Good: niacin

mg cholesterol	15
mg sodium	75
mg potassium	255

PASTA WITH GRILLED SALMON AND STIR-FRIED VEGETABLES

See cover photo.

This makes an unusual and elegant main course. If you cannot barbecue the salmon, simply broil it, cook it in a non-stick skillet, or roast it (page 139).

Makes 6 servings

1 lb	salmon fillet, skin removed, cut in 6 pieces	500 g
1 tbsp	honey	15 mL
1 tsp	sesame oil	5 mL
½ tsp	hot chili paste	2 mL

Sauce:

1 tbsp	olive oil	15 mL
3	cloves garlic, finely chopped	3
2 tbsp	finely chopped fresh ginger root	25 mL
¼ tsp	hot red pepper flakes	1 mL
2	leeks or small onions, trimmed and cut in 1-inch/2.5 pieces	2
1	carrot, thinly sliced on diagonal	1
1	sweet red pepper, cut in 1-inch/ 2.5 cm pieces	1
1	bunch bok choy, spinach or Swiss chard, chopped	1
¼ cup	rice vinegar	50 mL
1 tbsp	sesame oil	15 mL
1 tbsp	honey	15 mL
½ tsp	pepper	2 mL
	Salt to taste	
1 lb	penne or other tube pasta	500 g
6	green onions, cut in 1-inch/ 2.5 cm pieces	6
¼ cup	chopped fresh cilantro or parsley	50 mL

IS YOUR PASTA READY?

To tell when pasta is ready, taste it; if it does not have an uncooked centre core, it is ready. (People say that you can tell whether pasta is done by throwing it against a wall, but this is not a good plan. The pasta will stick to the wall both before and after it is ready, and if you don't get it off the wall quickly, it will dry and the paint will come off with it. Finally, if your children see you do this, your walls will never be the same again!)

1. Pat salmon dry. In small bowl, combine 1 tbsp/15 mL honey, 1 tsp/5 mL sesame oil and chili paste. Rub into salmon.

2. For sauce, heat olive oil in large, deep non-stick skillet or wok. Add garlic, ginger and hot pepper flakes. Cook gently until fragrant, but do not brown.

3. Add leeks and carrot. Cook, stirring constantly, for 5 minutes. If mixture looks dry, add ¼ cup/50 mL water.

4. Add pepper and bok choy. Cook for 5 minutes, or until just wilted. Add vinegar, 1 tbsp/15 mL sesame oil, 1 tbsp/15 mL honey, pepper and salt. Cook for another 5 minutes.

5. Preheat broiler, barbecue or non-stick skillet. Cook salmon for 3 to 5 minutes per side, or until just cooked through.

6. Meanwhile, bring large pot of water to boil. Add pasta and cook until tender but firm. Drain well.

7. Add green onions to sauce and heat if necessary. Toss drained pasta with sauce. Add cilantro. Taste and adjust seasonings if necessary. Serve pasta and top each serving with salmon.

PER SERVING

Calories	501
g carbohydrate	74
g fibre	7
g total fat	12
g saturated fat	2
g protein	27

Excellent: vitamin A; vitamin C; niacin; riboflavin; iron; vitamin B_6; folacin; vitamin B_{12}
Good: thiamine; calcium

mg cholesterol	38
mg sodium	104
mg potassium	1162

LINGUINE WITH GRILLED SEAFOOD AND PESTO TOMATO SAUCE

This dish is so flavourful that every bite tastes like a burst of spring. If you do not want to use shellfish, use fresh swordfish, halibut, salmon or tuna. The tomato sauce and the pesto sauce can be made ahead, but cook the pasta at the last moment and then combine.

Makes 6 servings

½ lb	cleaned large shrimp	250 g
½ lb	scallops	250 g
2 tbsp	olive oil, divided	25 mL
½ cup	pesto (page 45)	125 mL
3	cloves garlic, finely chopped	3
1	onion, chopped	1
pinch	hot red pepper flakes	pinch
1	28-oz/796 mL tin plum tomatoes, with juices	1
1 lb	linguine	500 g

1. Pat shrimp and scallops dry. Butterfly shrimp, cutting them in two pieces. Cut each scallop into two rounds.

2. In large bowl, combine seafood with 1 tbsp/15 mL oil and large spoonful pesto. Reserve.

3. Heat remaining 1 tbsp/15 mL oil in large, deep non-stick skillet or Dutch oven. Add garlic, onion and hot pepper flakes and cook gently for a few minutes without browning. Add tomatoes and bring to boil. Cook gently until thickened, breaking up tomatoes as you stir. Puree sauce at this point if desired. Reserve.

4. Preheat broiler or barbecue and grill seafood. Add seafood to tomato sauce and reheat gently. Do not overcook. (Seafood can also be cooked directly in sauce.)

5. Meanwhile, bring large pot of water to boil. Add linguine and cook until tender but firm. Drain pasta well. Toss with sauce. Taste and adjust seasonings if necessary. Top each serving with spoonful of pesto.

PER SERVING

Calories	444
g carbohydrate	67
g fibre	5
g total fat	8
g saturated fat	1
g protein	26

Excellent: niacin; vitamin B_{12}
Good: iron; vitamin B_6; folacin

mg cholesterol	70
mg sodium	375
mg potassium	625

RIGATONI WITH TUNA, PEPPERS AND TOMATO SAUCE

This is a great way to use canned tuna. If this (or any other) sauce is too watery, add croutons or toasted breadcrumbs to the dish before serving. They will absorb moisture and disappear in the sauce.

Makes 6 servings

1 tbsp	olive oil	15 mL
3	cloves garlic, finely chopped	3
¼ tsp	hot red pepper flakes	1 mL
2	sweet red peppers, preferably roasted (page 154), peeled and diced	2
1	28-oz/796 mL tin plum tomatoes, pureed with juices	1
1	7-oz/198 g tin white tuna (water-packed), drained and flaked	1
2 tbsp	chopped black olives	25 mL
1 tbsp	capers	15 mL
2 tbsp	balsamic vinegar	25 mL
½ tsp	pepper	2 mL
	Salt to taste	
1 lb	rigatoni or other tube pasta	500 g
1 cup	homemade croutons (page 60)	250 mL
¼ cup	chopped fresh parsley	50 mL

1. Heat oil in large, deep non-stick skillet. Add garlic and hot pepper flakes and cook gently until fragrant, but do not brown.

2. Add sweet peppers, tomatoes and tuna. Cook for 8 to 10 minutes, or until thickened. Add olives, capers, vinegar, pepper and salt.

3. Meanwhile, bring large pot of water to boil. Add pasta and cook until tender but firm. Drain well and toss with sauce and croutons. Taste and adjust seasonings if necessary. Sprinkle with parsley.

CAPERS

Capers are the buds of the caper plant, which grows in the Mediterranean, usually near water. For some reason, many people think capers are "fishy," perhaps because they are often served with fish. They have a piquant flavour that cuts the richness of things like smoked salmon. They come packed either in vinegar or salt, and in both cases should be rinsed well before using. I prefer to use small capers.

PER SERVING

Calories	414
g carbohydrate	72
g fibre	6
g total fat	5
g saturated fat	1
g protein	19

Excellent: vitamin C; niacin; vitamin B$_{12}$
Good: vitamin A; iron; vitamin B$_6$; folacin

mg cholesterol	11
mg sodium	434
mg potassium	536

SPAGHETTI WITH MEATBALLS

This old-fashioned recipe is always a favourite. Kids love it, because the meatballs are little and cute.
You can use ground turkey or chicken in place of the beef.

Makes 6 to 8 servings

½ lb	extra-lean ground beef	250 g
1	egg	1
½ cup	breadcrumbs	125 mL
½ tsp	salt	2 mL
¼ tsp	pepper	1 mL
1 tbsp	olive oil	15 mL
1	onion, chopped	1
2	cloves garlic, finely chopped	2
1	carrot, diced	1
1	stalk celery, diced	1
1	28-oz/796 mL tin plum tomatoes, with juices	1
1 lb	spaghetti	500 g
¼ cup	grated Parmesan cheese	50 mL
2 tbsp	chopped fresh basil or parsley	25 mL

1. Combine ground beef with egg, breadcrumbs, salt and pepper. Form mixture into about 24 small meatballs. Place on waxed paper-lined baking sheet and reserve.

2. In large, deep non-stick skillet or Dutch oven, heat oil. Add onion, garlic, carrot and celery. Cook gently for about 10 minutes.

3. Add tomatoes, breaking them up with spoon. Cook over medium heat until thickened, about 10 minutes.

4. Add meatballs to boiling sauce. Cover, reduce heat and cook gently for 20 to 25 minutes, until meatballs are cooked through. Stir occasionally. (Add a little water or tomato juice at any time if mixture seems dry.) Taste and adjust seasonings if necessary.

5. Meanwhile, bring large pot of water to boil. Add spaghetti and cook until tender but firm. Drain well and combine with sauce. Sprinkle with cheese and basil. Serve immediately.

PER SERVING

Calories	450
g carbohydrate	68
g fibre	5
g total fat	10
g saturated fat	3
g protein	22

Excellent: vitamin A; niacin; vitamin B_{12}
Good: iron; vitamin B_6; folacin

mg cholesterol	59
mg sodium	558
mg potassium	563

MEATLESS MAIN COURSES

Vegetable Paella

Vegetarian Muffuletta

Stir-fried Tofu with Vegetables

Black Bean Chèvre Quesadillas

Mixed Bean Chili

Baked Polenta Casserole

Sweet and Sour Vegetable Stew

"Cassoulet" of Onions

Springtime Stir-fried Rice and Vegetables

Quickbread Pizza

Falafel Vegetable Burgers

Potato and Broccoli Egg White Frittata

Ribollita

Grilled Tofu Kebabs

VEGETABLE PAELLA

Although paella is traditionally made with morsels of chicken, sausage and seafood, it is equally delicious and beautiful-looking made with vegetables. When you drain the tomatoes, reserve the liquid and use it in soups or sauces.

You can add one 19-oz/540 mL tin of chickpeas to this if you wish.

Makes 8 servings

1 tbsp	olive oil	15 mL
2	onions, diced	2
2	cloves garlic, finely chopped	2
2	carrots, diced	2
1	large bulb fennel or celery, trimmed and cut in chunks	1
1	sweet red pepper, cut in chunks	1
¼ lb	mushrooms, quartered	125 g
1	28-oz/796 mL tin plum tomatoes, drained and chopped	1
2 cups	uncooked rice	500 mL
pinch	crushed saffron or turmeric, optional	pinch
¼ tsp	pepper	1 mL
	Salt to taste	
3 cups	homemade vegetable stock (page 62) or water, hot	750 mL
1 cup	fresh or frozen corn niblets	250 mL
1 cup	fresh or frozen peas	250 mL
¼ lb	snow peas, trimmed	125 g

1. Heat oil in large casserole or Dutch oven. Add onions and garlic and cook gently for 5 minutes.

2. Add carrots, fennel, red pepper and mushrooms. Cook for about 5 minutes. Add ¼ cup/50 mL water at any time if pan seems dry. Stir in tomatoes and rice. Cook for a few minutes.

3. Add saffron, pepper and salt to hot stock. Add stock to rice and bring to boil. Cover and cook gently for 20 minutes, or until rice is cooked. (You can also bake dish for 35 to 40 minutes in preheated 350°F/180°C oven.)

4. Sprinkle top of rice with corn, peas and snow peas. Cover and cook or bake for 5 to 8 minutes. Toss gently and serve.

See photo opposite page 64.

FENNEL

Fennel has a texture like celery and a sweet, delicate, anise/licorice flavour. The licorice taste is usually more pronounced when the fennel is raw, but very mild when it is cooked. Use the bulb part only, as the stalks tend to be stringy and tough. The dill-like leaves can be used for garnish or seasoning. Uncooked, fennel can be served in salads, as part of a vegetable tray with dips or even on a fruit platter for dessert. And fennel is great cooked in soups, pasta sauces and vegetable side dishes.

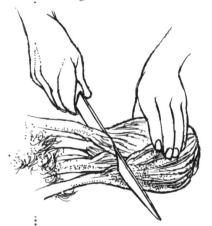

PER SERVING	
Calories	280
g carbohydrate	57
g fibre	4
g total fat	3
g saturated fat	trace
g protein	8

Excellent: vitamin A; vitamin C
Good: niacin; vitamin B$_6$; folacin

mg cholesterol	0
mg sodium	229
mg potassium	670

See photo opposite page 65.

VEGETARIAN MUFFULETTA

A muffuletta is a big sandwich that originated in New Orleans. It is usually filled with cold cuts, cheese and an olive-based salad and is delicious but high in fat. This version is also stacked with great things but has a much lower fat content. The sandwich can be served immediately, but it is a bit easier to cut if it is wrapped and refrigerated for at least one hour before slicing.

**LOWER-FAT
SANDWICH SPREADS**

- pesto (page 45)
- salsas (see index)
- yogurt cheese (page 228), plain or mixed with salsa or pesto
- salad dressings
- rouille (page 154)
- hummos (page 37)
- white bean spread (page 36)
- peanut sauce (page 86)
- eggplant spread (page 34)
- pureed roasted red peppers (page 154)
- cranberry orange sauce with ginger (page 182)
- chutney

Makes 8 servings

2	eggplants, about 1 lb/500 g each, cut in ¼-inch/5 mm slices	2
1	19-oz/540 mL tin chickpeas, rinsed and drained	1
2 tbsp	lemon juice	25 mL
1 tbsp	sesame oil	15 mL
1 tsp	ground cumin	5 mL
1	clove garlic, minced	1
½ tsp	salt	2 mL
½ tsp	pepper	2 mL
½ tsp	hot chili paste	2 mL
1	10-inch/25 cm round loaf Italian bread	1
1	sweet red pepper, roasted (page 154), peeled and cut in chunks	1
1	sweet yellow pepper, roasted, peeled and cut in chunks	1
1	bunch fresh arugula or watercress, trimmed	1
⅓ cup	pesto sauce (page 45)	75 mL

1. Preheat barbecue or broiler and grill eggplant until browned on both sides. Reserve.

2. Puree chickpeas, lemon juice, sesame oil, cumin, garlic, salt, pepper and chili paste. Taste and adjust seasonings and/or thin with water if necessary.

3. Cut bread in half horizontally and remove some of insides (save for breadcrumbs or croutons). Spread bottom half of bread with chickpea puree and layer on eggplant slices with roasted peppers and arugula. Spread top half of bread with pesto and place firmly on sandwich. Wrap tightly. Cut into wedges to serve.

PER SERVING

Calories	371
g carbohydrate	71
g fibre	7
g total fat	4
g saturated fat	1
g protein	13

Excellent: vitamin C; thiamine; niacin; iron; folacin
Good: vitamin A; vitamin B$_6$

mg cholesterol	1
mg sodium	772
mg potassium	610

STIR-FRIED TOFU WITH VEGETABLES

I enjoy tofu best when it's cooked with Asian seasonings. If you can't find extra-firm tofu, press regular tofu before using (see sidebar).

Serve this with steamed rice (page 50).

Makes 4 to 6 servings

Sauce:

½ cup	homemade vegetable stock (page 62) or water	125 mL
2 tbsp	soy sauce	25 mL
1 tbsp	frozen orange juice concentrate	15 mL
1 tbsp	rice wine or sake	15 mL
1 tbsp	granulated sugar	15 mL
2 tsp	grated orange peel, divided	10 mL
¼ tsp	pepper	1 mL
1 tbsp	cornstarch	15 mL
1 tsp	sesame oil	5 mL

To Cook:

1 tbsp	vegetable oil	15 mL
3	cloves garlic, finely chopped	3
1 tbsp	finely chopped fresh ginger root	15 mL
3	green onions, sliced	3
½ tsp	hot chili paste, optional	2 mL
1 tbsp	black bean sauce (page 156)	15 mL
1	onion, cut in eight pieces	1
1	stalk celery, sliced	1
¼ lb	mushrooms, sliced	125 g
1	sweet red pepper, diced	1
¼ lb	snow peas, trimmed	125 g
1 lb	extra-firm tofu, cut in 1½-inch/4 cm cubes	500 g

TOFU

Tofu, or bean curd, is curded soybean milk that has been pressed into custard-like cakes. Look for whole pieces covered with water and check the expiry date before buying. Keep the tofu in the refrigerator, and change the water once a day.

I like to buy the extra-firm tofu, but if you can't find it, wrap regular tofu in a tea towel and weigh it down for 30 minutes to press out any excess liquid.

PER SERVING

Calories	238
g carbohydrate	25
g fibre	7
g total fat	7
g saturated fat	1
g protein	20

Excellent: vitamin C; calcium
Good: folacin

mg cholesterol	0
mg sodium	442
mg potassium	587

1. Combine stock, soy sauce, orange juice concentrate, rice wine, sugar, 1 tsp/5 mL orange peel, pepper, cornstarch and sesame oil. Blend well and reserve.

2. Heat vegetable oil in wok or large non-stick skillet until very hot. Add garlic, ginger, green onions, remaining 1 tsp/5 mL orange peel, hot chili paste and black bean sauce. Stir-fry for 10 to 15 seconds, or until fragrant.

3. Add onion, celery, mushrooms and red pepper and toss lightly over high heat for 1 minute. Add snow peas. Stir-fry for 30 seconds.

4. Stir up sauce mixture and add to vegetables. Cook, stirring constantly, for about 45 seconds, or until thickened.

5. Pat tofu dry and add to vegetables. Toss gently and cook for a few minutes to heat and coat with sauce.

BLACK BEAN CHÈVRE QUESADILLAS

See photo opposite page 96.

You can cut these into wedges and serve them as appetizers. Or place wedges on top of a lightly dressed green salad with some tomato salsa (page 43), and serve as a main course.

These can be made ahead and reheated. (I like to barbecue them for extra flavour.) They can also be made open-faced and served like a pizza.

Makes 6 servings

1 cup	cooked black beans (page 68)	250 mL
1	tomato, chopped and drained	1
1	sweet red pepper, preferably roasted (page 154), peeled and chopped	1
1	chipotle or jalapeño, chopped, optional	1
1	clove garlic, minced	1
½ cup	chopped fresh cilantro or parsley	125 mL
2 tbsp	chopped fresh chives or green onions	25 mL
2 tbsp	chopped fresh basil	25 mL
1½ cups	grated light Monterey Jack or Cheddar cheese	375 mL
½ cup	crumbled chèvre (goat cheese) or feta cheese	125 mL
6	10-inch/25 cm flour tortillas or 8-inch/20 cm pita breads, split	6

1. Combine black beans, tomato, red pepper, chipotle, garlic, cilantro, chives, basil, Monterey Jack and chèvre.

2. Place tortillas on counter in single layer. Spread filling evenly over one half of each tortilla.

3. Fold unfilled half of tortilla over filled side and press together gently.

4. Preheat barbecue and grill quesadillas for 2 to 3 minutes per side until lightly browned. Or bake in single layer on baking sheet in preheated 400°F/200°C oven for 7 to 10 minutes. Or cook for a few minutes per side in non-stick skillet that has been very lightly brushed with vegetable oil.

TORTILLAS

I use two types of tortillas in this book — flour and corn. They are not always interchangeable, but both are delicious. I always keep them on hand in the freezer. Flour tortillas are widely available now and can be used raw or cooked. I use them for pizza crusts (page 127), fajitas (page 171), appetizer rollups (page 46) and quesadillas (see recipe). I even make grilled cheese sandwiches with them. I often use corn tortillas baked as chips (page 87) or warmed as a bread, but they can also be used as taco shells or made into tortilla baskets (page 121).

PER SERVING

Calories	340
g carbohydrate	43
g fibre	4
g total fat	11
g saturated fat	6
g protein	18

Excellent: vitamin C; calcium
Good: niacin; riboflavin; iron; folacin

mg cholesterol	27
mg sodium	546
mg potassium	285

MIXED BEAN CHILI

This is delicious made with only one type of bean, but my favourite is a combination of black turtle beans, white navy beans, white kidney beans and/or black-eyed peas. You can also use 4 cups/1 L cooked or canned beans instead of the dried.

I usually serve this plain or with steamed white or brown rice and a salad. Provide bowls of soft yogurt cheese (page 228) or thick yogurt, diced tomatoes, grated light Cheddar or Monterey Jack cheese, chopped cilantro or diced mild green chiles — and let guests add their own garnishes.

Makes 8 to 10 servings

2 cups	mixed dried beans	500 mL
1 tbsp	vegetable oil	15 mL
2	onions, chopped	2
4	cloves garlic, finely chopped	4
3 tbsp	chili powder	45 mL
1 tsp	ground cumin	5 mL
1 tsp	paprika	5 mL
1 tsp	dried oregano	5 mL
1	28-oz/796 mL tin plum tomatoes, pureed with juices	1
3	chipotles or jalapeños, diced	3
1 tbsp	adobo sauce from chipotles, optional	15 mL
½ tsp	pepper	2 mL
	Salt to taste	
2 tbsp	chopped fresh cilantro or parsley	25 mL

1. Cover beans generously with cold water and soak overnight in refrigerator. Drain beans well and place in large pot. Cover with water, bring to boil and cook gently for 30 minutes.

2. Meanwhile, heat oil in Dutch oven. Add onions and garlic and cook gently for 5 minutes until tender and fragrant. Add chili powder, cumin, paprika and oregano. Cook for about 30 seconds until well combined. Stir in tomatoes, chipotles and adobo sauce. Cook for 10 minutes.

3. Drain beans well and add to sauce mixture. Add water if necessary so that beans are covered by about 1 inch/2.5 cm liquid.

4. Cook, covered, for 1 to 2 hours, or until beans are tender and mixture is quite thick. (Uncover if necessary to reduce liquid.) Add pepper, salt and cilantro. Season to taste.

CANNED VS. DRIED BEANS

You can substitute canned beans for dried ones. Recipes will require less preparation and cooking time, but the texture of the dish may suffer, and the canned beans are higher in sodium. I always rinse the beans to remove as much salt as possible.

I like to use canned beans in purees and pureed soups, but in salads, side dishes and chili dishes, where the texture of the beans makes a big difference, I prefer to cook my own dried beans.

TORTILLA BASKETS

Place a corn tortilla in an ovenproof bowl, with another bowl nested on top. Bake at 400°F/200°C for 10 to 15 minutes, until the tortilla holds its bowl shape.

BAKED POLENTA CASSEROLE

Polenta is to Italians what hot cereal is to Canadians and what grits are to the southern states. It is a relatively new taste for North Americans, but we are quickly adopting it as it is easily available (simply made from cornmeal) and very good!

When you are making polenta, it is a good idea to stir it with a long-handled wooden spoon, as it tends to "spit" at you from the pot. To protect yourself even further, wear an oven mitt on your stirring hand.

Makes 8 to 10 servings

Polenta:

4½ cups	water	1.125 L
½ tsp	salt	2 mL
¼ tsp	pepper	1 mL
1½ cups	cornmeal (regular or instant)	375 mL

Tomato Sauce:

1 tbsp	olive oil	15 mL
1	onion, chopped	1
2	cloves garlic, finely chopped	2
pinch	hot red pepper flakes	pinch
2	28-oz/796 mL tins plum tomatoes, with juices	2
½ tsp	pepper	2 mL
	Salt to taste	
2 tbsp	chopped fresh parsley	25 mL
½ lb	light ricotta cheese, cut in chunks	250 g
¼ cup	pesto sauce (page 45)	50 mL
¾ cup	grated part-skim mozzarella cheese	175 mL
2 tbsp	grated Parmesan cheese	25 mL

MEATLESS MAIN COURSE SALADS

Slight adaptions maybe necessary (such as using vegetable stock or water instead of chicken stock).

- Tabbouleh Salad (page 72)
- Mixed Grain Salad (page 73)
- Black Bean, Corn and Rice Salad (page 74)
- Sushi Salad (page 75)
- Grilled Bread and Cherry Tomato Salad (page 81)
- Spaghettini with Salad Greens (page 82)

1. Prepare polenta in advance. Bring water, salt and pepper to boil. Very slowly add cornmeal in thin stream, stirring constantly with whisk. Reduce heat slightly. Cook on very low heat for 5 minutes for quick-cooking polenta and 15 to 20 minutes for regular, until thickened and tender. Stir occasionally. Taste and adjust seasonings if necessary.

2. Pour polenta into 8 x 4-inch/1.5 L loaf pan that has been lined with waxed paper. Chill for a few hours or overnight.

3. Prepare sauce by heating oil in Dutch oven. Add onion, garlic and hot pepper flakes and cook gently until mixture is very fragrant and onions are tender.

4. Add tomatoes and cook for 20 to 30 minutes, until thick. Puree sauce. Add pepper, salt and parsley. Taste and adjust seasonings if necessary.

5. To assemble, spoon about 1 cup/250 mL tomato sauce in bottom of 13 x 9-inch/3.5 L baking dish. Unmould polenta and cut into ½-inch/1 cm slices. Cut each slice in half on the diagonal. Arrange overlapping slices on top of sauce. Dot with ricotta and pesto. Spoon over remaining tomato sauce and top with mozzarella and Parmesan.

6. Bake in preheated 375°F/190°C oven for 30 to 35 minutes, until top is slightly golden and casserole is bubbling. Allow to rest for 5 to 10 minutes before serving.

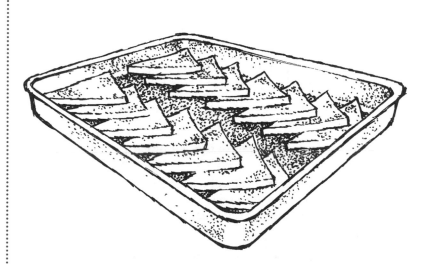

PER SERVING

Calories	231
g carbohydrate	33
g fibre	4
g total fat	7
g saturated fat	3
g protein	11

Good: vitamin A; vitamin C; niacin; calcium; vitamin B$_6$

mg cholesterol	16
mg sodium	611
mg potassium	588

SWEET AND SOUR VEGETABLE STEW

This dish is based on a side dish that Mark McEwen, the talented chef of North 44°, once made at my school. The flavours are unusual and exciting. Serve it with couscous or basmati rice, and add other vegetables if you like, such as cauliflower, green beans or broccoli.

Makes 6 to 8 servings

2 tsp	olive oil	10 mL
2	cloves garlic, finely chopped	2
1 tbsp	chopped fresh ginger root	15 mL
3	large leeks, trimmed and thickly sliced	3
2	carrots, sliced ½ inch/1 cm thick	2
1	bulb fennel, trimmed and cut in large chunks	1
2	potatoes, peeled and cut in large chunks	2
2	sweet potatoes, peeled and cut in large chunks	2
1 lb	butternut squash, peeled and cut in large chunks	500 g
¼ cup	rice vinegar or cider vinegar	50 mL
¼ cup	honey	50 mL
1 tsp	hot chili paste	5 mL
1 tsp	five-spice powder	5 mL
1	28-oz/796 mL tin plum tomatoes, pureed with juices	1
2	ears corn, cut in half lengthwise and then in 1-inch/2.5 cm pieces	2
1	19-oz/540 mL tin chickpeas, rinsed and drained,or 2 cups/ 500 mL cooked chickpeas	1
1 tsp	sesame oil	5 mL
¼ cup	chopped fresh cilantro or parsley	50 mL
¼ cup	chopped fresh basil	50 mL

FIVE-SPICE POWDER
Five-spice powder is slightly anise or licorice flavoured; in many recipes, curry powder can be used instead, although the taste will be quite different. Make your own five-spice powder by combining equal amounts of ground anise or fennel seeds, ground coriander, ground cinnamon, ground pepper and ground cloves.

PER SERVING

Calories	399
g carbohydrate	86
g fibre	10
g total fat	5
g saturated fat	1
g protein	11

Excellent: vitamin A; vitamin C; thiamine; niacin; iron; vitamin E; vitamin B$_6$; folacin
Good: riboflavin; calcium

mg cholesterol	0
mg sodium	433
mg potassium	1405

1. Heat olive oil in Dutch oven. Add garlic, ginger and leeks. Cook gently until leeks wilt. (Add a few spoonfuls of water if pan appears dry.)

2. Add carrots, fennel, potatoes, sweet potatoes and squash. Combine well and cook for about 20 minutes.

3. Add vinegar, honey, chili paste and five-spice powder. Bring to boil.

4. Add tomatoes, corn and chickpeas. Cook for 10 to 15 minutes longer, uncovered, until thick and stew-like.

5. Add sesame oil, cilantro and basil. Taste and adjust seasonings if necessary.

"CASSOULET" OF ONIONS

Although I had always thought of a cassoulet as a casserole of beans and rich meats, lately I have seen cassoulets made with lobster and salmon, so why not a vegetarian version? Instead of the dried beans, you can use two 19-oz/540 mL tins canned beans, rinsed and drained.

Makes 8 servings

1 lb	dried navy beans, cranberry beans or white kidney beans (about 2 cups/500 mL)	500 g
1 tbsp	olive oil	15 mL
8	large onions, thickly sliced	8
4	cloves garlic, finely chopped	4
12	cloves garlic, peeled	12
¼ tsp	hot red pepper flakes	1 mL
1	28-oz/796 mL tin plum tomatoes, pureed with juices	1
1 cup	dry white wine, vegetable stock or water	250 mL
2 tsp	chopped fresh rosemary, or ½ tsp/2 mL dried	10 mL
2 tsp	chopped fresh thyme, or ½ tsp/2 mL dried	10 mL
½ tsp	pepper	2 mL
	Salt to taste	

Topping:

1 cup	fresh breadcrumbs	250 mL
2 tbsp	chopped fresh parsley	25 mL
1 tbsp	olive oil	15 mL

COOKING DRIED BEANS

Dried beans are high in fibre, contain protein and have very little fat. To be prepared for cooking, they must be reconstituted. I usually soak beans for 3 to 4 hours at room temperature or overnight in the refrigerator. Rinse and drain the soaked beans, then cover with lots of cold water. Bring to a boil, skim off any scum that rises to the surface, reduce the heat and simmer gently until tender. If you want the beans to be creamy in texture, cover them; if you want them firmer, don't cover them. Beans usually require 1 to 1½ hours to become tender, but the time varies with the age and variety of bean.

Although I prefer the above method there is a quick-soak method of cooking beans. Bring dried beans covered generously with water to a boil. Remove from heat and allow to sit 1 hour. Drain, cover with water again and cook until tender, about 1 hour.

DRIED BEANS

• Cannellini beans, white kidney beans and great northern beans are all similar and can be used interchangeably. They can also be found canned in supermarkets.

• Navy beans or pea beans are white, small and round. I love to use them in baked beans, bean soups and salads.

• Red kidney beans are most often associated with chili dishes and bean salads. They are widely available in tins.

• Black turtle beans are used in chili dishes, soups and salads. They can sometimes be found in tins.

1. Rinse beans and soak in cold water for few hours at room temperature or overnight in refrigerator. Drain and rinse beans. Place in large pot and cover with cold water. Bring to boil. Skim off any froth that rises to surface. Reduce heat and simmer gently for 1 hour. Drain well.

2. Meanwhile, heat 1 tbsp/15 mL oil in Dutch oven. Add onions, chopped and whole garlic and hot pepper flakes and cook gently for about 20 minutes, until onions soften. (Onions will wilt eventually!)

3. Add tomatoes, wine, rosemary, thyme, pepper and salt and bring to boil. Cook gently, covered, for 30 minutes.

4. Add beans and combine well. (If mixture is very wet, cook, uncovered, for about 15 minutes, or until just moist.) Taste and adjust seasonings if necessary.

5. Place bean mixture in large shallow casserole (about 3 qt/3 L). Combine breadcrumbs with parsley and 1 tbsp/15 mL olive oil. Sprinkle over beans. Bake in preheated 350°F/180°C oven for 30 minutes.

PER SERVING

Calories	327
g carbohydrate	58
g fibre	14
g total fat	5
g saturated fat	1
g protein	15

Excellent: thiamine; iron; vitamin B_6; folacin
Good: vitamin C; niacin; calcium

mg cholesterol	0
mg sodium	200
mg potassium	987

SPRINGTIME STIR-FRIED RICE AND VEGETABLES

This is a beautiful dish that is full of flavour. You can use brown rice instead of the white rice and you can vary the vegetables. If you wish, place a small piece of grilled salmon or sea bass on each serving.

Makes 6 to 8 servings

2 cups	long-grain rice, preferably basmati	500 mL
2¾ cups	cold water	675 mL
2 tsp	olive oil	10 mL
1	clove garlic, finely chopped	1
2 tbsp	finely chopped fresh ginger root	25 mL
1	shallot or small onion, finely chopped	1
1	carrot, thinly sliced on diagonal	1
¼ lb	green beans, sliced on diagonal	125 g
1	sweet red pepper, sliced	1
1	bunch asparagus, trimmed and sliced on diagonal	1
½ cup	fresh or frozen corn niblets	125 mL
½ cup	fresh or frozen peas	125 mL
3	green onions, sliced	3
¼ cup	rice vinegar or cider vinegar	50 mL
2 tbsp	chopped fresh cilantro or parsley	25 mL

1. Rinse rice well. Place in large saucepan and add cold water. Bring to boil. Reduce heat to medium and cook, uncovered, just until water has evaporated. Cover and cook on very low heat for 10 minutes.

2. Meanwhile, heat oil in wok or large, deep skillet. Add garlic, ginger and shallot. Cook gently for a few minutes until tender and fragrant.

3. Add carrot and cook for 2 minutes. Add green beans, red pepper and asparagus and stir-fry for 2 minutes. Add corn, peas and green onions and heat thoroughly. Remove from heat.

4. Just before serving, add rice to vegetables and combine gently. Stir in vinegar and cilantro. Taste and adjust seasonings if necessary.

GREEN ONIONS, SCALLIONS AND SHALLOTS

Green onions and scallions are the same thing (they are usually called scallions in the United States). Shallots are entirely different and look more like garlic than onions. They taste a little like a cross between onion and garlic but have a very distinctive flavour. I substitute one small onion and a half clove garlic for cooked shallots. If raw shallots are called for (as in a salad dressing), I usually use green onions instead.

PER SERVING

Calories	290
g carbohydrate	60
g fibre	4
g total fat	2
g saturated fat	trace
g protein	8

Excellent: vitamin A; vitamin C; folacin
Good: vitamin B_6

mg cholesterol	0
mg sodium	29
mg potassium	340

Provençal Fish Stew with Rouille
(page 154)

Mussels with Black Bean Sauce
(page 156)

QUICKBREAD PIZZA

This quickbread pizza is one of my favourites. It's great for kids as they don't have to wait for the crust to rise!

You can use a plain or spicy tomato sauce (pages 102 and 186) on this, but I love the taste and texture of fresh tomatoes.

Makes 8 servings

4	large tomatoes, halved, seeded and chopped	4
⅓ cup	chopped fresh basil or parsley	75 mL
2	cloves garlic, minced	2
¼ tsp	pepper	1 mL
	Salt to taste	

Quickbread Crust:

2 cups	all-purpose flour	500 mL
1¼ cups	whole wheat flour	300 mL
⅓ cup	cornmeal	75 mL
1 tbsp	granulated sugar	15 mL
1 tbsp	chopped fresh rosemary, or ½ tsp/2 mL dried	15 mL
½ tsp	salt	2 mL
2 tsp	baking powder	10 mL
1 tsp	baking soda	5 mL
1⅔ cups	low-fat yogurt	400 mL
3 tbsp	olive oil	45 mL
1 cup	grated part-skim mozzarella cheese	250 mL
¼ cup	grated Parmesan cheese	50 mL

1. Combine tomatoes, basil, garlic, pepper and salt. Reserve.

2. For crust, combine flours with cornmeal, sugar, rosemary, salt, baking powder and baking soda. Stir together well. Combine yogurt with oil. Pour over dry ingredients and knead dough lightly into ball. Brush 15 x 10-inch/2 L baking dish lightly with oil. Press dough evenly into pan.

3. Sprinkle half of mozzarella over dough. Drain tomato mixture and spread over cheese. Sprinkle with remaining mozzarella and Parmesan.

4. Bake in preheated 400°F/200°C oven for 20 to 25 minutes, or until pizza is puffed and cheese is lightly browned. Cut into squares.

PER SERVING

Calories	354
g carbohydrate	52
g fibre	5
g total fat	10
g saturated fat	4
g protein	15

Excellent: niacin; calcium
Good: thiamine; riboflavin; iron

mg cholesterol	13
mg sodium	531
mg potassium	442

FALAFEL VEGETABLE BURGERS

I love the taste and texture of Israeli falafels, and have combined the most delicious aspects of them in these vegetarian burgers. Serve them in pita breads with the sauce, or cut them into quarters and serve them as appetizers with the tahini sauce or Middle Eastern Dressing for dipping (see sidebar). You can also serve the burgers with sliced tomatoes and cucumbers.

Makes 8 burgers

4 cups	cooked chickpeas, or 2 19-oz/ 540 mL tins, rinsed and well drained	1 L
1	10-oz/284 mL tin mushrooms, drained and patted dry	1
4	slices bread, moistened and squeezed dry	4
1 tsp	baking soda	5 mL
2	cloves garlic, minced	2
1	small onion, finely chopped	1
1	small carrot, grated	1
½ cup	chopped fresh parsley	125 mL
1 tbsp	ground cumin	15 mL
1 tsp	ground coriander	5 mL
1 tsp	hot red pepper sauce, optional	5 mL
1 tsp	salt	5 mL
1 tsp	pepper	5 mL

MIDDLE EASTERN DRESSING

Combine 1 minced clove garlic, ¾ tsp/4 mL ground cumin, ¾ tsp/4 mL paprika, ½ tsp/2 mL cayenne, ½ cup/125 mL soft yogurt cheese (page 228) or thick yogurt and 1 tbsp/15 mL lemon juice. Stir in 2 tbsp/ 25 mL chopped fresh cilantro or parsley and 2 tbsp/25 mL mayonnaise (optional).

Makes about ½ cup/125 mL.

Tahini Sauce:

½ cup	soft yogurt cheese (page 228) or thick yogurt	125 mL
2 tbsp	tahini	25 mL
1 tbsp	lemon juice	15 mL
1	clove garlic, minced	1
¼ tsp	hot red pepper sauce	1 mL
	Salt to taste	
2 tbsp	chopped fresh mint, or ½ tsp/2 mL dried	25 mL
2 tbsp	chopped fresh cilantro or parsley	25 mL

1. In food processor, combine chickpeas, mushrooms, bread and baking soda until finely chopped but not quite a paste (chop in batches if necessary). Add garlic, onion, carrot, parsley, cumin, coriander, hot pepper sauce, salt and pepper. Mix lightly and shape mixture gently into 8 patties.

2. Bake burgers in single layer in preheated 350°F/180°C oven for 30 minutes. Or brush large non-stick skillet with oil, heat and cook burgers on both sides, until brown and crisp.

3. To make sauce, combine yogurt cheese, tahini, lemon juice, garlic, hot pepper sauce and salt in food processor or blender. Blend in mint and cilantro. Taste and adjust seasonings if necessary. Serve burgers with sauce.

MEATLESS MAIN COURSE VEGETABLE DISHES

Slight adaptions maybe necessary (such as using vegetable stock or water instead of chicken stock).

PER SERVING (1 burger)

Calories	228
g carbohydrate	36
g fibre	5
g total fat	5
g saturated fat	1
g protein	12

Excellent: iron; folacin
Good: vitamin A; thiamine; niacin

mg cholesterol	2
mg sodium	611
mg potassium	416

POTATO AND BROCCOLI EGG WHITE FRITTATA

If you love eggs the way I do, it is great to have an omelette or frittata once in a while that is cholesterol free. (You could also use two whole eggs and six egg whites in this recipe — as long as you end up with ten parts of an egg!)

This is great hot or cold, served in a wedge on a salad with a salsa. Leftovers are wonderful in sandwiches or cut up and used as a garnish in salads.

Makes 6 to 8 servings

1 lb	broccoli, rapini or Swiss chard, trimmed and diced	500 g
4 tsp	olive oil, divided	20 mL
1	onion, chopped	1
2	cloves garlic, finely chopped	2
2	potatoes (about 1 lb/500 g), peeled and diced	2
¼ tsp	hot red pepper flakes	1 mL
¼ cup	chopped fresh parsley	50 mL
10	egg whites	10
¼ cup	water	50 mL
¼ tsp	pepper	1 mL
½ tsp	salt	2 mL

1. Bring large pot of water to boil. Add broccoli and cook for about 5 minutes. Drain well.

2. Heat 2 tsp/10 mL oil in large non-stick skillet. Add onion and garlic and cook gently until tender, but do not brown. Pat potatoes dry and add to skillet with hot pepper flakes. Cook until potatoes are tender, about 10 minutes. Add broccoli and parsley and combine well. Cool.

NON-STICK SKILLETS
Non-stick skillets have improved immeasurably in the past several years. The new pans have baked-on non-stick coatings that are virtually impossible to remove. The pans are based on very heavy metals and are often guaranteed for twenty years or more. Follow the manufacturer's directions.

3. In large bowl, mix egg whites with water, pepper and salt just until slightly frothy. Add vegetables and combine.

4. Wipe out skillet and heat remaining 2 tsp/10 mL oil. When oil is hot, add egg mixture. Allow to cook on bottom. With knife, loosen edges of frittata so that some of uncooked egg runs down to bottom.

5. Frittata can be baked in preheated 350°F/180°C oven for 15 minutes or, more exciting, slide it onto cookie sheet and then invert back into skillet to cook second side, about 5 minutes. Slide onto serving platter and cut into wedges.

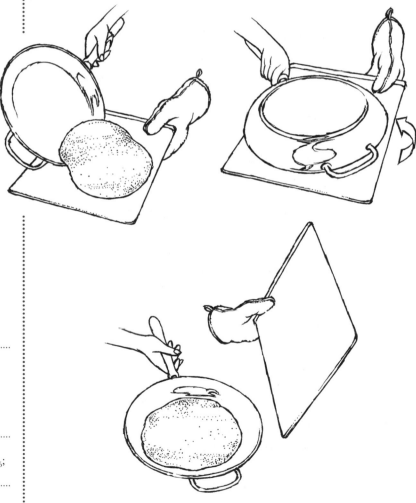

PER SERVING

Calories	128
g carbohydrate	17
g fibre	3
g total fat	3
g saturated fat	1
g protein	9

Excellent: vitamin C
Good: riboflavin; vitamin B$_6$; folacin

mg cholesterol	0
mg sodium	301
mg potassium	478

RIBOLLITA

Ribollita is recooked minestrone. It is a favourite dish in Tuscany, where it is made to use up leftover minestrone and the famous Tuscan bread. But many people like it better than the minestrone itself, and they make minestrone especially for it. I usually make this in a casserole, a method I learned from my friend Luigi Berra while I was staying with his family in Greve, just outside of Florence, but the bread is sometimes just added to the soup and cooked gently until thick.

If you are making this with leftover minestrone, adjust the amount of bread and cheese depending on how much leftover soup you have. Improvise!

Makes 8 to 10 servings

1 tbsp	olive oil	15 mL
1	onion, chopped	1
3	cloves garlic, finely chopped	3
pinch	hot red pepper flakes	pinch
1	carrot, diced	1
1	stalk celery, diced	1
1	medium zucchini, diced	1
3 cups	chopped cabbage	750 mL
4 cups	homemade vegetable stock (page 62) or water	1 L
2	28-oz/796 mL tins plum tomatoes, with juices	2
1	19-oz/540 mL tin white kidney beans, rinsed and drained, or 2 cups/500 mL cooked beans	1
1	bunch Swiss chard or rapini, chopped	1
1 cup	small soup pasta	250 mL
½ tsp	pepper	2 mL
	Salt to taste	
¼ cup	chopped fresh basil or parsley	50 mL
8	thick slices Italian bread	8
½ cup	grated Parmesan cheese	125 mL

1. Heat oil in large Dutch oven. Add onion, garlic and hot pepper flakes. Cook gently for a few minutes until tender.

2. Add carrot, celery, zucchini and cabbage. Cook for about 5 minutes to wilt vegetables slightly.

3. Add stock and tomatoes and bring to boil, breaking up tomatoes with spoon. Cook for 30 minutes until vegetables are tender.

4. Add beans, Swiss chard and pasta and cook for 15 minutes longer. Stir in pepper, salt and basil. Taste and adjust seasonings if necessary.

5. Line 13 x 9-inch/3.5 L baking dish with layer of bread. Spoon soup over top and sprinkle with cheese. Repeat layers.

6. Bake in preheated 350°F/180°C oven for 20 to 25 minutes, until golden brown and bubbling.

PER SERVING

Calories	327
g carbohydrate	57
g fibre	10
g total fat	5
g saturated fat	2
g protein	15

Excellent: vitamin A; vitamin C; niacin; iron; folacin
Good: thiamine; riboflavin; calcium; vitamin E; vitamin B_6

mg cholesterol	5
mg sodium	757
mg potassium	1038

GRILLED TOFU KEBABS

The first time I ate grilled tofu was at Greens restaurant in San Francisco. It tasted so different from any other tofu dish I had eaten. You can make this as kebabs (soak wooden skewers in water for at least 1 hour before using), or leave the tofu in one piece, marinate and grill it like a cut of meat. When I make kebabs, I like to use two skewers for each one. This stops the food from rolling around when it is being turned. Serve the kebabs on a bed of steamed rice or couscous.

Makes 4 servings (8 kebabs)

1 lb	extra-firm tofu or regular tofu, pressed (page 118), cut in 16 cubes	500 g
1	red onion, cut in 16 chunks	1
1	zucchini, cut in 16 chunks	1
16	mushroom caps	16
1	sweet red pepper, cut in 16 chunks	1

Marinade:

¼ cup	hoisin sauce	50 mL
2 tbsp	black bean sauce	25 mL
2 tbsp	rice vinegar	25 mL
2 tbsp	ketchup	25 mL
2 tbsp	honey	25 mL
1 tbsp	soy sauce	15 mL
1 tsp	sesame oil	5 mL

1. Place tofu in one large flat dish and vegetables in another large dish.

2. Combine all ingredients for marinade. Divide marinade between tofu and vegetables, pour over and toss gently.

3. Using two skewers for each kebab, thread tofu and vegetables on skewers. You should end up with 8 kebabs.

4. Line baking sheet with foil and brush with vegetable oil. Arrange kebabs on oiled pan and broil for a few minutes per side until browned. Or barbecue kebabs.

FRIED RICE

My sister, Jane Krangle, uses up leftover rice by making this simple fried rice dish that we all love.

Heat 1 tsp/5 mL vegetable oil in a large, non-stick skillet. Add 1 chopped clove garlic and 2 chopped green onions. Cook gently until soft (add 2 tbsp/25 mL water if vegetables start to stick). Add 1 beaten egg and cook, stirring, breaking up curds. Add 3 cups/750 mL cooked rice and ½ cup/125 mL peas. Cook, stirring constantly, until hot. Add 1 tbsp/15 mL soy sauce. Taste and adjust seasonings if necessary.

Makes 3 to 4 servings.

PER SERVING

Calories	250
g carbohydrate	35
g fibre	8
g total fat	4
g saturated fat	trace
g protein	21

Excellent: vitamin C; calcium
Good: niacin; vitamin B$_6$; folacin

mg cholesterol	0
mg sodium	522
mg potassium	787

FISH AND SEAFOOD

Sesame-crusted Salmon on Greens

Roasted Salmon with Lentils

Steamed Salmon with Korean Dressing

Oven-poached Halibut with Herb Vinaigrette

Hoisin-glazed Sea Bass or Salmon

Asian Tuna or Swordfish Burgers

Seared Tuna with Japanese Noodle Salad

Baked Red Snapper with Hot Chiles

Oven-baked Fish and Chips

Sweet and Sour Swordfish

Swordfish Teriyaki

Gefilte Fish with Beet Horseradish Salad

Provençal Fish Stew with Rouille

Mussels with Black Bean Sauce

Risotto with Seafood and Peppers

Fish Fillets with Rosemary

SESAME-CRUSTED SALMON ON GREENS

This is one of my favourite dishes. I usually serve it with steamed basmati rice, quinoa (page 220) or couscous.

Makes 6 servings

6	4-oz/125 g fillets fresh salmon, skin removed	6
1 tbsp	honey	15 mL
1 tbsp	soy sauce	15 mL
1 tsp	honey-style mustard	5 mL
1 tbsp	sesame seeds	15 mL

Orange Ginger Dressing:

1	clove garlic, minced	1
1 tsp	minced fresh ginger root	5 mL
3 tbsp	orange juice	45 mL
2 tbsp	soy sauce	25 mL
2 tbsp	rice vinegar or balsamic vinegar	25 mL
2 tsp	sesame oil	10 mL
2 tsp	honey	10 mL
¼ tsp	hot red pepper sauce	1 mL
12 cups	mixed greens	3 L
1 lb	asparagus, trimmed, cooked and cut in 2-inch/5 cm pieces	500 g
1	sweet red pepper, cut in strips	1
1	orange, peeled and sectioned	1
2 tbsp	chopped fresh cilantro or parsley	25 mL
2 tbsp	chopped fresh chives or green onions	25 mL

1. Pat salmon dry. In small bowl, combine honey, soy sauce and mustard. Rub over salmon. Sprinkle with sesame seeds.

2. Brush non-stick ovenproof skillet lightly with oil. Add salmon and cook for 1 minute per side. Transfer to preheated 425°F/ 220°C oven. Cook for 7 to 8 minutes, or until just cooked.

3. To make orange ginger dressing, whisk together garlic, ginger, orange juice, soy sauce, vinegar, sesame oil, honey and hot pepper sauce. Taste and adjust seasonings if necessary. Toss dressing with greens, asparagus, red pepper, orange, cilantro and chives. Serve salad topped with salmon.

SESAME OIL
The sesame oil used in these recipes is the toasted Asian sesame oil. It is dark in colour and very fragrant. (Do not confuse it with the golden sesame oil found in health food stores.) Once opened, store it in the refrigerator.

Sesame oil is seldom used in large quantities or as a "cooking oil," as the flavour is very intense. It is usually used as a last-minute seasoning in stir-fries, salad dressings, dips, etc.

PER SERVING

Calories	242
g carbohydrate	16
g fibre	3
g total fat	10
g saturated fat	1
g protein	25

Excellent: vitamin A; vitamin C; thiamine; niacin; riboflavin; vitamin B_6; folacin; vitamin B_{12}
Good: iron

mg cholesterol	57
mg sodium	496
mg potassium	1049

ROASTED SALMON WITH LENTILS

This is my rendition of a popular French bistro dish.

Makes 6 servings

1½ cups	dried green lentils	375 mL
4 tsp	olive oil, divided	20 mL
1	onion, chopped	1
2	cloves garlic, finely chopped	2
1 tsp	ground cumin	5 mL
¼ tsp	hot red pepper flakes	1 mL
1	carrot, finely diced	1
1	stalk celery, finely diced	1
1 cup	tinned plum tomatoes, pureed with juices	250 mL
¼ cup	chopped fresh parsley	50 mL
½ tsp	pepper	2 mL
	Salt to taste	
1½ lb	fresh salmon fillet, skin removed, cut in 6 pieces	750 g
1 tsp	chopped fresh rosemary	5 mL

1. Place lentils in large pot and cover generously with water. Bring to boil and cook gently for 25 to 35 minutes, until just tender. Drain well.

2. Meanwhile, heat 3 tsp/15 mL oil in large non-stick skillet and add onion and garlic. Cook gently for 5 minutes. Add cumin and hot pepper flakes. Cook for 30 seconds.

3. Add carrot, celery and tomatoes to skillet. Cook until carrots are just tender and liquid from tomatoes has reduced.

4. Add drained lentils, parsley, pepper and salt to skillet. Taste and adjust seasonings if necessary. Keep warm.

5. Brush a second non-stick skillet with remaining 1 tsp/5 mL oil. Sprinkle salmon with rosemary. Cook for 1 to 2 minutes per side, or until slightly browned and crusty.

6. Transfer salmon to baking sheet lined with parchment paper (or leave in skillet if it is ovenproof). Bake in preheated 400°F/200°C oven for 7 to 9 minutes, or until just cooked through. Serve salmon on bed of lentils.

LENTILS

There are many types of lentils. Red and green ones are easily found in health food stores, bulk stores and supermarkets. Red lentils (sometimes called pink or orange) are smaller than green/brown lentils. I use the red lentils in soups, as they cook quickly, lose their shape and thicken mixtures. I use green lentils in salads and side dishes because they keep their texture.

Lentils do not need to be soaked, so they are easy and quick to cook. I do not like canned green lentils very much, as they have a mushy texture.

PER SERVING

Calories	361
g carbohydrate	34
g fibre	8
g total fat	10
g saturated fat	2
g protein	34

Excellent: vitamin A; thiamine; niacin; riboflavin; iron; vitamin B$_6$; folacin; vitamin B$_{12}$

mg cholesterol	57
mg sodium	129
mg potassium	1208

STEAMED SALMON WITH KOREAN DRESSING

This is an adaptation of a recipe I learned from Madhur Jaffrey when I was taking cooking classes at Darina Allen's wonderful school at Ballymaloe near Cork, Ireland. Madhur Jaffrey vacationed there while she taught, and I vacationed there while I learned. Jaffrey is an accomplished actress, which enhances her teaching ability, and she has a unique way of putting a magical spell over her students. Eventually I convinced her that Toronto was also a great place for a vacation, and when she taught at my school the students were as spellbound with her as I was.

Although you can bake this salmon, you can probably put together a makeshift steaming unit using equipment from your cupboards as shown.

This dish can also be made with a black bean sauce (page 156). It is delicious served hot or cold.

Makes 4 servings

¼ lb	rice vermicelli or regular vermicelli	125 g
¾ lb	fresh spinach, trimmed and washed	375 g
1 tbsp	finely chopped fresh ginger root	15 mL
3	green onions, chopped	3
4	salmon fillets (about 4 oz/ 125 g each), skin removed	4
1	lemon, cut in 8 slices	1
¼ tsp	pepper	1 mL

Korean Dressing:

1½ tbsp	soy sauce	20 mL
2 tbsp	water	25 mL
2 tsp	sesame oil	10 mL
1	clove garlic, minced	1
1 tsp	minced fresh ginger root	5 mL
2 tsp	granulated sugar	10 mL
pinch	hot red pepper flakes	pinch
¼ cup	chopped fresh chives	50 mL
¼ cup	chopped fresh cilantro or parsley	50 mL
1 tbsp	sesame seeds, toasted (page 34), optional	15 mL

1. To assemble steaming unit, fit rack in bottom of wok or large deep skillet (rack should sit about 1 inch/2.5 cm from bottom). Find shallow glass or ceramic ovenproof dish that fits on rack. There should be a lid for the wok or use foil.

2. If you are using rice vermicelli, cover with boiling water and allow to stand for 3 minutes. If you are using regular vermicelli, cook in boiling water for 4 minutes. Drain well and rinse with cold water. Reserve.

3. Arrange spinach leaves over bottom of baking dish. Place vermicelli on spinach. Sprinkle with half the chopped ginger and green onions. Arrange fish on top in single layer. Sprinkle with remaining ginger and green onions. Arrange 2 lemon slices on each fillet. Sprinkle with pepper.

4. Add water to wok or skillet, just to top of rack (water should not touch baking dish). Bring water to boil.

5. Set baking dish with fish on rack and cover. Cook at medium-high heat for 8 to 10 minutes if fish is about 1 inch/ 2.5 cm thick.

6. Meanwhile, prepare dressing by combining soy sauce, water, sesame oil, garlic, minced ginger, sugar and hot pepper flakes.

7. When salmon is ready, pour dressing over and sprinkle with chives, cilantro and sesame seeds.

PER SERVING

Calories	311
g carbohydrate	31
g fibre	3
g total fat	9
g saturated fat	1
g protein	26

Excellent: vitamin A; thiamine; niacin; riboflavin; iron; vitamin B_6; folacin; vitamin B_{12}

mg cholesterol	57
mg sodium	419
mg potassium	1021

Oven-poached Halibut with Herb Vinaigrette

I once had a dish like this in a posh New York restaurant. I was with five friends and we all ordered different things so that we could sample as many dishes as possible. It was one of those "take a bite and pass it on" meals. A poached halibut with herb vinaigrette was the best item we tried that night, but I didn't get enough of it. So now I make it all the time and eat a whole portion by myself!

Try to find fresh halibut if you can, because the texture is silkier than frozen. This dish can be served warm or cold.

Makes 6 servings

Herb Vinaigrette:

¼ cup	Champagne or sherry vinegar, or lemon juice	50 mL
¼ cup	water	50 mL
½ tsp	granulated sugar	2 mL
½ tsp	dry mustard	2 mL
1	shallot, minced, optional	1
½ tsp	pepper	2 mL
2 tbsp	olive oil	25 mL
¼ tsp	hot red pepper sauce	1 mL
2 tbsp	chopped fresh cilantro or parsley	25 mL
2 tbsp	chopped fresh chives or green onions	25 mL
2 tbsp	chopped fresh parsley	25 mL
2 tbsp	chopped fresh basil	25 mL
6	pieces fresh halibut (about 4 oz/125 g each)	6
1 tbsp	lemon juice	15 mL
¼ tsp	pepper	1 mL
4	large carrots, grated	4
1	bunch watercress, optional	1

FRESH FISH

Fresh fish should not have any kind of strong odour. The fish should feel firm and the skin should be smooth and slippery. The eyes should be bright and the gills red.

If the store has packaged your fish in a plastic bag, unwrap it as soon as you get home and place it in a glass or stainless-steel dish. Cover lightly and keep in the coolest part of the refrigerator, over a pan of ice and water. Use the fish as soon as possible, within a day or two.

1. To prepare vinaigrette, whisk together vinegar, water, sugar, mustard, shallot and pepper. Whisk in oil, hot pepper sauce, cilantro, chives, parsley and basil. Reserve.

2. Place halibut in dish in single layer and sprinkle with lemon juice and pepper. Marinate in the refrigerator for approximately 10 minutes.

3. Line baking dish with parchment paper. Spread carrots over paper. Arrange fish on top. Cover with second piece of parchment. Bake in preheated 400°F/200°C oven for 10 minutes per inch/2.5 cm of thickness, or until fish just begins to flake when separated with knife. (Halibut fillets are usually ¾ inch/2 cm thick and therefore take 8 to 10 minutes to cook.)

4. Remove fish from oven and place carefully on serving platter. Scatter carrots on top. Pour vinaigrette over. Arrange watercress around edge of platter.

FROZEN FISH

I buy fresh fish as much as possible, but if you buy frozen fish, defrost it in the refrigerator or microwave, or cook it from the frozen state (cooking guidelines on page 150). Defrosting fish at room temperature destroys the texture and causes the fish to become dry. It could also be dangerous, as bacteria grow faster at room temperature. Never refreeze thawed fish.

PER SERVING

Calories	181
g carbohydrate	6
g fibre	1
g total fat	6
g saturated fat	1
g protein	24

Excellent: vitamin A; niacin; vitamin B_6; vitamin B_{12}

mg cholesterol	36
mg sodium	96
mg potassium	649

HOISIN-GLAZED SEA BASS OR SALMON

Hoisin sauce adds a sweet, mysterious flavour to dishes. You can use halibut, swordfish or tuna in this recipe, as well as boneless, skinless chicken breasts and thinly cut lamb chops.

This dish is good cold and perfect for picnics; leftovers can be added to rice or couscous salads.

Makes 4 servings

2 tbsp	hoisin sauce	25 mL
1 tbsp	soy sauce	15 mL
1 tsp	sesame oil	5 mL
¼ tsp	pepper	1 mL
4	4-oz/125 g sea bass or salmon fillets, about 1 inch/2.5 cm thick	4

1. In small bowl, combine hoisin sauce, soy sauce, sesame oil and pepper.

2. Pat fish dry and coat with sauce.

3. Preheat barbecue or broiler and cook fish for about 5 minutes per side. (You can also bake fish for 10 to 12 minutes in preheated 425°F/220°C oven.)

HOISIN SAUCE
Hoisin sauce is a sweet bean paste that is readily available in most supermarkets. Keep opened jars in the refrigerator. It is great as a glaze or in barbecue sauces and is traditionally used on the Mandarin pancakes served with Chinese roast duck. I like the Koon Chun brand the best.

PER SERVING

Calories	132
g carbohydrate	3
g fibre	0
g total fat	4
g saturated fat	1
g protein	22

Excellent: niacin
Good: vitamin B$_6$

mg cholesterol	47
mg sodium	359
mg potassium	296

See photo opposite page 97.

ASIAN TUNA OR SWORDFISH BURGERS

Many people want to eat more fish, but they want it to be more like meat. Ground tuna and swordfish make great fish burgers because of their firm, meaty texture. Serve these in the buns with grilled slices of red onion. Some fish merchants will grind the fish for you. Use it quickly, as ground meat, fish and chicken deteriorate quickly.

Makes 6 servings

2 tsp	olive oil	10 mL
1	clove garlic, finely chopped	1
1 tbsp	finely chopped fresh ginger root	15 mL
3	green onions, chopped	3
1 lb	fresh tuna or swordfish	500 g
2	egg whites, or 1 whole egg	2
½ cup	fresh breadcrumbs	125 mL
½ tsp	salt	2 mL
¼ tsp	pepper	1 mL
2 tbsp	hoisin sauce	25 mL
1 tbsp	soy sauce	15 mL
1 tsp	sesame oil	5 mL
6	sesame seed buns	6

1. Heat olive oil in skillet. Add garlic, ginger and green onions and cook gently until fragrant. Cool.

2. Cut fish into chunks and pat dry. Place in food processor and chop coarsely. Add egg whites and breadcrumbs and combine well. Blend in cooled garlic mixture, salt and pepper. Shape into 6 patties about ½ inch/1 cm thick.

3. To make glaze, in small bowl, combine hoisin sauce, soy sauce and sesame oil.

4. Just before serving, preheat broiler or barbecue. Cook burgers for 1 to 2 minutes, turn and brush with glaze. Turn and brush twice more, cooking burgers for a total of about 5 minutes per side until cooked through but still juicy. Serve in sesame seed buns.

Lemon Rosemary Fish Burgers: Omit ginger and glaze. Add 1 tbsp/15 mL lemon juice and 1 tsp/5 mL chopped fresh rosemary (or pinch dried) to burgers. Serve burgers in crusty Italian buns or pitas with barbecued eggplant and red peppers.

PER SERVING

Calories	335
g carbohydrate	36
g fibre	2
g total fat	9
g saturated fat	2
g protein	25

Excellent: vitamin A; thiamine; niacin; vitamin B_{12}
Good: riboflavin; iron; vitamin B_6

mg cholesterol	29
mg sodium	730
mg potassium	301

SEARED TUNA WITH JAPANESE NOODLE SALAD

Fresh tuna has become very popular in the past couple of years. It is usually served rare, and it tastes and looks unbelievably meaty.

Although this recipe has a long list of ingredients, it is easy to make. Because the tuna is served rare, make sure your fish is very fresh. Be careful not to overcook it if you want that pink centre, as it seems to go from medium rare to well done in a blink! This recipe can also be made with salmon or swordfish.

You can prepare the tuna on its own and serve it separately, and the noodle salad can also be served alone. Buy the noodles in health food stores or Asian markets.

Makes 6 servings

1 lb	fresh tuna fillet, 1 inch/ 2.5 cm thick	500 g
1 tbsp	sesame oil	15 mL
1 tbsp	pepper	15 mL
½ tsp	salt	2 mL
½ tsp	vegetable oil	2 mL

Japanese Noodle Salad:

½ lb	Japanese whole wheat or buckwheat noodles, or regular whole wheat noodles	250 g
1	large carrot, cut in thin strips	1
1	medium zucchini, cut in thin strips	1
1	sweet red pepper, cut in thin strips	1
1	sweet yellow pepper, cut in thin strips	1
2 oz	snow peas, sliced thinly on diagonal	60 g
3	green onions, cut in thin strips	3

ASIAN NOODLES

• Rice vermicelli (also called rice stick noodles) do not need to be cooked. Simply cover with boiling water and allow to soak for 5 to 7 minutes. Drain well. (If you are not using the whole package, place the dry noodles in a plastic bag and break some off inside the bag, so they don't fly all over the kitchen.)

• Japanese whole wheat or buckwheat noodles can be found in health food stores or Asian markets. They should be cooked in lots of boiling water until tender but firm.

• Fresh Chinese noodles usually come vacuum-packed; the precooked noodles should be rinsed under hot water before being added to a dish. Substitute regular spaghetti if you wish, but cook it first.

Dressing:

1	small clove garlic, minced	1
1 tbsp	minced fresh ginger root	15 mL
1 tbsp	rice wine or sake	15 mL
1 tbsp	soy sauce	15 mL
1 tbsp	rice vinegar or cider vinegar	15 mL
1 tbsp	sesame oil	15 mL
1 tbsp	lemon juice	15 mL
½ tsp	hot red pepper sauce	2 mL
⅓ cup	chopped fresh cilantro or parsley	75 mL
2 tbsp	chopped fresh mint	25 mL
2 tbsp	chopped fresh basil	25 mL

1. Pat tuna dry. Rub with sesame oil, pepper and salt.

2. Brush non-stick skillet with vegetable oil and heat. Sear tuna for 2 to 3 minutes per side, or until well browned outside but pink on inside. Allow to rest for 10 minutes. Slice thinly on diagonal (fish should be rare).

3. Cook noodles in large pot of boiling water until tender but firm. Rinse with cold water and drain well.

4. Bring pot of water to boil. Add carrot, zucchini and sweet peppers and cook for 2 minutes. Lift out and refresh with cold water. Pat dry. Boil snow peas and green onions for 10 seconds, or until brightened. Chill under cold water and pat dry. Toss vegetables with noodles.

5. Combine all ingredients for dressing and toss with noodles and vegetables.

6. To serve, arrange noodle salad on each plate. Top with slices of seared tuna.

PER SERVING

Calories	324
g carbohydrate	37
g fibre	7
g total fat	9
g saturated fat	2
g protein	25

Excellent: vitamin A; vitamin C; thiamine; niacin; vitamin B_6; vitamin B_{12}
Good: riboflavin; iron

mg cholesterol	29
mg sodium	380
mg potassium	513

BAKED RED SNAPPER WITH HOT CHILES

We developed this recipe for our "Some Like It Hot" class, and it was an instant success. You can prepare it ahead of time and bake it just before serving, or bake it ahead and serve it at room temperature or cold.

Red snapper works perfectly in this recipe, but you can also use any fresh white-fleshed fish that your fish merchant recommends.

If my baking pan is large enough to accommodate the whole fish, I leave the head and tail on, because a fish looks much more important that way!

Makes 8 servings

1	4-lb/2 kg red snapper, cleaned	1
2 tbsp	minced fresh ginger root	25 mL
1 tbsp	hot chili paste	15 mL
2	cloves garlic, minced	2
¼ cup	chopped fresh cilantro or parsley	50 mL
1 tsp	sesame oil	5 mL
3	green onions, chopped	3
½ tsp	salt	2 mL
1 tbsp	olive oil	15 mL
1	lemon, sliced, optional	1
	Sprigs fresh cilantro or parsley, optional	

1. If fish is too large for baking dish, cut off head and tail. Pat fish dry inside and out. Cut 4 diagonal slits in each side of fish.

2. In food processor (or in blender with a little water), blend together ginger, chili paste and garlic. Add cilantro, sesame oil, green onions and salt. Puree.

3. Reserve about 1 tbsp/15 mL chile puree. Stuff remaining puree into slits in fish. Combine reserved puree with olive oil and rub over fish. Place on large baking sheet lined with foil.

4. Bake fish in preheated 425°F/220°C oven for 10 minutes per inch/2.5 cm of thickness. (If fish is 3 inches/7.5 cm thick, cook for about 30 minutes.) Garnish with lemon and cilantro.

FRESH CHILE PEPPERS

Even though there are guidelines on how to tell the difference between a hot and mild chile, be careful. Where the chile is grown, how much water and sunlight the plant receives, even where the individual chile is located on the plant can all make a difference.

JALAPEÑOS

Jalapeños are thumb-shaped, dark-green and medium-hot. Fresh, canned and pickled can be used interchangeably, although the flavours may be slightly different. Individual jalapeños vary greatly, so taste them before adding them to a dish.

PER SERVING	
Calories	129
g carbohydrate	2
g fibre	trace
g total fat	4
g saturated fat	1
g protein	21

Excellent: vitamin B$_{12}$
Good: niacin; vitamin B$_6$

mg cholesterol	37
mg sodium	191
mg potassium	469

OVEN-BAKED FISH AND CHIPS

This dish is healthful and delicious, with its crispy breading and "light" French fries. Use any thin, white-fleshed fish fillets. Serve with coleslaw (page 77).

Makes 6 servings

3 lb	baking potatoes	1.5 kg
3 tbsp	olive oil or vegetable oil, divided	45 mL
½ tsp	salt	2 mL
¼ tsp	pepper	1 mL
1 tsp	chopped fresh rosemary (or ¼ tsp/1 mL dried)	5 mL
1½ lb	white-fleshed fish fillets	750 g
½ cup	all-purpose flour	125 mL
2	egg whites or 1 whole egg	2
¾ cup	dry breadcrumbs	175 mL
¾ cup	cornflake crumbs	175 mL

1. Peel or scrub potatoes and cut into thick French-fry shapes. Pat dry and toss with 1 tbsp/15 mL oil, salt, pepper and rosemary. Arrange in single layer on non-stick baking sheet or baking pan lined with parchment paper. Bake in preheated 425°F/220°C oven for 40 minutes.

2. Meanwhile, cut fish into 6 serving-sized pieces. Pat dry.

3. Place flour in shallow dish. Beat egg whites in another shallow dish and combine breadcrumbs and cornflake crumbs in third dish.

4. Dust each piece of fish with flour. Dip into egg whites and allow excess to run off. Dip into crumb mixture and pat crumbs in firmly.

5. While potatoes are cooking, brush second baking sheet with 1 tbsp/15 mL oil or line with parchment paper. Arrange fish in single layer on baking sheet and drizzle with remaining 1 tbsp/15 mL oil. Put second baking sheet with fish in oven when potatoes have cooked for 40 minutes. Bake fish for 5 minutes, turn carefully and bake for 5 more minutes, or until fish is cooked through.

CHIPOTLES

Chipotles are very hot, dried, smoked jalapeños. They come in tins, packed in hot adobo sauce, but are also sometimes sold dried. When you open a tin, freeze any you don't use.

SERRANOS

Serranos are small and green; they are hotter than jalapeños.

HABAÑEROS

Habañeros (or Scotch Bonnets or Cascabels) are the hottest of all. They are small and round and can be green, yellow or red.

PER SERVING

Calories	422
g carbohydrate	59
g fibre	3
g total fat	8
g saturated fat	1
g protein	27

Excellent: thiamine; niacin; vitamin B_6; vitamin B_{12}
Good: iron; folacin

mg cholesterol	49
mg sodium	488
mg potassium	1069

SWEET AND SOUR SWORDFISH

This recipe from southern Italy is rich in flavour but lean in fat and calories. We serve it in our Lite Italian cooking course, and people love it. Everything except the final cooking can be done ahead of time. Use halibut if you can't find swordfish.

Makes 8 servings

2 tsp	olive oil	10 mL
3	large onions, thinly sliced	3
2	cloves garlic, finely chopped	2
pinch	hot red pepper flakes	pinch
¼ cup	raisins	50 mL
2 tsp	granulated sugar	10 mL
¼ cup	balsamic vinegar	50 mL
¼ cup	dry white wine or water	50 mL
	Salt to taste	
8	4-oz/125 g pieces swordfish, about 1 inch/2.5 cm thick	8
2 tbsp	chopped fresh parsley	25 mL

1. Heat oil in large non-stick skillet. Add onions, garlic, hot pepper flakes and raisins and sprinkle with sugar. Cook until onions begin to brown.

2. Add balsamic vinegar, wine and salt. Cook until onions are very tender and juices have almost disappeared. Taste and adjust seasonings if necessary.

3. Pat swordfish dry. Place in baking dish and spoon onions on top. Bake in preheated 425°F/220°C oven for 10 to 12 minutes, depending on thickness of fish. Sprinkle with parsley.

COOKING TIME FOR FISH

The Canadian Department of Fisheries came up with guidelines for cooking fish, which James Beard published and made famous. Cook fish on medium-high heat (broiling, frying, barbecuing, baking, steaming or poaching) for 10 minutes per inch of thickness. That means if you are cooking a whole fish that is 3 inches/7.5 cm thick, you'll cook it for 30 minutes at 425°F/220°C. If your fish is frozen, cook it for 20 minutes per inch, and if it is partially defrosted, cook it for 15 minutes per inch. Fish should just flake when gently prodded.

PER SERVING

Calories	192
g carbohydrate	11
g fibre	1
g total fat	6
g saturated fat	1
g protein	23

Excellent: niacin; vitamin B_{12}
Good: vitamin B_6

mg cholesterol	44
mg sodium	105
mg potassium	466

SWORDFISH TERIYAKI

Most people like their swordfish steaks thick for barbecuing, but I prefer them very thin, and have convinced my students that this is a delicious way to enjoy them. If the person in the fish store won't cut them thinly for you, simply buy a regular piece and slice it yourself.

Serve this with steamed brown rice, couscous or rice noodles. The sauce is also great on salmon, chicken and meat.

Makes 6 servings

3 tbsp	soy sauce	45 mL
3 tbsp	water	45 mL
⅓ cup	rice wine	75 mL
⅓ cup	granulated sugar	75 mL
1	clove garlic, smashed	1
1	1-inch/2.5 cm piece fresh ginger root, smashed	1
3	strips lemon peel	3
	Small handful fresh cilantro or parsley stems	
1½ lb	swordfish, sliced about ¼ inch/ 5 mm thick (6 large flat pieces)	750 g
¼ cup	chopped fresh cilantro or parsley	50 mL

1. Combine soy sauce, water, rice wine, sugar, garlic, ginger, lemon peel and cilantro stems in saucepan and bring to boil. Lower heat and cook until mixture is cooked down by about half and is thick and syrupy. Cool. Strain.

2. Pat fish dry and preheat barbecue. Cook fish for 1 minute and turn. Brush with glaze. Cook fish for 2 minutes and turn again. Brush with glaze. Cook fish for 1 more minute (it should be cooked through but still moist and juicy after 4 to 5 minutes of cooking, since it is so thin) and turn. Brush and turn once more. Serve topped with chopped cilantro.

PER SERVING

Calories	182
g carbohydrate	10
g fibre	trace
g total fat	5
g saturated fat	1
g protein	23

Excellent: niacin; vitamin B_{12}
Good: vitamin B_6

mg cholesterol	44
mg sodium	415
mg potassium	377

GEFILTE FISH WITH BEET HORSERADISH SALAD

Gefilte fish is a traditional Jewish specialty that happens to be low in calories.

If your fish merchant will not grind the fish for you, simply chop the fish finely in the food processor, in batches of 1 lb/ 500 g each. You can use many different blends of fish, but I like the whitefish/pickerel combination the best.

At a Seder this is always served as an appetizer, but I often eat it for lunch or a light supper. It's usually served cold, so it is easy to make ahead. The cooking juices should gel and can be served with the fish.

HORSERADISH

Horseradish is a pungent root that can be grated and added to sauces and mashed potatoes, or it can be combined with cooked beets for a relish. You can buy it already grated (either white with vinegar or red with beets), but if you make your own it will be much more piquant.

When grating horseradish, be careful, as the vapours can be harsh and make your eyes tear. (When my brother-in-law Wayne Krangle grates horseradish condiments for Passover, he always wears goggles!)

Makes 16 to 20 servings

2 lb	heads and bones from lean fish	1 kg
3	onions, sliced	3
2	carrots, sliced	2
4 qt	water	4 L
4 tsp	salt, divided	20 mL
2 tsp	pepper, divided	10 mL
3 lb	ground fish fillets (combination of whitefish and pickerel)	1.5 kg
3 tbsp	granulated sugar	45 mL
3	eggs, lightly beaten	3
¾ cup	ice water	175 mL
¼ cup	matzo meal	50 mL

Beet Horseradish Salad:

¼ cup	lemon juice	50 mL
1 tbsp	grated horseradish	15 mL
¼ tsp	pepper	1 mL
	Salt to taste	
1 tbsp	chopped fresh dill	15 mL
2 tbsp	chopped fresh chives or green onions	25 mL
2 lb	beets, cooked, peeled and diced	1 kg
1	head lettuce, shredded	1

HORSERADISH RELISH

My cousin Barbara Glickman makes this wonderful relish. It'll knock your socks off.

Peel 2 lb/1 kg horseradish root and cut into chunks. Peel half a raw beet (about 3 oz/90 g) and cut into chunks.

In a food processor, finely chop the horseradish and beet. Combine with 2 tsp/10 mL granulated sugar, 1½ cups/375 mL white vinegar (just enough to cover) and a pinch of salt. Pack into jars and seal.

Makes about 5 cups/1.25 L.

1. Place fish heads, bones, onions, carrots and water in pot and bring to boil. Skim if necessary. Add 2 tsp/10 mL salt and 1 tsp/5 mL pepper. Cook gently for about 20 minutes.

2. Combine ground fish with remaining salt and pepper, sugar, eggs, ice water and matzo meal. Shape mixture into 16 to 20 patties.

3. Gently place fish patties in simmering liquid. Cover, lower heat and cook very gently for 1½ hours. Uncover and cook for 30 minutes longer.

4. Remove fish from liquid and cool. (Fish keeps well refrigerated for up to 5 days.) Strain liquid and either freeze for future use or return to pot and reduce to 3 cups/750 mL (reduced stock will usually gel when it is cold and can be used as garnish or "sauce").

5. For beet salad, combine lemon juice, horseradish, pepper, salt, dill and chives. Toss beets with dressing. Taste and adjust seasonings if necessary.

6. To serve, place some lettuce on each plate. Top with beets and arrange fish on top.

PER SERVING

Calories	147
g carbohydrate	8
g fibre	1
g total fat	4
g saturated fat	1
g protein	19

Excellent: niacin; vitamin B_{12}
Good: thiamine; folacin

mg cholesterol	102
mg sodium	367
mg potassium	514

PROVENÇAL FISH STEW WITH ROUILLE

See photo opposite page 128.

Rouille is a garlic-red pepper mayonnaise-type mixture that is used to flavour dishes. It can also be used as a spread in sandwiches or as a dip.

You can serve this in small quantities as an appetizer, but I love it as a main course with potatoes or rice added to each serving. (I add ¼ cup/50 mL cooked rice or a diced small cooked potato to each bowl and then ladle the stew on top.)

Use a lean white-fleshed fish such as striped bass, halibut or red snapper in this dish.

Makes 8 servings

3 lb	heads and tails of lean white-fleshed fish, chopped	1.5 kg
8 cups	water	2 L
1 tbsp	olive oil	15 mL
2	onions, chopped	2
2	leeks or small onions, trimmed and chopped	2
1	bulb fennel or 2 stalks celery, trimmed and chopped	1
pinch	hot red pepper flakes	pinch
3	cloves garlic, chopped	3
1	28-oz/796 mL tin plum tomatoes, with juices	1
pinch	saffron, optional	pinch
½ tsp	pepper	2 mL
	Salt to taste	
1 lb	scallops	500 g
1 lb	lean white-fleshed fish fillets	500 g

ROASTING PEPPERS

Roasting peppers gives them an earthy, smoky taste. If you can, place the whole peppers on a barbecue (grill a bunch at one time), turning them every few minutes until all sides are blackened. Or you can cut the peppers in half, place them skin side up on a baking sheet and grill them under the broiler until they blacken. You can can also roast one pepper at a time over a gas element.

Let the blackened peppers cool and then peel off the skin and remove the stems, cores and seeds. Then slice or dice them and add to the dish.

PEELING PEPPERS

Seventeen years ago when I studied Italian cooking with Marcella Hazan in Bologna, we peeled every pepper before using it in any dish. I couldn't believe it at the time, but now I always peel peppers, too. You don't really have to peel peppers, but they are so much sweeter and milder that the extra time seems well spent.

If the peppers are not being cooked in a dish, roast and peel them. If you are cooking the peppers, simply peel them with a vegetable peeler (you will quickly learn to buy square-shaped peppers with smooth sides!).

Rouille:

2	cloves garlic, minced	2
1	sweet red pepper, roasted and peeled	1
½ tsp	hot chili paste	2 mL
½ tsp	Dijon mustard	2 mL
½ cup	soft yogurt cheese (page 228) or thick yogurt	125 mL
1 tbsp	mayonnaise, optional	15 mL
	Salt and pepper to taste	
8	slices French bread, toasted	8
2 tbsp	chopped fresh parsley	25 mL

1. Place fish heads and tails in large Dutch oven and cover with cold water. Bring to boil, skim off froth and simmer gently for 25 minutes. Strain and reserve stock.

2. Heat olive oil in Dutch oven. Add onions, leeks, fennel, hot pepper flakes and chopped garlic. Cook for about 8 minutes, stirring.

3. Add tomatoes, saffron and 5 cups/1.25 L reserved stock. Bring to boil. Add pepper and salt. Cook for 30 minutes.

4. If scallops are large, cut through their thickness and add to soup with fish fillets. Cook for 10 minutes, or until fish is just cooked. Taste and adjust seasonings if necessary.

5. Meanwhile, to prepare rouille, puree garlic with roasted red pepper, hot chili paste, mustard, yogurt cheese and mayonnaise. Taste and add salt and pepper if necessary. Spread rouille on bread.

6. Serve soup in bowls with some fish and scallops. Place slice of bread with rouille on top. Sprinkle with parsley.

FREEZING ROASTED PEPPERS

Line a baking sheet with plastic wrap, foil or waxed paper and spread out roasted peppers in a single layer (I leave them in large pieces). Freeze, lift off paper and then pack in freezer bags or containers. This way the pieces will stay separate and you can defrost small amounts at a time.

PER SERVING

Calories	257
g carbohydrate	25
g fibre	2
g total fat	5
g saturated fat	1
g protein	28

Excellent: vitamin C; niacin; vitamin B_{12}
Good: riboflavin; iron; vitamin B_6; folacin

mg cholesterol	46
mg sodium	434
mg potassium	1076

MUSSELS WITH BLACK BEAN SAUCE

See photo opposite page 129.

You can serve mussels as an appetizer or as a main course (this recipe serves 6 to 8 as a main course; 8 to 10 as an appetizer). You can also serve these over pasta or rice or just with lots of crusty bread. I always put a few extra bowls on the table to collect the empty shells, and I provide spoons for the juices.

Cultivated mussels are milder in flavour than wild ones, but they are much easier to clean. To clean wild mussels, scrub them well and remove the beards. To clean cultivated mussels, simply wash and remove the beards. When you are cleaning the mussels, discard any that do not close tightly when touched, any with broken shells and any that are very heavy (they may be full of sand). After the mussels are cooked, discard any that do not open.

Makes 6 to 8 servings

4 lb	mussels	2 kg

Black Bean Sauce:

2 tsp	vegetable oil	10 mL
3	cloves garlic, finely chopped	3
1 tbsp	finely chopped fresh ginger root	15 mL
3	green onions, chopped	3
½ tsp	hot chili paste	2 mL
2 tbsp	fermented black beans, rinsed and chopped	25 mL
1 tsp	grated lemon peel	5 mL
2	leeks or small onions, trimmed and thinly sliced	2
2	sweet red peppers, thinly sliced	2
½ cup	homemade chicken stock (page 59) or fish stock (page 53), dry white wine or water	125 mL
2 tbsp	rice vinegar or cider vinegar	25 mL
1 tbsp	soy sauce	15 mL
2 tsp	sesame oil	10 mL
¼ cup	chopped fresh cilantro or parsley	50 mL

BLACK BEANS AND BLACK BEAN SAUCE
The black beans used in Asian recipes are fermented and salted, and they are commonly used in small amounts as a seasoning, not a food. Do not confuse them with the dried or tinned black turtle beans used in chili dishes and soups.

If they are old and dried out, fermented beans can be soaked in boiling water for about 10 minutes before being drained and chopped. You can also buy black bean sauce — fermented beans combined with ingredients like garlic, oil, sugar and rice wine. My favourite brand is Lee Kum Kee black bean and garlic sauce. Once the jar has been opened, store it in the refrigerator.

1. Clean mussels and discard any that have broken shells or that do not close when lightly tapped.

2. Heat vegetable oil in wok or Dutch oven. Add garlic, ginger, green onions, chili paste, black beans and lemon peel. Cook for 30 seconds, or until very fragrant.

3. Add leeks and peppers and cook for 2 minutes, or until vegetables are slightly wilted.

4. Add stock, vinegar, soy sauce and sesame oil to wok. Stir well and bring to boil.

5. Add mussels and return to boil. Cover and cook for 5 to 7 minutes, or until mussels have opened and are thoroughly cooked. Stir well. Sprinkle with cilantro.

PER SERVING

Calories	143
g carbohydrate	12
g fibre	2
g total fat	5
g saturated fat	1
g protein	12

Excellent: vitamin C; iron; folacin; vitamin B_{12}
Good: vitamin A; thiamine; niacin

mg cholesterol	25
mg sodium	319
mg potassium	308

RISOTTO WITH SEAFOOD AND PEPPERS

Although I like to be able to make things in advance, risotto really cannot be made ahead (page 224). So invite people you feel comfortable having in your kitchen, and serve appetizers while they help you stir.

I like to serve risotto as the first sit-down course so that I don't have to leave people sitting at the table for 20 minutes while I make it. But the seafood and onions can be prepared ahead.

When I make risotto I always make lots, but there still never seems to be any left over! If you do have leftover risotto, it can be reheated in small portions in the microwave. Or better still, shape into patties and cook them in a non-stick pan in a bit of olive oil until they are crusty on the outside and soft and creamy on the inside.

Makes 6 to 8 servings

3 tbsp	olive oil, divided	45 mL
3	cloves garlic, finely chopped	3
¼ tsp	hot red pepper flakes	1 mL
1	sweet red pepper, diced	1
1	sweet yellow pepper, diced	1
½ lb	cleaned shrimp, diced	250 g
½ lb	scallops, diced	250 g
¼ cup	chopped fresh parsley	50 mL
¼ cup	chopped fresh basil	50 mL
4 cups	homemade chicken stock (page 59), or 1 10-oz/284 mL tin chicken broth plus water	1 L
½ cup	dry white wine	125 mL
1	onion, chopped	1
1½ cups	short-grain Italian rice, preferably Arborio	375 mL
	Salt and pepper to taste	

1. Heat 1 tbsp/15 mL oil in large non-stick skillet. Add garlic and hot pepper flakes. Cook until fragrant, about 30 seconds. Add red and yellow peppers and cook until wilted, about 10 minutes.

2. Add shrimp and scallops and stir well. Cook just until cooked through, about 2 to 3 minutes. Stir in parsley and basil. Reserve. (This can be done ahead.)

3. About 20 minutes before serving, combine stock and wine. Bring to boil and keep at simmer.

4. Heat remaining 2 tbsp/25 mL oil in large saucepan or Dutch oven. Add onion and cook gently for 5 minutes until tender and fragrant.

5. Stir in rice and coat well. Add ½ cup/125 mL stock and cook over medium-high heat, stirring constantly, until liquid evaporates or is absorbed. When pan is dry, repeat. Continue until rice is barely tender and almost all liquid is used. This should take about 15 minutes. (Rice will cook a bit more after you add seafood.)

6. Reheat seafood and stir into rice. Cook for 3 to 4 minutes. Taste and season with salt and pepper if necessary. Serve immediately.

CLEANING SHRIMP

Although you can buy shrimp already cleaned and shelled, you pay a premium for them, and if they have been frozen without their shells, they can dry out. I usually buy a 5-lb/2.5 kg block of frozen shrimp in their shells and defrost and clean them as I need them. Hold part of the chunk under cold water until it breaks off and then return the rest to the freezer, well wrapped. Defrost the shrimp you are using in the refrigerator, or in a sink or bowl of cold water.

To clean shrimp, remove the shells and then wiggle the tail part off gently. Run a knife along the top of the shrimp and devein by pulling out the black intestinal tract if there is one. Pat the shrimp dry.

PER SERVING

Calories	365
g carbohydrate	47
g fibre	2
g total fat	9
g saturated fat	1
g protein	21

Excellent: vitamin C; niacin; vitamin B$_{12}$
Good: vitamin A

mg cholesterol	71
mg sodium	142
mg potassium	481

FISH FILLETS WITH ROSEMARY

This simple recipe works with any fish that barbecues or broils well, such as halibut, salmon, sea bass, tuna, red snapper, monkfish or swordfish.

Makes 4 servings

4	fish fillets (about 4 oz/125 g each)	4
1 tbsp	olive oil	15 mL
1 tbsp	chopped fresh rosemary, or ½ tsp/2 mL dried	15 mL
½ tsp	pepper	2 mL
½ tsp	salt	2 mL

1. Pat fish dry and remove skin.

2. Brush fish with olive oil. Sprinkle with rosemary and pepper. Marinate in refrigerator for up to 8 hours.

3. Just before cooking, sprinkle salt over both sides of fish. Preheat barbecue or broiler and grill fish for 4 to 5 minutes per side. (You can also cook this in a hot non-stick skillet brushed with olive oil.)

MANGO RED PEPPER SALSA

Serve this salsa with grilled fish, pork or lamb.

Combine 1 roasted, peeled and diced sweet red pepper (page 154), 2 tbsp/ 25 mL finely chopped mild green chiles, 1 tsp/5 mL finely chopped jalapeño and 2 peeled and diced mangos (or 1½ cups/375 mL diced fresh or canned pineapple). Stir in ⅓ cup/75 mL chopped fresh cilantro or parsley, 1 tbsp/15 mL lime juice and salt and pepper to taste.

Makes about 2 cups/500 mL.

PER SERVING

Calories	155
g carbohydrate	trace
g fibre	0
g total fat	6
g saturated fat	1
g protein	24

Excellent: niacin; vitamin B$_{12}$
Good: vitamin B$_6$

mg cholesterol	36
mg sodium	348
mg potassium	513

Caribbean Vegetable and Chicken Curry *(page 168)*
Double Cornbread with Mild Green Chiles *(page 246)*

Roast Turkey Breast with Rosemary and Garlic *(page 182)*
Rapini with Raisins and Pine Nuts *(page 204)*
Spicy Mashed Sweet Potatoes *(page 214)*
Roasted Root Vegetables *(page 217)*
Cranberry Orange Sauce with Ginger *(page 182)*

POULTRY

Moroccan Chicken

Asian Chicken Chili

Chicken Pot Pie

Chicken Burgers Teriyaki

Breaded Chicken Fingers

Caribbean Vegetable and Chicken Curry

Barbecued Chicken Fingers

Chicken Fajitas

Chicken Breasts with Black Bean Sauce

St. Lucia Barbecued Chicken

Stir-fried Chicken and Vegetables

Skewered Chicken on a Bun

Chicken with Forty Cloves of Garlic

Chicken with Raspberry Vinegar

Roast Chicken with Bulgur Stuffing

Linda Stephen's Grilled Cilantro Chicken with Pad Thai

Roast Turkey Breast with Rosemary and Garlic

MOROCCAN CHICKEN

This spicy chicken is so good cold that I often make more than I need so I can use the leftovers in a salad. I roast the chicken breasts on the bone for extra juiciness, but I do remove the skin first so that the marinade can penetrate better.

Makes 6 servings

⅓ cup	honey	75 mL
1 tsp	sesame oil	5 mL
2 tbsp	lemon juice	25 mL
½ tsp	grated lemon peel	2 mL
3	cloves garlic, minced	3
½ tsp	ground cumin	2 mL
1 tsp	paprika	5 mL
¼ tsp	cinnamon	1 mL
¼ tsp	cayenne, optional	1 mL
¼ tsp	pepper	1 mL
6	skinless single chicken breasts, bone-in	6
¼ tsp	salt	1 mL
1 tbsp	sesame seeds	15 mL

1. In large bowl, combine honey, sesame oil, lemon juice, lemon peel, garlic, cumin, paprika, cinnamon, cayenne and pepper.

2. Add chicken to marinade. Turn to coat well. Refrigerate for 1 to 12 hours, turning a few times.

3. Line baking sheet with foil. Arrange chicken on foil bone side down. Spoon over any extra marinade and sprinkle with salt and sesame seeds. Bake in preheated 400°F/200°C oven for 30 to 40 minutes, or until cooked through.

SPICES

Spices are the seeds, bark and roots of certain plants. Ground spices lose their flavour quickly, so it is best to buy them in small quantities, or buy them whole and grind them as you need them. (Experts say that spices lose their flavour within a year of being ground.)

Store spices in a cool, dry place, and use them cautiously at first, so you can decide whether you like them with a particular food. There are some traditional matches such as nutmeg with spinach or cinnamon with apples, but follow your own instincts. It is personal taste that results in new recipes being invented. Spices can make your food exciting and replace the flavour lost by limiting fat and salt.

PER SERVING

Calories	208
g carbohydrate	17
g fibre	trace
g total fat	3
g saturated fat	1
g protein	28

Excellent: niacin; vitamin B_6
Good: vitamin B_{12}

mg cholesterol	68
mg sodium	175
mg potassium	345

ASIAN CHICKEN CHILI

This dish combines Eastern flavours with Western ideas. It can be made ahead of time and is a perfect nineties recipe — old-fashioned comfort food updated with international ingredients and a lighter style.

Serve it over steamed rice or couscous.

Makes 8 to 10 servings

1 tbsp	vegetable oil	15 mL
3	cloves garlic, finely chopped	3
2 tbsp	finely chopped fresh ginger root	25 mL
6	green onions, chopped	6
2	sweet red peppers, diced	2
2 tsp	hot chili paste, or to taste	10 mL
1 lb	boneless, skinless chicken breasts, diced	500 g
1	28-oz/796 mL tin plum tomatoes, drained and pureed	1
4 cups	cooked red kidney beans, or 2 19-oz/540 mL tins, rinsed and drained	1 L
2 tbsp	soy sauce	25 mL
1 tbsp	rice wine	15 mL
1 tsp	sesame oil	5 mL
½ cup	chopped fresh cilantro or parsley	125 mL

1. Heat oil in large deep skillet or wok. Add garlic, ginger and green onions. Cook gently for 30 seconds, until fragrant. Add red peppers and chili paste and cook for a few minutes.

2. Add chicken and combine well. Cook, stirring constantly, for about 5 minutes, until chicken pieces are white on outside.

3. Add tomatoes. Bring to boil. Reduce heat and simmer gently for 30 minutes, or until mixture is quite thick and almost all juices have evaporated.

4. Stir in beans, soy sauce and rice wine. Cook for 10 minutes.

5. Stir in sesame oil and cilantro. Taste and adjust seasonings if necessary.

PER SERVING

Calories	229
g carbohydrate	27
g fibre	10
g total fat	4
g saturated fat	1
g protein	22

Excellent: vitamin C; niacin; iron; vitamin B$_6$; folacin
Good: vitamin A; thiamine

mg cholesterol	33
mg sodium	358
mg potassium	780

CHICKEN POT PIE

*Chicken pot pie is great with a biscuit or phyllo pastry crust,
but I love it topped with mashed potatoes. Try it with some of
the other mashed-potato recipes in the book, too. You can also
make this with leftover turkey.*

Makes 8 to 10 servings

2 tbsp	olive oil	25 mL
½ lb	mushrooms, quartered	250 g
2	leeks or onions, trimmed and chopped	2
1 cup	diced carrots	250 mL
⅓ cup	all-purpose flour	75 mL
2 cups	homemade chicken stock (page 59), or milk	500 mL
1 tbsp	chopped fresh thyme, or ½ tsp/2 mL dried	15 mL
¼ tsp	hot red pepper sauce	1 mL
½ tsp	pepper	2 mL
	Salt to taste	
4 cups	diced cooked chicken breasts	1 L
½ cup	fresh or frozen corn niblets	125 mL
1 cup	fresh or frozen peas	250 mL
¼ cup	diced pimento or roasted sweet red pepper (page 154)	50 mL

Cheddar Mashed Potato Topping:

2 lb	baking potatoes, peeled and cut in 2-inch/5 cm pieces	1 kg
¾ cup	milk, hot	175 mL
¼ tsp	pepper	1 mL
	Salt to taste	
¾ cup	grated light Cheddar cheese	175 mL
1 tsp	paprika	5 mL

HANDLING CHICKEN
Keep chicken refrigerated
and use it quickly, or
freeze it. Chicken can be
easily contaminated with
salmonella and other
bacteria, so it must be
handled carefully. Defrost it
in the refrigerator or in the
microwave but never at
room temperature, as that's
when bacteria can grow
the fastest.

Be sure to prepare
chicken on an easy-to-
sanitize area, and wash the
counter, utensils and your
hands carefully afterwards.

1. Heat oil in large saucepan or Dutch oven. Add mushrooms, leeks and carrots. Cook for a few minutes. Sprinkle with flour. Cook gently for 5 minutes, but do not brown.

2. Whisk in stock and bring to boil. Reduce heat and add thyme, hot pepper sauce, pepper and salt. Simmer gently for 10 minutes, stirring occasionally.

3. Stir in chicken, corn, peas and pimento. Taste and adjust seasonings if necessary.

4. To make topping, cook potatoes in large pot of boiling water until tender. Drain well and pat dry. Mash. Beat in milk, pepper, salt and cheese. Taste and adjust seasonings if necessary. (Add more milk if necessary so that you can spread potatoes.)

5. Lightly oil 3 qt/3 L casserole dish. Spoon chicken mixture into dish. Pipe or spoon potato mixture over chicken and sprinkle with paprika.

6. Bake in preheated 400°F/200°C oven for 30 to 35 minutes, or until hot and bubbly.

CHICKEN BURGERS TERIYAKI

The teriyaki sauce adds a wonderful flavour to these chicken burgers, and it can also be used on lamb burgers or fish burgers.

Makes 6 servings

1 lb	boneless, skinless chicken breasts, trimmed of all fat	500 g
2	egg whites, or 1 whole egg	2
¾ cup	fresh breadcrumbs	175 mL
1	clove garlic, minced	1
1 tsp	minced fresh ginger root	5 mL
2 tbsp	chopped fresh cilantro or parsley	25 mL
2 tbsp	chopped fresh chives or green onions	25 mL
¼ tsp	salt	1 mL
3 tbsp	lemon ginger teriyaki sauce (see sidebar)	45 mL
6	hamburger buns or pita breads	6
3 cups	shredded lettuce	750 mL

1. Cut chicken into cubes and pat dry. Place in work bowl of food processor fitted with steel knife and chop on/off until finely chopped. (If you do not have food processor, mince meat finely with knife or buy it preground and use same day.)

2. Add egg whites, breadcrumbs, garlic, ginger, cilantro, chives and salt. Blend in.

3. Shape mixture into 6 patties. Refrigerate until ready to cook.

4. Preheat barbecue or broiler. Grill patties for 3 minutes per side. Brush generously with teriyaki sauce. Keep turning and brushing with sauce every 2 minutes for about 10 minutes, or until burgers are cooked through.

5. Serve in buns with shredded lettuce.

GROUND CHICKEN
Ground chicken is even more perishable than chicken pieces, so use it the same day or freeze it. Most store-bought ground chicken is made with both light and dark meat, and possibly skin and fat. Therefore, if you have a food processor, grind boneless, skinless chicken breasts yourself, so you know the ground chicken is fresh and lean, or ask your butcher to do this for you.

LEMON GINGER TERIYAKI SAUCE
In a saucepan, combine 3 tbsp/45 mL soy sauce, 3 tbsp/45 mL water, ⅓ cup/ 75 mL rice wine, ¼ cup/ 50 mL granulated sugar, 2 minced cloves garlic, 1 tbsp/15 mL minced fresh ginger root, ¼ tsp/1 mL hot chili paste and 1 tbsp/15 mL lemon juice. Bring to a boil and cook on medium-high heat until syrupy, about 5 minutes. Makes about ⅓ cup/75 mL.

PER SERVING

Calories	307
g carbohydrate	40
g fibre	2
g total fat	5
g saturated fat	1
g protein	25

Excellent: niacin
Good: thiamine; riboflavin; iron; vitamin B_6; folacin

mg cholesterol	44
mg sodium	655
mg potassium	345

BREADED CHICKEN FINGERS

In my constant attempt to cook things that my children will like, I keep trying to make chicken fingers that are not deep-fried and are somewhat healthful.

Instead of breadcrumbs you could use your children's favourite crackers or cereal to make the crumbs (or use half crackers or cereal and half breadcrumbs). Make the crumbs in the food processor or place the crackers or cereal in a plastic bag and crush with a rolling pin.

You can also bake whole chicken breasts this way (just bake for about 10 minutes longer). Serve with one of the dipping sauces.

Makes 4 to 6 servings

1 tsp	vegetable oil	5 mL
1 lb	boneless, skinless chicken breasts	500 g
1/3 cup	soft yogurt cheese (page 228) or thick yogurt	75 mL
1 tbsp	ketchup	15 mL
1 tsp	Dijon mustard	5 mL
1/2 tsp	Worcestershire sauce	2 mL
1/4 tsp	pepper	1 mL
1 1/2 cups	breadcrumbs or cracker crumbs	375 mL

1. Brush baking sheet with vegetable oil and place in preheated 400°F/200°C oven.

2. Cut each chicken breast into 4 or 5 strips. Pat dry.

3. Place yogurt cheese, ketchup, mustard, Worcestershire and pepper in bowl and combine well. Add chicken pieces and coat well.

4. Place cracker crumbs on large plate. One at a time, roll chicken fingers in crumbs and pat in.

5. Place chicken in single layer on baking sheet and bake for 15 minutes. Turn and bake for 10 to 12 minutes longer, or until crisp and cooked through.

PLUM DIPPING SAUCE

Combine 1/4 cup/50 mL plum sauce, 1 tsp/5 mL soy sauce and 1/2 tsp/2 mL ground ginger.

Makes about 1/4 cup/50 mL

HONEY GARLIC SAUCE

Combine 1/4 cup/50 mL honey, 1 tbsp/15 mL soy sauce and 1 minced clove garlic.

Makes about 1/4 cup/50 mL.

PER SERVING

Calories	288
g carbohydrate	29
g fibre	1
g total fat	4
g saturated fat	1
g protein	33

Excellent: niacin; vitamin B_6
Good: riboflavin; iron; vitamin B_{12}

mg cholesterol	68
mg sodium	416
mg potassium	420

CARIBBEAN VEGETABLE AND CHICKEN CURRY

See photo opposite page 160.

Barbecuing the chicken adds flavour to this dish, but you can also just add the uncooked chicken along with the potatoes. Serve this over rice or couscous. For a vegetarian version, omit the first four ingredients.

Makes 8 servings

6	boneless, skinless single chicken breasts	6
2 tbsp	Dijon mustard	25 mL
2 tsp	sesame oil	10 mL
3 tbsp	curry powder, divided	45 mL
1 tbsp	vegetable oil	15 mL
3	cloves garlic, finely chopped	3
2 tbsp	finely chopped fresh ginger root	25 mL
1	small hot chile pepper, finely chopped	1
pinch	allspice	pinch
pinch	cinnamon	pinch
pinch	nutmeg	pinch
1	onion, coarsely chopped	1
1	leek, trimmed and coarsely chopped	1
½ cup	homemade vegetable stock (page 62), or homemade chicken stock (page 59) or water	125 mL
1	28-oz/796 mL tin plum tomatoes, pureed with juices	1
2	potatoes, peeled and cut in chunks	2
1	large sweet potato, peeled and cut in chunks	1
2	carrots, sliced	2
1 lb	butternut squash, peeled and cut in chunks	500 g
¾ cup	pineapple juice, tomato juice or canned coconut milk	175 mL

PLANTAINS

Plantains are becoming more and more available. They are served as a vegetable, although they look like bananas. They are often sliced thinly and deep-fried and served as an appetizer or garnish, but I love to add them to stews and curries. I buy the ripe yellow/black ones rather than the green. Instead of peeling them as you would a banana, slit the skin lengthwise and then peel.

2	plantains, peeled and cut in chunks, optional	2
1	19-oz/540 mL tin chickpeas, rinsed and drained, or 2 cups/ 500 mL cooked chickpeas	1
½ cup	chopped fresh cilantro or parsley	125 mL

1. Pat chicken dry. In small bowl, combine mustard, sesame oil and 1 tbsp/15 mL curry powder. Coat chicken with mixture.

2. Preheat barbecue or broiler and grill chicken for 5 minutes per side (chicken will not be completely cooked). Cut into 2-inch/5 cm chunks. Reserve.

3. Heat oil in large, deep skillet or Dutch oven. Add garlic, ginger and hot chile pepper. Cook for 30 seconds. Add remaining 2 tbsp/25 mL curry powder, allspice, cinnamon and nutmeg. Cook for 30 seconds longer. Add onion, leek and stock. Cook until liquid evaporates.

4. Add pureed tomatoes and bring to boil. Add potatoes and sweet potato and cook, covered, for 10 minutes.

5. Add carrots, squash, pineapple juice, plantains, chickpeas and chicken and cook, covered, for 30 minutes longer.

6. Taste and adjust seasonings if necessary. Sprinkle with cilantro.

CURRY POWDER

Curry powder is a blend of spices used to flavour East Indian dishes. Traditionally there is a different blend for every kind of meat, fish or vegetable, but for convenience, most spice companies make an all-purpose blend. Bolst's is a good brand.

To make your own curry powder, combine 1 tsp/5 mL ground cumin, 2 tbsp/25 mL ground coriander, 1 tsp/ 5 mL turmeric, ¼ tsp/1 mL salt, ½ tsp/2 mL cinnamon, ¼ tsp/1 mL ground cloves, 1 tsp/5 mL cardamom and about 1 tsp/5 mL cayenne (more or less to taste).

Makes about ¼ cup/50 mL

PER SERVING

Calories	317
g carbohydrate	41
g fibre	6
g total fat	6
g saturated fat	1
g protein	27

Excellent: vitamin A; vitamin C; niacin; iron; vitamin B_6
Good: thiamine; folacin

mg cholesterol	55
mg sodium	389
mg potassium	895

BARBECUED CHICKEN FINGERS

This recipe is a hit with both children and adults. It can be served warm or cold, and you can cook whole chicken breasts instead of fingers.

I serve these chicken fingers over rice as a main course, or as an appetizer with a yogurt dip for the kids and a spicy salsa dip (page 43) for adults.

Makes 4 adult servings; 6 child-sized servings

1 lb	boneless, skinless chicken breasts	500 g
2 tbsp	honey	25 mL
2 tbsp	lemon juice	25 mL
1 tbsp	ketchup or commercial chili sauce	15 mL
¼ tsp	ground cumin	1 mL
½ tsp	salt	2 mL

1. Cut each chicken breast into 4 or 5 strips. Pat dry.

2. In bowl, combine honey, lemon juice, ketchup and cumin. Add chicken and marinate in refrigerator for up to 8 hours.

3. Just before cooking, stir salt into chicken mixture. Preheat barbecue or broiler. Grill chicken pieces for 5 to 7 minutes per side, depending on thickness, until just cooked through.

PER ADULT SERVING

Calories	151
g carbohydrate	8
g fibre	trace
g total fat	2
g saturated fat	trace
g protein	26

Excellent: niacin; vitamin B_6

mg cholesterol	70
mg sodium	330
mg potassium	239

CHICKEN FAJITAS

This Eastern-flavoured adaptation of fajitas is perfect for a Super Bowl or World Series party instead of chili or whatever you had last year! If you cannot find flour tortillas, just use pita bread and fill the pockets with the chicken, vegetables and lettuce.

Makes 8 servings

8	small boneless, skinless single chicken breasts (3 oz/90 g each)	8
1 tbsp	hoisin sauce	15 mL
1 tbsp	honey	15 mL
1 tbsp	sesame oil	15 mL
1 tsp	hot chili paste	5 mL
2	cloves garlic, minced	2
1 tbsp	minced fresh ginger root	15 mL
1 lb	eggplant, cut in ¼-inch/ 5 mm slices	500 g
2	large onions, sliced	2
8	10-inch/25 cm flour tortillas	8
⅓ cup	hoisin sauce	75 mL
2 cups	shredded lettuce	500 mL
¼ cup	chopped fresh cilantro or parsley	50 mL

1. Pat chicken dry. Combine 1 tbsp/15 mL hoisin sauce, honey, sesame oil, chili paste, garlic and ginger. Combine half of sauce with chicken and marinate in refrigerator until ready to cook.

2. Brush remaining marinade on eggplant and onion slices. Preheat broiler or barbecue and grill eggplant and onions on both sides until browned and cooked through.

3. Grill chicken on both sides until browned and cooked through, but do not overcook. Cut vegetables and chicken into 2-inch/5 cm pieces and toss together if you wish, or leave in large pieces.

4. To warm tortillas, wrap in foil and place in preheated 350°F/180°C oven for 5 to 10 minutes.

5. To assemble, spread spoonful of hoisin sauce over middle of each tortilla. Place some of chicken and vegetable mixture in centre. Top with lettuce and cilantro. Fold up bottom and roll up fajita to enclose filling.

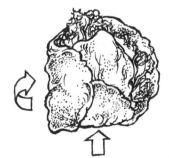

PER SERVING

Calories	349
g carbohydrate	46
g fibre	3
g total fat	7
g saturated fat	1
g protein	26

Excellent: niacin; vitamin B$_6$
Good: riboflavin; iron

mg cholesterol	53
mg sodium	523
mg potassium	440

CHICKEN BREASTS WITH BLACK BEAN SAUCE

Students often bring me wonderful recipes, and this dish, from Irene Tam, is one of the best. It has become one of our favourite meals as it is so easy to prepare and the flavours are so dynamic. The sauce is also great with pork tenderloin or salmon (salmon should only be cooked for about 10 minutes). Serve this with steamed rice or couscous and a few simply cooked vegetables. It is good hot or cold, so it is also perfect for picnics.

If you are using boneless chicken breasts, use a little less black bean sauce. Otherwise the dish may be too strong.

Makes 6 servings

6	skinless single chicken breasts, bone-in	6
2 tbsp	black bean sauce (page 156)	25 mL
1 tsp	frozen orange juice concentrate	5 mL
2 tbsp	water	25 mL
½ tsp	hot chili paste	2 mL
1 tsp	sesame oil, optional	5 mL
2 tbsp	chopped fresh cilantro or parsley	25 mL

1. Pat chicken breasts dry.

2. In small bowl, combine black bean sauce, orange juice concentrate, water, hot chili paste and sesame oil.

3. Rub black bean mixture all over chicken. Arrange chicken, bone side down, on baking sheet lined with foil.

4. Bake in preheated 375°F/190°C oven for 45 minutes, or until chicken is cooked through. Sprinkle with cilantro before serving.

SKINNING CHICKEN
I usually remove the skin from chicken before cooking. I often leave the breast on the bones, however, as the bones help to keep the meat juicy when there is no skin. If you are using skinless, boneless chicken breasts, be extremely careful not to overcook them, as they can easily become dry and tough. Be sure to keep any raw skin and bones for chicken stock (page 59).

PER SERVING

Calories	142
g carbohydrate	3
g fibre	trace
g total fat	2
g saturated fat	trace
g protein	27

Excellent: niacin; vitamin B_6
Good: vitamin B_{12}

mg cholesterol	73
mg sodium	147
mg potassium	289

St. Lucia Barbecued Chicken

Barbecued chicken is a favourite dish in St. Lucia. When I barbecue chicken, if the sauce is sugar- or tomato-based, I like to bake the chicken first. That way I only have to brown and flavour the chicken on the barbecue, and it won't burn. The chicken is also good just baked; the final grilling step is optional.

Makes 8 to 10 servings

St. Lucia Barbecue Sauce:

1	28-oz/796 mL tin plum tomatoes, drained and pureed	1
1 cup	finely chopped fresh or canned pineapple	250 mL
¼ cup	brown sugar	50 mL
¼ cup	Dijon mustard	50 mL
2 tbsp	cider vinegar	25 mL
1 tbsp	Worcestershire sauce	15 mL
2 tbsp	minced fresh ginger root	25 mL
6	cloves garlic, minced	6
1	onion, finely chopped	1
2	hot fresh chile peppers, minced	2
1 tsp	ground cumin	5 mL
1 tsp	paprika	5 mL
4 lb	skinless chicken pieces, bone-in	2 kg

1. In saucepan, combine all ingredients except chicken. Bring to boil and cook for 15 minutes, uncovered. Sauce should be thick. Cool.

2. Pat chicken pieces dry and coat with sauce. Place meaty side up in baking dish and bake in preheated 350°F/180°C oven for 30 minutes.

3. If you want to barbecue chicken, remove chicken from baking dish, transfer sauce to saucepan and boil until thick. Barbecue chicken for 5 to 10 minutes per side, brushing with reduced sauce. If you aren't barbecuing, simply bake chicken for 10 to 20 minutes longer in sauce, or until thoroughly cooked.

GRILLING

Barbecuing has become very popular lately. It adds flavour to food without adding fat and everyone loves the smoky taste. A lot of people are dedicated to using charcoal barbecues, but I think gas barbecues are easy to use, and the food tastes great. Built-in indoor barbecues are becoming more and more common, but you can also buy countertop electric grills that give you better flavour than a broiler without the expense of a built-in grill.

STIR-FRIED CHICKEN AND VEGETABLES

This is a recipe I teach in my university survival course, and it is very popular. At the beginning of the course, the teenage students are all so serious that I have to keep reminding them that cooking is fun and that I don't give out grades! Luckily there are always one or two more experienced cooks who testify that if you know how to cook, you become the most popular kid on campus, and invitations to dinner at your place become really hot tickets! That seems to win them over every time.

Serve this with steamed rice.

Makes 4 to 5 servings

1 lb	boneless, skinless chicken breasts	500 g
1 tbsp	soy sauce	15 mL
1 tbsp	cornstarch	15 mL

Sauce:

⅔ cup	homemade chicken stock (page 59) or water	150 mL
2 tbsp	hoisin sauce	25 mL
2 tsp	sesame oil	10 mL
1 tbsp	rice wine or sake	15 mL
1 tbsp	cornstarch	15 mL

To Cook:

1 tbsp	vegetable oil	15 mL
2	cloves garlic, finely chopped	2
1 tbsp	finely chopped fresh ginger root	15 mL
3	green onions, chopped	3
1 tsp	hot chili paste	5 mL
1	sweet red pepper, cut in strips	1
1	carrot, thinly sliced	1
1	bunch broccoli, cut in 1-inch/ 2.5 cm pieces	1
2 tbsp	chopped fresh cilantro or green onions	25 mL

1. Cut chicken into 1–inch/2.5 cm chunks. In large bowl, combine 1 tbsp/15 mL soy sauce and 1 tbsp/15 mL cornstarch. Add chicken to marinade and reserve.

2. To make sauce, in separate bowl, combine stock, hoisin sauce, sesame oil, rice wine and 1 tbsp/15 mL cornstarch. Reserve.

3. To cook, heat vegetable oil in wok or large, deep skillet. Add garlic, ginger, green onions and hot chili paste. Cook for 30 seconds.

4. Add chicken to skillet and cook until lightly browned. Add red pepper, carrot, broccoli and ¼ cup/50 mL water. Cover and cook for 3 to 5 minutes, or until chicken is just cooked through and broccoli is bright green.

5. Stir sauce well and add to chicken/vegetable mixture. Bring to boil, stirring constantly. Taste and adjust seasonings if necessary. Serve sprinkled with cilantro.

WOKS

Woks are useful for low-fat cooking, as you cook a lot of food in very little oil. Buy a large one so there is plenty of room to stir things around. Choose a wok with handles on both sides and buy one with a lid, so that you can also use it for steaming.

When cooking with a wok, make sure the wok is very hot before you add the food to it.

To help prevent sticking, season your new wok by washing it well. Fill it half full with a neutral-tasting vegetable oil, then heat the wok on the stove and cool off a few times, brushing the unoiled areas occasionally. Pour out the oil and wipe out the wok. After using, wash it only with water. Reseason as necessary.

PER SERVING

Calories	278
g carbohydrate	19
g fibre	4
g total fat	8
g saturated fat	1
g protein	32

Excellent: vitamin A; vitamin C; niacin; vitamin B$_6$; folacin
Good: riboflavin; iron; vitamin B$_{12}$

mg cholesterol	66
mg sodium	501
mg potassium	823

SKEWERED CHICKEN ON A BUN

This chicken dish is great on its own, but it is also irresistible served with a luscious, garlicky tzatziki (page 39). You can use whole chicken breasts rather than cubes.

I like to serve this in sesame hot dog buns or submarine buns, but try whole wheat buns, pita breads or rolled-up flour tortillas too.

This dish is also good cold. If you are using bamboo skewers, soak them in cold water for 1 hour before using.

Makes 4 servings

1 lb	boneless, skinless chicken breasts	500 g
2 tbsp	lemon juice	25 mL
½ tsp	salt	2 mL
½ tsp	pepper	2 mL
¼ tsp	ground cumin	1 mL
¼ tsp	dried oregano	1 mL
pinch	hot red pepper flakes, optional	pinch
2	cloves garlic, minced	2
4	hot dog buns	4

1. Cut chicken into 1½-inch/4 cm cubes.

2. In bowl, combine lemon juice, salt, pepper, cumin, oregano, hot pepper flakes and garlic. Add chicken pieces and marinate for up to 1 hour in refrigerator.

3. Thread chicken onto 4 skewers. Preheat broiler or barbecue and grill chicken for 5 to 7 minutes per side, or until just cooked through. Check often to prevent burning. Remove chicken from skewers and serve in buns.

CHOPPING AND COOKING GARLIC

Cooked garlic is gentle in flavour, and the longer it cooks, the softer and sweeter it becomes.

When cooking garlic, do not let it brown too much, or it will become bitter. Cook it on low heat, in a little oil, until it becomes fragrant; add some water if garlic appears to be sticking. If you do not want to use oil at all, start the cooking in a little water or chicken stock. If you are cooking garlic and onions together, add the onion to the hot skillet first to cool off the pan a little.

The more finely garlic is chopped, the more flavour it releases. I use a garlic press to mince garlic when it is going to be eaten raw in a salad dressing, dip or spread. But minced garlic sticks and burns when it is added to a hot skillet, so I chop the garlic with a knife if I am sautéeing it.

PER SERVING

Calories	276
g carbohydrate	28
g fibre	1
g total fat	4
g saturated fat	1
g protein	30

Excellent: niacin; vitamin B$_6$
Good: thiamine; iron

mg cholesterol	70
mg sodium	545
mg potassium	276

CHICKEN WITH FORTY CLOVES OF GARLIC

Some people are actually afraid of the forty cloves of garlic in this recipe (once in class I tripled it, and students really went ballistic!). But it is as I always say — the longer garlic cooks, the milder and sweeter it becomes.

This is a good make-ahead dish, as it tastes even better after sitting in its juices overnight and being reheated. Serve the chicken over mashed potatoes with some of the juices and lots of garlic. Although it is not traditional, the chèvre cream is sensational with this.

Makes 6 servings

1	3-lb/1.5 kg chicken, cut in pieces, skin removed	1
1 tbsp	olive oil	15 mL
40	cloves garlic, peeled	40
10	shallots, peeled, optional	10
3 tbsp	cognac or brandy	45 mL
½ tsp	salt	2 mL
½ tsp	pepper	2 mL
¾ cup	dry white wine or homemade chicken stock (page 59)	175 mL
2 tbsp	chopped fresh chives or green onions, optional	25 mL

1. Pat chicken pieces dry. Heat oil in large, deep non-stick skillet. Brown chicken pieces well, in batches if necessary so as not to crowd pan, about 8 minutes per side.

2. Add garlic cloves and shallots and shake pan well to move cloves under chicken a bit. Cook for another 10 to 15 minutes, until garlic and shallots brown lightly.

3. Discard any fat from pan. Pour in cognac and flambé with long match if desired (pages 262-63).

4. Add salt, pepper and wine. Bring to boil, cover, reduce heat and simmer gently for 30 minutes. Sprinkle with chives before serving.

CHÈVRE CREAM

In a small saucepan, combine ½ cup/125 mL milk and 3 oz/90 g chèvre (goat cheese). Heat gently and whisk until smooth. Stir in 1 tsp/5 mL each chopped fresh thyme and rosemary (or ¼ tsp/1 mL each dried), 2 tbsp/25 mL chopped fresh chives or green onions, ¼ tsp/1 mL pepper and salt to taste.

Makes about ½ cup/125 mL.

PER SERVING

Calories	192
g carbohydrate	7
g fibre	trace
g total fat	6
g saturated fat	1
g protein	25

Excellent: niacin; vitamin B$_6$

mg cholesterol	76
mg sodium	280
mg potassium	355

CHICKEN WITH RASPBERRY VINEGAR

This recipe has always been one of my favourites. Serve it with rice or couscous. Instead of raspberry vinegar you can use sherry vinegar, balsamic vinegar or lemon juice.

Makes 4 to 6 servings

1 lb	skinless, boneless chicken breasts	500 g
½ cup	all-purpose flour	125 mL
4 tsp	olive oil, divided	20 mL
½ tsp	salt	2 mL
¼ tsp	pepper	1 mL
1 tbsp	chopped fresh rosemary, or ½ tsp/2 mL dried	15 mL
¼ cup	raspberry vinegar	50 mL
¼ cup	dry white wine or homemade chicken stock (page 59)	50 mL
½ lb	snow peas, trimmed	250 g
2 cups	cherry tomatoes	500 mL

1. Cut chicken into 2-inch/5 cm cubes. Pat dry and dust lightly with flour.

2. Heat 2 tsp/10 mL oil in large non-stick skillet or wok. Cook chicken for 4 to 5 minutes, until just cooked through. During cooking, sprinkle chicken with salt, pepper and rosemary.

3. Remove chicken and reserve. Add vinegar and wine to pan and cook on medium-high heat, scraping bottom to loosen any flavourful bits of chicken. Cook until sauce reduces slightly.

4. Return chicken pieces to pan and turn to coat well and heat. Transfer to serving platter and keep warm.

5. Return pan to heat and add remaining oil. Add snow peas and cook for 1 minute. Add tomatoes and cook only until heated through. Arrange vegetables around chicken or combine everything together.

LEMON-ROASTED CHICKEN

If you want a plain old-fashioned roast chicken, buy the best chicken you can find (organic or free-range), sprinkle it with coarse salt and a bit of pepper and put a pierced lemon in the cavity. Roast it at 400°F/200°C for 1 to 1¼ hours (for a 3- to 4-lb/1.5 to 2 kg chicken).

PER SERVING

Calories	238
g carbohydrate	14
g fibre	3
g total fat	6
g saturated fat	1
g protein	29

Excellent: vitamin C; niacin; vitamin B_6
Good: thiamine; iron

mg cholesterol	66
mg sodium	368
mg potassium	583

ROAST CHICKEN WITH BULGUR STUFFING

Roast chicken or turkey is delicious stuffed with an unusual rice or grain. This bulgur stuffing can be cooked separately and served on its own as a side dish.

Makes 6 servings

2 tsp	olive oil	10 mL
2	onions, chopped	2
1	clove garlic, finely chopped	1
2	stalks celery, chopped	2
¼ cup	chopped dried apricots	50 mL
2 tbsp	raisins	25 mL
1 tbsp	pine nuts, toasted (page 245)	15 mL
1 cup	bulgur	250 mL
2 cups	homemade chicken stock (page 59), hot	500 mL
½ tsp	salt	2 mL
½ tsp	pepper	2 mL
¼ cup	chopped fresh parsley	50 mL
1	3-lb/1.5 kg chicken	1
1 tbsp	soy sauce	15 mL
1 tbsp	apricot jam	15 mL

1. For stuffing, heat oil in large saucepan or Dutch oven. Add onions and garlic and cook gently for 5 minutes. Add celery, apricots, raisins and pine nuts. Cook for 1 minute.

2. Add bulgur, stock, salt and pepper and bring to boil. Reduce heat, cover and cook gently on low heat for 10 minutes, until bulgur is just tender and liquid has been absorbed. Add parsley. Taste and adjust seasonings if necessary. Cool.

3. Pat chicken dry inside and out. Stuff with bulgur mixture and place any remaining stuffing in lightly oiled casserole dish. Truss chicken if you wish.

4. Combine soy sauce with apricot jam. Brush on chicken. Bake in preheated 400°F/200°C oven for 1½ hours, or until juices run clear (check chicken after 45 minutes and if it is browning too much, reduce oven temperature to 325°F/160°C and cover lightly with tent of foil). After chicken has cooked for 45 minutes, place dish of extra stuffing, covered, in oven to heat. Carve chicken and serve with stuffing.

TRUSSING A CHICKEN

This is just one way to truss a chicken:

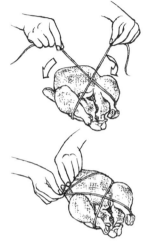

PER SERVING
(stuffing and chicken, no skin)

Calories	312
g carbohydrate	29
g fibre	6
g total fat	9
g saturated fat	2
g protein	30

Excellent: niacin; vitamin B$_6$
Good: iron; folacin; vitamin B$_{12}$

mg cholesterol	73
mg sodium	291
mg potassium	549

PER SERVING
(stuffing and chicken, with skin)

Calories	406
g carbohydrate	31
g fibre	6
g total fat	17
g saturated fat	4
g protein	33

Excellent: niacin; vitamin B$_6$
Good: riboflavin; folacin; vitamin B$_{12}$; iron

mg cholesterol	88
mg sodium	442
mg potassium	581

Linda Stephen's Grilled Cilantro Chicken with Pad Thai

Linda Stephen began teaching at my school more than fifteen years ago, and she has a devoted following of students who love her warm, generous and very organized style of teaching. In 1986 she spent a year working in Australia, where she fell in love with Thai cuisine. She then studied cooking in Thailand and now has a great ability to simplify Thai recipes as well as invent her own.

The marinade for this chicken is also delicious spread on steak or lamb chops, and sometimes Linda slices the chicken or meat and serves it in or on the Pad Thai noodles. Pad Thai often contains bits of tofu, shrimp and chicken, but this version is meatless. You can serve it with the cilantro chicken or other meats, or as a vegetarian dish on its own.

Makes 6 servings

Chicken:

4	cloves garlic	4
2	shallots or 1 small onion	2
1 cup	fresh cilantro or parsley	250 mL
2 tbsp	Thai fish sauce (nam pla) or soy sauce	25 mL
¼ cup	lime juice	50 mL
1 tbsp	pepper	15 mL
6	boneless, skinless single chicken breasts	6

Pad Thai Noodles:

½ lb	rice vermicelli noodles (fettuccine width)	250 g
¼ cup	tomato sauce	50 mL
2 tbsp	Thai fish sauce (nam pla) or soy sauce	25 mL
2 tbsp	lime juice	25 mL
2 tbsp	brown sugar	25 mL
½ tsp	hot chili paste	2 mL
1 tbsp	vegetable oil	15 mL
3	cloves garlic, finely chopped	3
2	eggs, lightly beaten	2
1 cup	fresh bean sprouts	250 mL
2 tbsp	finely chopped roasted peanuts	25 mL
2	green onions, thinly sliced	2
2 tbsp	chopped fresh cilantro or parsley	25 mL

1. To prepare chicken, combine garlic, shallots, cilantro, fish sauce, lime juice and pepper in blender or food processor and blend until smooth. Pour into shallow dish. Add chicken pieces and turn to coat evenly with marinade. Marinate in refrigerator for a few hours or overnight.

2. Preheat barbecue or broiler. Cook chicken for 6 to 8 minutes per side, or until outside is brown and inside is no longer pink. Baste with marinade during cooking. Discard any leftover marinade.

3. Meanwhile, to prepare Pad Thai, place noodles in large bowl and cover with boiling water. Allow to stand for 8 to 10 minutes, until softened but still firm. Drain well.

4. In small bowl, combine tomato sauce, fish sauce, lime juice, sugar and chili paste. Reserve.

5. Heat oil in large skillet or wok. Add garlic and cook gently until fragrant but not brown. Stir in reserved sauce and heat thoroughly.

6. Add beaten eggs. Allow to set slightly and then stir into mixture. Add noodles and toss gently. Add bean sprouts.

7. Turn noodles onto serving platter. Garnish with peanuts, green onions and chopped cilantro. Serve with hot or cold chicken.

PER SERVING

Calories	370
g carbohydrate	40
g fibre	2
g total fat	7
g saturated fat	1
g protein	34

Excellent: niacin; vitamin B_6
Good: riboflavin; iron; folacin; vitamin B_{12}

mg cholesterol	145
mg sodium	643
mg potassium	492

ROAST TURKEY BREAST WITH ROSEMARY AND GARLIC

See photo opposite page 161.

This is a great way to prepare a small turkey dinner. When you cook a whole turkey, the breast meat often becomes dry by the time the dark meat is thoroughly cooked. But when the breast is cooked by itself, it stays tender and juicy, as it does not have to be cooked too long.

Leftover roast turkey is never quite as good reheated; instead, use it in sandwiches, fajitas, soups, casseroles and stir-fries.

Makes 8 servings

1	skinless turkey breast, bone in, about 3 lb/1.5 kg	1
2	cloves garlic, cut in slivers	2
	Tiny sprigs fresh rosemary, or ½ tsp/2 mL dried	
3 tbsp	honey	45 mL
1 tbsp	Dijon mustard	15 mL
1 tbsp	olive oil	15 mL
1 tbsp	lemon juice	15 mL
½ tsp	pepper	2 mL
	Salt to taste	

1. Trim any fat from turkey. Make small slits in top of breast and insert garlic slivers and rosemary. (If you don't have fresh rosemary, add dried rosemary to the honey mixture.)

2. In small bowl, combine honey, mustard, oil, lemon juice and pepper. Brush all over turkey breast. Sprinkle with salt.

3. Place turkey in baking dish, meaty side up. Roast in preheated 350°F/180°C oven for 45 to 60 minutes, depending on size of breast. Baste every 10 to 15 minutes until done. To carve, slice meat off bone on diagonal.

CRANBERRY ORANGE SAUCE WITH GINGER

Use this traditional sauce with roast turkey, or in turkey or chicken sandwiches. It can be made a day ahead and keeps well in the refrigerator for at least four days.

In a saucepan, combine ¾ lb/375 g cranberries, 1 cup/250 mL orange juice, 1 cup/250 mL brown sugar and 1 tbsp/15 mL grated fresh ginger root. Bring mixture to a boil, reduce heat and simmer gently for 10 minutes, stirring occasionally. Cranberries will pop open and mixture will thicken.

Makes about 2 cups/500 mL.

PER SERVING

Calories	214
g carbohydrate	5
g fibre	0
g total fat	5
g saturated fat	1
g protein	35

Excellent: niacin; vitamin B_6
Good: vitamin B_{12}

mg cholesterol	80
mg sodium	94
mg potassium	364

MEAT

Moroccan Meatballs with Chickpeas and Couscous

Meatloaf with Irish Mashed Potatoes

Stir-fried Barbecued Beef and Noodles

Middle Eastern Burgers with Yogurt Mint Sauce

Aunt Pearl's Tzimmes (Carrot Stew)

Texas Chili

Beef Sukiyaki

Korean Flank Steak

Sirloin Steak with Mustard Pepper Crust

Veal Cutlets in Tomato Sauce Casserole

Cantonese-style Grilled Leg of Lamb

Roast Lamb with Rosemary and Potatoes

Pork Tenderloin with Apricot Glaze

Southern Barbecued Pork Roast

Stir-fried Pork

MOROCCAN MEATBALLS WITH CHICKPEAS AND COUSCOUS

I developed this recipe for a budget-cooking article I did for my Quick Cuisine column in the Toronto Star. You could also shape the mixture into patties and grill them for different and delicious hamburgers. Serve in pita breads with this tomato sauce or garlicky tzatziki (page 39).

Makes 6 servings

Meatballs:

¾ lb	extra-lean ground beef	375 g
¾ cup	cooked chickpeas, rinsed, well drained and finely chopped	175 mL
2 tbsp	finely chopped onion	25 mL
1	clove garlic, finely chopped	1
1	egg white	1
⅓ cup	dry breadcrumbs	75 mL
½ tsp	ground cumin	2 mL
½ tsp	salt	2 mL
¼ tsp	pepper	1 mL
1 tbsp	vegetable oil	15 mL

Tomato Sauce:

1	onion, chopped	1
2	cloves garlic, finely chopped	2
¼ tsp	hot red pepper flakes	1 mL
1 tsp	ground cumin	5 mL
1 tsp	turmeric	5 mL
1	28-oz/796 mL tin plum tomatoes, pureed with juices	1
¼ tsp	pepper	1 mL
	Salt to taste	

COUSCOUS
Although some people think of couscous as a grain, it is really pasta — made from a grain (semolina). Even kids love it. It is a traditional food of the Middle East. Originally, couscous took hours to cook, as it had to be steamed and dried many times, but today most couscous sold is the instant-cooking type.

Couscous:

1½ cups	couscous	375 mL
2¼ cups	boiling water	550 mL
¼ tsp	cinnamon	1 mL

1. To make meatballs, combine ground beef, chickpeas, onion, garlic, egg white, breadcrumbs, cumin, salt and pepper. Shape mixture into 1½-inch/4 cm balls – you should have about 30.

2. Heat oil in large, deep skillet and brown meatballs on all sides. Remove from pan.

3. Discard all but 2 tsp/10 mL oil from pan. Add onion, garlic and hot pepper flakes. Cook gently for 2 to 3 minutes. Stir in cumin and turmeric. Cook for 30 seconds.

4. Add pureed tomatoes and meatballs and bring to boil. Cook gently, covered, for 20 minutes. Cook uncovered for another 10 minutes. Add pepper and salt. Taste and adjust seasonings if necessary.

5. Meanwhile, place couscous in 9-inch/2.5 L square baking dish. Cover with boiling water and stir in cinnamon. Cover tightly with foil and allow to rest for 15 minutes. Serve with meatballs and sauce.

PER SERVING

Calories	384
g carbohydrate	55
g fibre	4
g total fat	9
g saturated fat	2
g protein	22

Excellent: niacin; iron; folacin; vitamin B_{12}
Good: thiamine; riboflavin; vitamin B_6

mg cholesterol	29
mg sodium	557
mg potassium	667

MEATLOAF WITH IRISH MASHED POTATOES

See photo opposite page 192.

Even extra-lean ground beef is high in fat, so I like to serve this meatloaf with lower-fat side dishes like mashed potatoes and spicy corn ragout (page 211). You might also want to try this recipe using ground chicken or turkey instead of the beef. Bake the loaf until a meat thermometer registers 165°F/72°C.

The mashed potato dish is the Irish specialty colcannon, and it is also wonderful on its own. The recipe is from my friend Simone Goldberg. We met when I co-chaired Share Our Strength's Taste of the Nation event in Toronto — an evening of food and wine that benefits hunger-relief. Simone organized the event in Ottawa. She is a wonderful cook and dedicated vegetarian, and her recipes are always worth sharing. She serves the potatoes with meatless dishes, of course, like tofu meatloaf or tofu shepherd's pie.

This recipe makes enough for 8 to 10 servings, but it freezes well and is delicious in sandwiches. Serve it with tomato sauce.

Makes 8 to 10 servings

2 tsp	olive oil	10 mL
1	onion, chopped	1
2	cloves garlic, finely chopped	2
2 lb	extra-lean ground beef	1 kg
3	egg whites, or 1 whole egg	3
1 tbsp	Dijon mustard	15 mL
1 tbsp	Worcestershire sauce	15 mL
½ tsp	hot red pepper sauce, optional	2 mL
1 tsp	salt	5 mL
½ tsp	pepper	2 mL
1½ cups	fresh breadcrumbs	375 mL
½ cup	tomato sauce, ketchup or commercial chili sauce	125 mL
2 tbsp	chopped fresh parsley	25 mL

SPICY TOMATO SAUCE

Serve this spicy Cajun-style sauce on meatloaf, breaded chicken, veal or fish. You can also use it as a barbecue sauce or on pasta. The sauce freezes well. Reduce the amount of hot pepper sauce and cayenne if you don't like things hot.

Heat 1 tsp/5 mL olive oil in large deep skillet. Add 1 finely chopped onion, 1 chopped stalk celery and 3 finely chopped cloves garlic. Cook on low heat for 5 minutes (if vegetables start to stick, add ¼ cup/50 mL water and allow water to evaporate). Add 2 tsp/10 mL pepper, 1 tbsp/15 mL paprika and ¼ tsp/1 mL cayenne. Cook for 1 minute. Add 1 28-oz/ 796 mL tin plum tomatoes, with juices, and ¼ tsp/1 mL hot red pepper sauce. Bring to a boil, reduce heat and simmer gently for 10 minutes. Puree. Taste and adjust seasonings if necessary. Makes about 2 cups/500 mL.

Topping:

¼ cup	tomato sauce or ketchup	50 mL
1 tbsp	Dijon mustard	15 mL
3 lb	baking potatoes, peeled and quartered	1.5 kg
4 cups	coarsely chopped cabbage	1 L
¾ cup	milk	175 mL
1½ cups	chopped green onions	375 mL
½ tsp	hot red pepper sauce	2 mL
¼ tsp	pepper	1 mL
	Salt to taste	

1. Heat oil in large skillet. Add onion and garlic and cook gently until tender.

2. In large bowl, combine ground beef, egg whites, mustard, Worcestershire sauce, hot pepper sauce, salt, pepper, breadcrumbs, tomato sauce and parsley. Add cooled onion mixture and knead ingredients together lightly until blended.

3. Line large loaf pan with parchment paper or foil and place mixture in pan. (Or shape mixture into loaf and bake on lined baking sheet.) Bake, covered (cover freeform loaf loosely with parchment paper or foil), in preheated 350°F/180°C oven for 45 minutes.

4. Combine tomato sauce and mustard for topping. Uncover meatloaf, brush with topping and bake, uncovered, for 25 minutes longer. Cool for 10 minutes before serving.

5. Meanwhile, cook potatoes in boiling water until tender, about 20 minutes. Cook cabbage in boiling water for 10 minutes. In small saucepan, heat milk and green onions for 5 minutes.

6. Drain potatoes, reserving cooking liquid, and mash. Mash in cabbage, milk, green onions, hot pepper sauce, pepper and salt. Add some reserved cooking liquid if necessary to make potatoes smooth. Taste and adjust seasonings if necessary. Serve potatoes with sliced meatloaf.

PER SERVING

Calories	360
g carbohydrate	37
g fibre	4
g total fat	12
g saturated fat	4
g protein	27

Excellent: niacin; iron; vitamin B_6; vitamin B_{12}
Good: vitamin C; thiamine; riboflavin; folacin

mg cholesterol	60
mg sodium	634
mg potassium	910

STIR-FRIED BARBECUED BEEF AND NOODLES

Flank steak is a very lean cut of beef, and using it in stir-fries makes a small portion seem like lots. In this recipe the steak is barbecued first, which adds a fabulous flavour, but it can be broiled, too. The dish can also be made with chicken breasts or even tofu.

If you just want to stir-fry the beef, slice it thinly and marinate in the soy sauce, sugar and sesame oil mixture for 30 minutes at room temperature. Then stir-fry in 1 tbsp/15 mL vegetable oil before continuing with the recipe.

Makes 8 servings

1 lb	flank or sirloin steak	500 g
2 tbsp	soy sauce	25 mL
1½ tsp	granulated sugar	7 mL
1 tbsp	sesame oil, divided	15 mL
1 tbsp	vegetable oil	15 mL
2	cloves garlic, finely chopped	2
1 tbsp	finely chopped fresh ginger root	15 mL
3	green onions, sliced	3
½ tsp	hot chili paste	2 mL
6	fresh shiitake or regular mushroom caps, sliced	6
1	onion, thinly sliced	1
1	bunch broccoli, Swiss chard or rapini, trimmed and cut in 2-inch/5 cm pieces	1
1	sweet red pepper, cut in strips	1
½ lb	spaghettini, cooked, or 13-oz/400 g package pre-cooked Chinese noodles, rinsed under hot water for 1 minute	250 g
½ cup	homemade chicken stock (page 59) or water	125 mL
2 tbsp	hoisin sauce	25 mL
2 tbsp	chopped fresh cilantro or parsley	25 mL

FRESH GINGER ROOT
Look for a firm root with taut skin and store it at room temperature. To keep it longer, place peeled pieces in a jar of sherry or vodka — they should keep indefinitely. Use the ginger-flavoured spirit instead of rice wine or sherry in stir-fries.

I usually chop ginger very finely, but if you have a heavy-duty garlic press you can stand thin pieces in it and press down as for garlic.

Ground ginger is great in baking, and although it doesn't taste at all like fresh ginger, in a pinch you could substitute 1 tsp/5 mL powdered for 1 tbsp/5 mL fresh. Candied ginger is delicious in muffins and quickbreads.

1. Pat steak dry. Combine soy sauce, sugar and 1 tsp/5 mL sesame oil. Pour over steak and marinate for 2 to 8 hours in refrigerator.

2. Barbecue steak for about 3 to 4 minutes per side, or until very rare (meat will cook further in sauce). Cool. Slice thinly and reserve.

3. Just before serving, heat vegetable oil in wok or large, deep skillet. Add garlic, ginger, green onions and hot chili paste. Cook for 30 seconds, or until fragrant.

4. Add mushrooms and onion. Cook until slightly wilted. Add broccoli, red pepper and noodles and stir together well. Add stock and hoisin sauce and bring to boil. Cook for 5 minutes.

5. Add beef and remaining sesame oil. Cook only until beef is thoroughly heated, about 3 to 5 minutes. Taste and adjust seasonings if necessary. Serve sprinkled with cilantro.

PER SERVING

Calories	269
g carbohydrate	30
g fibre	3
g total fat	8
g saturated fat	2
g protein	20

Excellent: vitamin C; niacin; vitamin B_{12}
Good: iron; vitamin B_6; folacin

mg cholesterol	23
mg sodium	235
mg potassium	490

MIDDLE EASTERN BURGERS WITH YOGURT MINT SAUCE

The bulgur in this burger adds wonderful flavour, an interesting texture and all the health benefits of using grains.

Makes 6 servings

1 tbsp	olive oil	15 mL
1	small onion, finely chopped	1
1	clove garlic, finely chopped	1
1 lb	extra-lean ground beef or lamb	500 g
½ cup	dry bulgur	125 mL
2	egg whites, or 1 whole egg	2
¼ tsp	cinnamon	1 mL
½ tsp	dried oregano	2 mL
1 tsp	salt	5 mL
¼ tsp	pepper	1 mL
pinch	cayenne	pinch

Yogurt Mint Sauce:

1	clove garlic, minced	1
½ cup	soft yogurt cheese (page 228) or thick yogurt	125 mL
2 tbsp	chopped fresh mint, or 2 tsp/5 mL dried	25 mL
2 tbsp	chopped fresh parsley	25 mL
6	8-inch/20 cm pita breads	6
3 cups	shredded lettuce	750 mL

1. Heat oil in small skillet. Add onion and garlic and cook gently until tender and fragrant. Cool slightly.

2. Combine meat, bulgur and egg whites. Beat in onion mixture, cinnamon, oregano, salt, pepper and cayenne. Form mixture into 6 patties.

3. Preheat broiler or barbecue and grill burgers for 7 to 8 minutes per side, depending on their thickness, until thoroughly cooked.

4. For sauce, combine garlic, yogurt cheese, mint and parsley. Taste and adjust seasonings if necessary.

5. Serve burgers in pita breads with shredded lettuce and sauce.

PER SERVING

Calories	377
g carbohydrate	46
g fibre	3
g total fat	10
g saturated fat	3
g protein	24

Excellent: niacin; riboflavin; iron; folacin; vitamin B$_{12}$
Good: thiamine; vitamin B$_6$

mg cholesterol	40
mg sodium	667
mg potassium	428

AUNT PEARL'S TZIMMES (CARROT STEW)

For as long as I can remember, my aunt, Pearl Duckman, made tzimmes for our Seder — no mean feat when you consider that we usually have almost one hundred people. That's a lot of carrots to peel! One year she was away, so I bravely volunteered to make the tzimmes. Everyone complained that it was okay but not nearly as good as Auntie Pearl's, and that maybe I needed thirty more years of practice. (It hasn't been thirty years yet, but everyone agrees that I'm getting better!)

Here's her recipe, brought down to a reasonable size. It serves about twenty as a side dish, but I love it for a main course all year round.

Makes 12 main-course or 20 side-dish servings

6 lb	carrots, peeled and cut in 1-inch/2.5 cm pieces	3 kg
¼	turnip, peeled and cut in 1-inch/2.5 cm pieces	¼
1	sweet potato, peeled and cut in 1-inch/2.5 cm pieces	1
2 lb	beef brisket or short ribs, trimmed of all fat and cut in 1-inch/2.5 cm pieces	1 kg
½ cup	brown sugar	125 mL
¾ cup	matzo meal (see sidebar)	175 mL
1 tsp	salt	5 mL
1 tsp	pepper	5 mL
2 tbsp	lemon juice	25 mL

1. Place layer of carrots, turnip and sweet potato in bottom of large Dutch oven. Add some meat. Sprinkle over some sugar, matzo, salt, pepper and lemon juice. Continue layering until all ingredients are used up.

2. Add enough water to come almost to top of ingredients – about 8 cups/2 L. Bring to boil on top of stove.

3. Transfer pan to preheated 275°F/140°C oven, cover and cook for about 12 hours (we usually do this overnight). Remove cover and bake for 1 to 2 hours longer, or until top browns a little and most of liquid evaporates. Stew should be quite thick. Taste and adjust seasonings if necessary.

MATZO MEAL

Matzo meal is ground matzo, an unleavened cracker bread that is traditional at Passover but can be purchased all year round. Matzo and matzo meal are available at Jewish delicatessens and most supermarkets. If you are not using matzo for religious or traditional reasons, you can substitute breadcrumbs or crushed soda cracker crumbs.

PER SERVING

Calories	266
g carbohydrate	41
g fibre	6
g total fat	6
g saturated fat	2
g protein	15

Excellent: vitamin A; niacin; vitamin B$_6$; vitamin B$_{12}$
Good: riboflavin; iron; folacin

mg cholesterol	29
mg sodium	358
mg potassium	672

TEXAS CHILI

This chili uses small cubes of meat, but you can also use ground meat. Serve it over rice. Top it with soft yogurt cheese (page 228) and chopped green onions, or wrap in flour tortillas.

Makes 12 servings

1 tbsp	vegetable oil	15 mL
1½ lb	lean stewing beef, diced	750 g
1½ lb	lean stewing pork, diced	750 g
½ cup	all-purpose flour	125 mL
4	large onions, finely chopped	4
6	cloves garlic, finely chopped	6
1	4-oz/114 mL tin mild green chiles, rinsed, drained and chopped	1
3 tbsp	chili powder	45 mL
1 tbsp	ground cumin	15 mL
1 tbsp	dried oregano	15 mL
1 tsp	cayenne	5 mL
½ tsp	pepper	2 mL
3 cups	beef stock, or 1 28-oz/796 mL tin plum tomatoes, crushed with juices	750 mL
1 cup	beer or water	250 mL
4 cups	cooked red kidney beans, or 2 19-oz/540 mL tins, rinsed and drained	1 L
1 cup	grated light Cheddar cheese	250 mL

1. Heat oil in large, deep non-stick skillet. Pat beef and pork dry and toss with flour. Brown in hot oil in batches. Remove and reserve each batch. Discard all but 1 tbsp/15 mL fat from pan. Return pan to heat.

2. Add onions and garlic and cook gently until tender and fragrant, about 10 minutes. Add mild chiles, chili powder, cumin, oregano, cayenne and pepper.

3. Return beef and pork to skillet and combine well. Add stock and beer and bring to boil. Cook gently, uncovered, for 2 to 3 hours, until meat is very tender and mixture is thick. Stir in beans. Taste and adjust seasonings if necessary.

4. Transfer chili to 3-qt/3 L casserole, top with cheese and bake in preheated 350°F/180°C oven for 30 minutes, or until thoroughly heated.

PER SERVING

Calories	344
g carbohydrate	25
g fibre	7
g total fat	11
g saturated fat	4
g protein	35

Excellent: thiamine; niacin; iron; vitamin B$_6$; folacin; vitamin B$_{12}$
Good: riboflavin

mg cholesterol	66
mg sodium	265
mg potassium	952

Meatloaf *(page 186)* **with Garlic Mashed Potatoes** *(page 215)*
Spicy Corn Ragout *(page 211)*
Spicy Tomato Sauce *(page 186)*

Korean Flank Steak *(page 194)*
Sesame Spinach *(page 207)*
Mixed Grain Pilaf *(page 221)*

BEEF SUKIYAKI

This is a soothing, nourishing, sweet-tasting broth full of delicious treasures. Vary the recipe according to your own taste. You can make this ahead up to the point of adding the softened noodles and the beef. Reheat before adding the noodles and raw beef, and be sure not to overcook.

Makes 6 servings

¾ lb	lean sirloin steak, trimmed of all fat, about 1 inch/2.5 cm thick	375 g
1	large onion, cut in thin rings	1
1 lb	spinach, Swiss chard or beet greens torn in pieces	500 g
¼ lb	bean sprouts	125 g
¼ lb	mushrooms, sliced	125 g
1	carrot, thinly sliced	1
½ lb	extra-firm tofu, cut in 1-inch/ 2.5 cm pieces	250 g
6	green onions, chopped	6
3 cups	beef stock, water or dashi (Japanese fish broth)	750 mL
3 tbsp	dry sherry, optional	45 mL
1 tbsp	granulated sugar	15 mL
3 tbsp	soy sauce	45 mL
3 oz	rice vermicelli noodles, soaked in hot water for 5 minutes, rinsed and well drained	90 g

1. Freeze meat for 20 minutes. Slice very thinly on diagonal.

2. Meanwhile, arrange onion in bottom of 4 qt/4 L saucepan or Dutch oven. Place spinach, bean sprouts, mushrooms, carrot, tofu and green onions on top.

3. Combine stock, sherry, sugar and soy sauce and pour over vegetables. Bring to boil and simmer gently for 5 to 10 minutes, or until onions are tender.

4. Stir in softened noodles and arrange beef on top. Cook for another 5 minutes. Taste and adjust seasonings if necessary.

PER SERVING

Calories	235
g carbohydrate	27
g fibre	5
g total fat	4
g saturated fat	1
g protein	24

Excellent: vitamin A; niacin; riboflavin; iron; vitamin B$_6$; folacin; vitamin B$_{12}$
Good: thiamine; calcium

mg cholesterol	28
mg sodium	531
mg potassium	951

KOREAN FLANK STEAK

See photo opposite page 193.

This is a delicious way to treat a reasonably priced lean cut of beef. Flank steak can be tough, so it benefits from marinating, but because it is quite thin it doesn't need to marinate for too long. Serve it with rice or rice vermicelli noodles (page 146) and sesame spinach (page 207).

This marinade also works well with a round steak cut about ³⁄₄ inch/2 cm thick (marinate it in the refrigerator for 8 to 12 hours) or with a blade or cross-rib steak (marinate for 18 to 24 hours).

Makes 4 to 6 servings

1 lb	flank steak, trimmed if necessary	500 g
¼ cup	soy sauce	50 mL
¼ cup	granulated sugar	50 mL
2 tsp	sesame oil	10 mL
2 tbsp	lemon juice	25 mL
4	cloves garlic, minced	4
½ tsp	pepper	2 mL

1. Pat steak dry and, very lightly, make horizontal slits in top of meat about ⅛ inch/2 mm deep.

2. Combine soy sauce, sugar, sesame oil, lemon juice, garlic and pepper. Combine with steak in flat dish or in heavy-duty plastic bag. Seal. Marinate in refrigerator, turning two or three times, for 4 to 8 hours or overnight.

3. Just before cooking, remove steak from marinade and pat dry. Place marinade in small saucepan and bring to boil. Cook for a few minutes until slightly syrupy.

4. Preheat barbecue and grill steak for 3 to 4 minutes per side for medium rare if steak is about 1 inch/2.5 cm thick. Brush once or twice with reduced marinade during cooking. Allow steak to rest for 5 minutes before carving. Slice thinly on diagonal.

MARINATING

We marinate meat to add flavour and, in some cases, to tenderize it. The smaller and thinner the meat, the less time it takes for the marinade to have an effect.

I marinate meat in the refrigerator, but if the meat is going to be cooked within an hour, it will probably be fine out of the refrigerator as long as the kitchen is cool. Place the marinating meat in a sealed plastic bag to make it easy to turn and clean up. Any leftover marinade could have raw meat juices in it, so it should be brought to a boil and cooked for a few minutes before being used as a sauce.

Salad dressings also work well as marinades. (see index under Salad dressings).

PER SERVING

Calories	245
g carbohydrate	10
g fibre	trace
g total fat	10
g saturated fat	4
g protein	27

Excellent: niacin; vitamin B$_{12}$
Good: vitamin B$_6$

mg cholesterol	46
mg sodium	610
mg potassium	387

SIRLOIN STEAK WITH MUSTARD PEPPER CRUST

Real meat lovers sometimes feel deprived when they are served a small steak, but if you slice a large sirloin steak very thinly on the diagonal, a 4-oz portion looks like a lot of meat.

You can also use flank steak in this recipe, but marinate it in the refrigerator for 4 to 8 hours or overnight, and cook for 3 to 4 minutes per side for rare. Or try this recipe with individual smaller steaks.

Makes 6 to 8 servings

2 tbsp	Dijon mustard	25 mL
1 tbsp	Worcestershire sauce	15 mL
1 tbsp	coarsely ground black pepper	15 mL
2	cloves garlic, minced	2
1/4 tsp	hot red pepper sauce	1 mL
1	1½-lb/750 g sirloin steak (1 inch/2.5 cm thick), preferably boneless, well trimmed	1

1. Combine mustard, Worcestershire, pepper, garlic and hot pepper sauce.

2. Pat steaks dry. Spread marinade over steaks and marinate in refrigerator for a few hours.

3. Preheat broiler or barbecue and grill steaks for 5 to 6 minutes per side for medium rare, or to an internal temperature of 120°F/50°C. Allow steaks to rest for few minutes before carving.

4. Carve steaks in thin slices slightly on diagonal (to make a wider slice). Serve 3 or 4 slices per person.

COOKING TIME FOR STEAKS AND CHOPS
When it comes to cooking steaks or chops, I use the method that grill chefs use, by pressing the top of the steak to feel the resistance. You can do this, too. Put your arm out in front of you, resting your forearm on a surface. Relax and feel your bicep muscle. That's what a rare steak feels like. Now lift your forearm as if you were making a muscle, but don't tense it. Feel your bicep. That's medium. Now tense your muscle and feel the bicep. That's well done.

PER SERVING

Calories	173
g carbohydrate	1
g fibre	trace
g total fat	6
g saturated fat	2
g protein	27

Excellent: niacin; vitamin B_{12}
Good: riboflavin; iron; vitamin B_6

mg cholesterol	65
mg sodium	117
mg potassium	365

VEAL CUTLETS IN TOMATO SAUCE CASSEROLE

Although this is a good way to use up leftover veal cutlets, soon you will be cooking them especially for this dish, as I do. You could simply serve the cutlets with some tomato sauce on top, but I always make this as a casserole.

You can prepare this with chicken, turkey or pork cutlets as well as veal. Because the meat is very thin, you only need 1 lb / 500 g for six servings. For a spicy version, add ½ tsp / 2 mL hot chili paste or more hot pepper flakes to the sauce. Use up leftovers in sandwiches on crusty bread.

Makes 6 servings

Tomato Sauce:

1 tbsp	olive oil	15 mL
1	onion, chopped	1
2	cloves garlic, finely chopped	2
pinch	hot red pepper flakes	pinch
1	stalk celery, chopped	1
1	carrot, chopped	1
2	28-oz/796 mL tins plum tomatoes, with juices	2
¼ tsp	pepper	1 mL
	Salt to taste	
1 lb	veal cutlets	500 g
½ cup	all-purpose flour	125 mL
4	egg whites, or 2 whole eggs, lightly beaten	4
2 cups	fine fresh breadcrumbs	500 mL
1 tbsp	olive oil	15 mL
¼ cup	chopped fresh parsley	50 mL

1. To prepare tomato sauce, heat 1 tbsp/15 mL olive oil in large skillet. Add onion, garlic and hot pepper flakes. Cook gently for 5 minutes. Add celery and carrot and cook for 5 minutes. Add tomatoes, pepper and salt. Cook for 20 minutes, until sauce thickens. Puree, taste and adjust seasonings if necessary.

2. Pat veal dry. Place flour in large flat dish. Place egg whites in another flat dish. Place breadcrumbs in third dish. Dust veal lightly with flour, dip in egg and then pat in breadcrumbs. Place veal on rack in single layer and keep in refrigerator until ready to cook.

3. Brush large baking sheet with 1 tbsp/15 mL olive oil. Heat baking sheet in preheated 375°F/190°C oven for 5 minutes. Arrange cutlets on hot pan in single layer and bake for 10 minutes. Turn and bake for another 10 to 15 minutes, or until cooked and browned.

4. Spoon some of sauce into shallow casserole. Arrange veal cutlets in sauce, overlapping if necessary. Pour remaining sauce on top. Bake for 20 to 30 minutes, or until very hot and bubbling.

PER SERVING

Calories	247
g carbohydrate	29
g fibre	4
g total fat	5
g saturated fat	1
g protein	23

Excellent: vitamin A; niacin; riboflavin; vitamin B$_6$; vitamin B$_{12}$
Good: vitamin C; thiamine; iron; folacin

mg cholesterol	59
mg sodium	594
mg potassium	984

CANTONESE-STYLE GRILLED LEG OF LAMB

Lamb is one of the most popular meats served in restaurants. Some people are still reluctant to cook it at home, because they think it will have a strong aroma and taste. But if you buy young lamb, trim it well and cook it medium rare, the result will be delicious and mild. Trimming the fat also reduces flareups on the barbecue. And because the meat is thin after being butterflied, it takes only about 30 minutes to cook. (If you cannot barbecue this, simply roast it.)

I like to serve this with ginger eggplant salad (see sidebar) and steamed rice.

Makes 8 to 10 servings

1	butterflied leg of lamb (about 3 lb/1.5 kg after boning), trimmed of all fat	1
¼ cup	hoisin sauce	50 mL
2 tbsp	Dijon mustard	25 mL
2 tbsp	ketchup	25 mL
2 tbsp	honey	25 mL
1 tbsp	soy sauce	15 mL
1 tsp	hot chili paste	5 mL
1 tsp	coarsely ground black pepper	5 mL
2	cloves garlic, minced	2
1 tbsp	minced fresh ginger root	15 mL

1. Cut lamb open so meat lies as flat as possible. Pat dry.

2. Combine hoisin sauce, mustard, ketchup, honey, soy sauce, hot chili paste, pepper, garlic and ginger. Smear mixture all over lamb.

3. Preheat barbecue and grill lamb for 10 to 15 minutes per side for rare, depending on thickness. If you are roasting, preheat oven to 400°F/200°C. Preheat baking sheet brushed lightly with vegetable oil. Place lamb on hot pan and roast for 30 to 40 minutes. Meat should register about 130°F/55°C on meat thermometer.

4. Allow meat to rest for 5 to 10 minutes before carving. Carve in thin slices against grain on diagonal.

GINGER EGGPLANT SALAD

Serve this as a side dish, condiment, dip or sauce with grilled meat or poultry. Barbecue or broil 1 lb/500 g eggplant slices, 1 large red pepper and 1 thickly sliced large red onion. Dice eggplant and onion. Peel and seed pepper and dice.

In large skillet, combine 2 tbsp/25 mL soy sauce, 2 tbsp/25 mL brown sugar, 1 tbsp/15 mL rice vinegar, 2 tbsp/25 mL orange juice, 2 cloves garlic, minced, 1 tsp/5 mL minced fresh ginger root and ¼ tsp/1 mL hot chili paste. Bring to a boil, add vegetables and heat. Stir in 2 tbsp/25 mL chopped fresh cilantro or parsley and 2 tsp/10 mL sesame oil.

Makes about 3 cups/750 mL.

PER SERVING

Calories	226
g carbohydrate	7
g fibre	trace
g total fat	8
g saturated fat	3
g protein	30

Excellent: niacin; riboflavin; vitamin B_{12}
Good: iron

mg cholesterol	105
mg sodium	329
mg potassium	230

ROAST LAMB WITH ROSEMARY AND POTATOES

The potatoes in this dish absorb all the delicious lamb juices.
Use any leftover lamb in a grilled meat salad.

Makes 10 to 12 servings

1	4-lb/2 kg leg of lamb, bone-in, well trimmed	1
2 tbsp	Dijon mustard	25 mL
4	cloves garlic, minced, divided	4
1 tsp	pepper, divided	5 mL
2 tbsp	chopped fresh rosemary, or 2 tsp/10 mL dried, divided	25 mL
3 lb	baking potatoes, peeled and very thinly sliced (6 to 8 large)	1.5 kg
2	large onions, sliced	2
½ tsp	salt	2 mL
1 cup	dry white wine, chicken stock or water	250 mL

1. Pat lamb dry. In small bowl, combine mustard, 2 cloves garlic, ½ tsp/2 mL pepper and 1 tbsp/15 mL rosemary. Spread over lamb. Allow to marinate while preparing potatoes.

2. Arrange potatoes, onions and remaining garlic in bottom of roasting pan. Sprinkle with remaining rosemary, pepper and salt. Pour wine over top.

3. Place lamb on top of potatoes. Roast in preheated 400°F/200°C oven for 80 to 90 minutes for rare. Meat thermometer should read 130°F/55°C. Turn roast once during cooking.

4. Allow roast to rest for 10 minutes before carving. Serve with potatoes and onions.

ROASTED SQUASH SAUCE

Roasted vegetable sauces are a great low-fat idea. This one is from Keith Jones, executive chef of Ottawa's Chateau Laurier.

Lightly brush a roasting pan with olive oil. Place 1 lb/500 g butternut squash (peeled, seeded and cut in a few large pieces) in the pan with 3 unpeeled cloves garlic and 1 peeled and quartered onion. Sprinkle with 1 tsp/5 mL chopped fresh rosemary (or ¼ tsp/ 1 mL dried) and ¼ tsp/1 mL pepper. Roast in a preheated 375°F/190°C oven for 45 minutes. Remove garlic as soon as it is cooked through.

Peel garlic and puree with squash, onion and 1½ cups/375 mL chicken stock. Season to taste with salt and pepper.

Makes about 2½ cups/625 mL.

PER SERVING

Calories	263
g carbohydrate	23
g fibre	2
g total fat	6
g saturated fat	3
g protein	27

Excellent: niacin; riboflavin; vitamin B$_{12}$
Good: thiamine; iron; vitamin B$_6$

mg cholesterol	87
mg sodium	191
mg potassium	559

PORK TENDERLOIN WITH APRICOT GLAZE

You can also use this glaze with porkloin roasts, pork chops and chicken.

Makes 6 to 8 servings

1½ lb	pork tenderloin	750 g
½ cup	apricot jam	125 mL
2 tbsp	Dijon mustard	25 mL
2 tbsp	balsamic vinegar or cider vinegar	25 mL
2 tsp	Worcestershire sauce	10 mL

1. Pat pork dry.

2. Combine jam, mustard, vinegar and Worcestershire sauce. Coat pork with glaze.

3. Place pork on rack set over foil-lined baking sheet. Roast in preheated 375°F/190°C oven for 40 to 50 minutes, or until cooked through (internal temperature about 160°F/70°C).

COOKING TIME FOR ROASTS

The cooking time for meat depends on the weight, thickness and shape of the cut. Although experienced cooks can usually take an educated guess, a meat thermometer is the only way to be sure. The thin-stemmed instant-read ones work the best. When you think the meat is ready, insert the thermometer into the centre of the roast, being careful not to let it touch the pan, a bone or a piece of fat. The thermometer will register in about 10 seconds. I like to cook beef and lamb to 130°F/55°C for rare. I usually cook pork to 160°F/70°C. Stuffed chicken or turkey should be cooked to 185°F/85°C to ensure that the raw juices in the stuffing are fully cooked.

PER SERVING

Calories	196
g carbohydrate	15
g fibre	trace
g total fat	4
g saturated fat	1
g protein	24

Excellent: thiamine; niacin
Good: riboflavin; vitamin B_6; vitamin B_{12}

mg cholesterol	57
mg sodium	123
mg potassium	476

SOUTHERN BARBECUED PORK ROAST

Pork roasts are quite lean now, and the slow roasting makes them very tender. I always make a lot of this dish as it freezes well and tastes just as good or better reheated. (Refrigerate the roast if you are not using it right away and reheat for 1 hour in 350°F/180°C oven.)

I like to serve this on top of mashed potatoes, rice or beans or polenta but it is also great in a sandwich.

Makes 10 to 12 servings

Barbecue Sauce:

2 tsp	vegetable oil	10 mL
1	onion, chopped	1
2	cloves garlic, finely chopped	2
2 cups	ketchup	500 mL
1 cup	cider vinegar	250 mL
1 cup	brown sugar	250 mL
3 tbsp	Worcestershire sauce	45 mL
1 tsp	hot red pepper sauce, optional	5 mL
1 tbsp	Dijon mustard	15 mL
1 cup	water	250 mL
3 lb	boneless lean pork roast (loin or leg), well trimmed	1.5 kg

1. To make barbecue sauce, heat oil in large saucepan. Add onion and garlic and cook gently until tender, about 5 minutes.

2. Add ketchup, vinegar, sugar, Worcestershire, hot pepper sauce, mustard and water. Bring to boil. Cook, stirring often, for about 20 minutes, or until sauce is about as thick as ketchup. Taste and adjust seasonings with salt, pepper and/or hot pepper sauce if necessary.

3. Rub pork with 1 cup/250 mL sauce. Place in roasting pan, add 1 cup/250 mL water, cover and cook in preheated 325°F/160°C oven for 3 hours.

4. Remove roast from pan. Skim fat from juices in pan. Combine ½ cup/125 mL defatted juices with reserved barbecue sauce (about 1½ cups/375 mL) and place in casserole dish. Slice or shred pork and add to sauce. Cover and bake for 1 hour.

PER SERVING

Calories	326
g carbohydrate	39
g fibre	1
g total fat	8
g saturated fat	3
g protein	26

Excellent: thiamine; niacin; vitamin B$_6$; vitamin B$_{12}$
Good: riboflavin; iron

mg cholesterol	65
mg sodium	798
mg potassium	890

STIR-FRIED PORK

Although I like to use fresh ingredients whenever possible, frozen broccoli spears are surprisingly good.

Makes 4 to 6 servings

¾ lb	pork loin, well trimmed	375 g
1 tbsp	soy sauce	15 mL
1 tbsp	rice wine or sake	15 mL
1 tbsp	water	15 mL
1 tsp	cornstarch	5 mL

Sauce:

¼ cup	homemade chicken stock (page 59) or water	50 mL
1 tbsp	hoisin sauce	15 mL
1 tbsp	cornstarch	15 mL
1 tsp	sesame oil, optional	5 mL

To Cook:

2 tsp	vegetable oil	10 mL
2	cloves garlic, finely chopped	2
3	green onions, chopped	3
1 tbsp	finely chopped fresh ginger root	15 mL
2 cups	broccoli florets	500 mL
2 cups	thinly sliced carrots	500 mL
1	14-oz/398 mL tin baby corn, rinsed and drained	1
¼ cup	homemade chicken stock or water	50 mL
¼ cup	chopped fresh cilantro or chives	50 mL

1. Slice pork as thinly as possible. In large bowl, combine pork with soy sauce, rice wine, water and 1 tsp/5 mL cornstarch. Stir well. Allow to marinate for 5 to 10 minutes.

2. To make sauce, in small bowl, combine ¼ cup/50 mL stock, hoisin sauce, 1 tbsp/15 mL cornstarch and sesame oil.

3. In wok or large, deep skillet, heat vegetable oil. Add garlic, green onions and ginger and cook for about 30 seconds. Add sliced pork and stir-fry just until it loses its raw appearance.

4. Add broccoli, carrots and corn. Stir well. Add stock. Cover. Cook for about 2 minutes, until vegetables are tender.

5. Stir sauce again. Add to wok. Bring to boil. Cook for 1 or 2 minutes until thickened. Sprinkle with cilantro.

PER SERVING

Calories	223
g carbohydrate	16
g fibre	3
g total fat	8
g saturated fat	2
g protein	21

Excellent: vitamin A; vitamin C; thiamine; niacin; vitamin B$_6$; vitamin B$_{12}$
Good: riboflavin; folacin

mg cholesterol	47
mg sodium	366
mg potassium	736

VEGETABLES AND SIDE DISHES

Broccoli or Rapini with Raisins and Pine Nuts

Glazed Cumin Carrots

Asparagus with Ginger

Roasted Red Onions with Balsamic Vinegar

Caramelized Beets and Onions

Corn with Garlic and Chives

Herb Barbecued Corn on the Cob

Spicy Corn Ragout

Sicilian Squash

Creamy Polenta with Corn and Roasted Garlic

Spicy Mashed Sweet Potatoes

Garlic Mashed Potatoes

Roasted Rosemary French Fries

Roasted Root Vegetables

Braised White Beans

White Bean Puree with Cumin

Middle Eastern Couscous

Mixed Grain Pilaf

Navajo Rice Pilaf

Rice with Pasta and Chickpeas

Risotto with Squash

BROCCOLI OR RAPINI WITH RAISINS AND PINE NUTS

See photo opposite page 161.

Broccoli is a versatile and popular vegetable, and this is a sophisticated way to prepare it. Rapini, a cross between broccoli and turnip greens, is becoming easier to find. Trim off the ends but use all the leafy parts as well as the stalks and florets.

Makes 4 servings

1	**large bunch broccoli or rapini (about 1½ lb/750 g), trimmed and cut in 2-inch/5 cm chunks**	1
1 tsp	**olive oil**	5 mL
1	**small onion, chopped**	1
1	**clove garlic, finely chopped**	1
¼ cup	**raisins**	50 mL
1 tbsp	**pine nuts, toasted (page 245)**	15 mL

1. Bring large pot of water to boil. Add broccoli. Return to boil and cook for 3 to 5 minutes, or until just tender. Drain and rinse with cold water to stop cooking and set colour and texture.

2. In large skillet, heat oil. Add onion and garlic and cook gently until tender (add bit of water if necessary to prevent browning). Add raisins and pine nuts and cook for a few minutes longer.

3. Add broccoli and toss gently until heated through and coated with onion mixture. Serve hot or at room temperature.

RAPINI

Rapini has long been available in specialty markets but is now becoming far more mainstream. It is actually a broccoli/turnip green combination; you just trim off the ends of the stems and use the leaves, stems and flowers.

Rapini has a slightly bitter but more interesting taste than broccoli. The Chinese variety is usually less bitter than the Italian. Use it in pasta dishes (page 97), soups (page 51) or as a vegetable side dish (page 203).

PER SERVING

Calories	101
g carbohydrate	18
g fibre	4
g total fat	3
g saturated fat	trace
g protein	5

Excellent: vitamin C; folacin
Good: vitamin A; vitamin B$_6$

mg cholesterol	0
mg sodium	39
mg potassium	535

SAUTÉED "WILD" MUSHROOMS

This is great on meats and pastas. I learnt the trick of making regular mushrooms taste like wild mushrooms from Marcella Hazan in Bologna.

Heat 1 tsp/5 mL olive oil in large skillet. Add 1 chopped onion and 3 finely chopped cloves garlic and cook gently until fragrant (add a little water if necessary). Add 1 lb/500 g sliced button mushrooms and one or two packages reconstituted (page 65), cleaned and chopped, dried, wild mushrooms (preferably porcini). Add strained soaking liquid and cook until all liquid evaporates or is absorbed by mushrooms. Season with salt, pepper and parsley.

Makes 1 to 1½ cups/250 to 375 mL.

GLAZED CUMIN CARROTS

Cumin, which gives this sweet dish its mysterious taste, is used in East Indian, Southwestern and Middle Eastern cooking, among others. If you don't have it, substitute ½ tsp/2 mL curry powder or chili powder. Use maple syrup or brown sugar instead of honey if you wish.

Makes 4 to 6 servings

2 lb	carrots	1 kg
2 tsp	vegetable oil	10 mL
1	clove garlic, finely chopped	1
1 tbsp	finely chopped fresh ginger	15 mL
1½ tsp	ground cumin	7 mL
1 tbsp	honey	15 mL
pinch	salt	pinch
1½ cups	homemade chicken stock (page 59), or water	375 mL

1. Peel carrots and cut into ¼-inch/5 mm slices on diagonal.

2. Heat oil in deep skillet and add garlic and ginger. Cook gently for 1 minute. Add cumin and cook for 30 seconds.

3. Add carrots, honey, salt and stock. Cook over medium heat, uncovered, until all liquid evaporates and carrots are tender and glazed. (If liquid evaporates before carrots are tender, simply add water.) Carrots should take about 20 to 25 minutes to cook. Taste and adjust seasonings if necessary.

ASPARAGUS WITH GINGER

This recipe is also delicious made with sugar snap peas or broccoli.

Makes 6 servings

1 tsp	sesame oil	5 mL
1 tbsp	finely chopped fresh ginger root	15 mL
3	green onions, chopped	3
1½ lb	asparagus, trimmed and cut in 2-inch/5 cm lengths	750 g
1 tbsp	soy sauce	15 mL
1 tbsp	balsamic vinegar	15 mL
½ tsp	honey	2 mL

1. Heat oil in wok or skillet. Add ginger and green onions and cook gently for 1 minute, or until fragrant.

2. Add asparagus and stir-fry for about 2 minutes, just until it loses its rawness.

3. Combine soy sauce, vinegar and honey. Add to skillet and cook for 1 minute, or just until asparagus is tender. Taste and adjust seasonings if necessary.

ASPARAGUS
When you buy asparagus, try to buy spears with tightly closed tips. I like fat, juicy asparagus stalks rather than the pencil-thin ones. I usually just trim (rather than break) about 1 inch/2.5 cm from the tough bottom ends and peel an inch or two up the stalks. Although this takes time, the peeled stalks are very tender, and I waste less asparagus this way.

I cook asparagus lying down in a skillet with an inch or two of water, rather than steaming it upright. The tips and peeled stalks will cook at the same rate. Cook the asparagus for 3 to 5 minutes, until it is bright green and a spear bends gently when it is held upright. After cooking, serve the asparagus immediately if you are serving it hot; if you are serving it cold, rinse in cold water to set the texture and colour and then pat dry.

PER SERVING

Calories	27
g carbohydrate	4
g fibre	1
g total fat	1
g saturated fat	trace
g protein	2

Excellent: folacin

mg cholesterol	0
mg sodium	146
mg potassium	125

SESAME SPINACH

Heat 1 tsp/5 mL sesame oil in a large skillet. Add 1 finely chopped clove garlic and 1 tbsp/15 mL water. Cook gently for a few minutes, until fragrant. Add 2 lb/1 kg trimmed and washed fresh spinach and keep turning until it wilts (don't worry, it will!). Season to taste with salt and pepper and sprinkle with 1 tsp/5 mL toasted sesame seeds.

Makes 4 servings.

See photo opposite page 193.

CLEANING SPINACH

Fresh spinach can be very sandy. To clean it, fill a sink with cold water and swish the spinach around in it for a minute or two. Then just let it soak for a few minutes. The sand will sink to the bottom and the leaves will rise to the top. Lift out the leaves gently; repeat if necessary.

ROASTED RED ONIONS WITH BALSAMIC VINEGAR

This dish will keep well in the refrigerator for a few days, so it can be made ahead. Use these diced in salads, sliced in sandwiches or cut in quarters as part of an appetizer platter. Serve them cold with cold entrees like sliced turkey, or hot with roast chicken.

Makes 8 servings

8	red onions (about 3 inches/ 7.5 cm in diameter)	8
⅓ cup	balsamic vinegar	75 mL
⅓ cup	water	75 mL
pinch	salt	pinch
pinch	pepper	pinch
¼ cup	chopped fresh basil or parsley	50 mL

1. Discard papery skin of onions but leave remaining skin intact.

2. Place onions in roasting pan in single layer and bake in preheated 375°F/190°C oven for 1¼ to 1½ hours, or until tender. Cool slightly.

3. Cut onions in half and discard any more papery skin. Place onions, cut side up, in serving dish.

4. Add vinegar and water to roasting pan. Deglaze pan by scraping up flavourful pan juices (discard any bits of onion skin sticking to pan). Cook, uncovered, until only a few syrupy tablespoons remain. Drizzle juice over cut surfaces of onions.

5. Sprinkle onions with salt, pepper and basil. Serve hot, cold or at room temperature.

CARAMELIZED BEETS AND ONIONS

This recipe was inspired by Linda Stephen, who teaches at my school and who loves beets. Cook beets in their skins for the best colour, flavour and nutrition.

This dish can be made ahead and reheated. The beets are delicious hot or cold, and they can also be chopped and eaten as a relish or sandwich filling.

Makes 4 to 6 servings

6	medium beets (about 1½ lb/750 g)	6
3 tbsp	granulated sugar	45 mL
3	onions, thickly sliced	3
⅓ cup	apple juice	75 mL
2 tbsp	red wine vinegar	25 mL
¼ tsp	pepper	1 mL
	Salt to taste	
2 tbsp	water	25 mL

1. Cut greens from beets, leaving about 1 inch/2.5 cm of stem. Wash beets but do not peel or cut up. Place in saucepan, cover with water and cook until tender, about 45 minutes. They can also be roasted in a preheated 400°F/200°C oven for 1 to 1½ hours or they can be cooked in microwave (page 79).

2. Meanwhile, sprinkle sugar over bottom of large, deep skillet. Brown over medium heat. Stir in onions and cook over low heat for about 10 minutes, until onions brown.

3. Add apple juice and vinegar and cook gently until onions are very tender. Reserve in skillet until beets are cooked.

4. Cool beets slightly under cold water and peel. Cut into thick French-fry shapes. Stir into onions. Add pepper, salt and water and reheat until any liquid has evaporated. Taste and adjust seasonings if necessary.

BEETS

Beets are sometimes overlooked. They are wonderfully sweet, and their colour makes them very exciting. If you cook them in the oven, their colour and flavour will not leach out into the cooking water. If you do boil beets, cook them in their skins and leave on an inch of stem. Peel them after they are cooked.

DAPHNE'S BEET SALAD

Daphne Smith came to us as a nurse when my son was born eleven years ago, and she agreed to stay on as a nanny partly because she loved our healthful cooking. She gave me this delicious recipe; I'd never eaten raw beets before, but these proved to be delicious.

Peel as many beets as you wish. Peel and core the same number of apples. Grate the apples and beets and combine. Eat as a salad or as a condiment with fish or meat.

PER SERVING

Calories	118
g carbohydrate	28
g fibre	4
g total fat	trace
g saturated fat	0
g protein	2

Excellent: folacin

mg cholesterol	0
mg sodium	67
mg potassium	554

CORN WITH GARLIC AND CHIVES

Frozen corn and fresh niblets cut from the cobs both work well in this. As frozen vegetables go, I like corn and peas the best. In fact, you could combine them in this recipe. To cut niblets off the cobs, cut the corn in half so that it can stand up on a cutting board. Holding it firmly, cut from top to bottom, as shown.

CORN

Frozen corn has already been blanched, so it only needs to be defrosted if you are using it in a salad; if you are using it in a cooked dish, you don't even have to bother defrosting it. Although you can also use canned corn, I think frozen is superior, and it doesn't contain as much salt. If you are using fresh corn, simply cut the niblets off the cobs. Cook the niblets in boiling water for 1 minute if the corn is not being cooked in the recipe.

Makes 4 to 6 servings

2 tsp	olive oil	10 mL
2	cloves garlic, finely chopped	2
4 cups	fresh or frozen corn niblets	1 L
pinch	pepper	pinch
	Salt to taste	
¼ cup	chopped fresh chives or green onions	50 mL

1. Heat oil in large skillet and cook garlic gently until very fragrant.

2. Add corn and cook for 3 to 5 minutes, until just cooked and heated thoroughly. Add pepper, salt and chives. Taste and adjust seasonings if necessary.

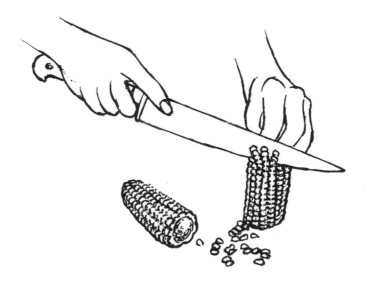

PER SERVING

Calories	151
g carbohydrate	33
g fibre	4
g total fat	2
g saturated fat	trace
g protein	5

Good: folacin

mg cholesterol	0
mg sodium	8
mg potassium	233

HERB BARBECUED CORN ON THE COB

See photo opposite page 97.

I always tell food stories in my classes, and this is one of my students' favourites.

When we drive home from the cottage in late August, we always buy fresh corn from the farmers' stands along the highway. Once my husband stopped behind another car, and I jumped out to buy the corn. While I was gone, the car in front of us left, my husband pulled up, and when I had bought my corn I turned around and got into a stranger's car (now parked in our former spot). The driver, trying not to scare me, said, "Dear, I think you are in the wrong car." My husband, not amused, said, "Trying out another family, honey?"

Everyone seems to have a different method for grilling corn on the cob. When I use it in salads or want a really barbecued taste, I husk the corn completely and cook it directly on the grill until it becomes slightly charred. When I want a more gentle flavour, I use this recipe. It is buttery and delicious, even though no fat is used.

FRESH HERBS

For years only restaurants had access to fresh herbs, and people wondered why the food sang when they ate out, while at home it just mumbled!

Although many books tell you to use three times the amount of fresh herbs as you would use dried, I never follow that rule. When I have fresh herbs I use lots, but I am very stingy with dried herbs.

Wash fresh herbs gently, dry them well and then wrap them in tea towels and store them in an airtight container in the refrigerator. Use them quickly and add them at the end of a recipe so that their delicate flavour doesn't cook away.

Makes 6 servings

6	ears fresh corn	6
	Sprigs of fresh herbs such as tarragon and chives	

1. Pull one side of husk away from corn without removing it completely. Loosen remaining husk. Do not remove silk.

2. Place sprig or two of fresh herbs against corn and reshape husks.

3. Preheat barbecue and place corn directly on grill. Cover with barbecue lid or place piece of foil loosely over corn. Grill for 3 to 5 minutes. Husks will blacken but corn inside will be tender.

PER SERVING

Calories	130
g carbohydrate	30
g fibre	4
g total fat	2
g saturated fat	trace
g protein	4

Excellent: folacin
Good: thiamine

mg cholesterol	0
mg sodium	20
mg potassium	299

See photo opposite page 192.

SPICY CORN RAGOUT

This is a great side dish to serve under a piece of meatloaf (page 186) or grilled chicken or salmon. It tastes delicious all year round, even when made with frozen corn, and is a wonderful way to add some sunshine to your plate in the middle of winter.

If you do not like spicy food, leave out the chipotle or jalapeño chile.

Makes 8 to 10 servings

2 tsp	olive oil	10 mL
2	cloves garlic, finely chopped	2
1	red onion, diced	1
2	sweet red peppers, diced	2
1	4-oz/114 mL tin mild green chiles, rinsed, drained and chopped	1
1	chipotle (page 149), pureed, or jalapeño, chopped, optional	1
8 cups	fresh or frozen corn niblets	2 L
1 cup	homemade chicken stock (page 59) or water	250 mL
¾ lb	fresh spinach, trimmed and chopped	375 g
¼ tsp	pepper	1 mL
	Salt to taste	
⅓ cup	chopped fresh cilantro or parsley	75 mL

1. Heat oil in large, deep skillet or Dutch oven. Add garlic and onion. Cook gently until tender and fragrant but do not brown.

2. Add red peppers, mild green chiles and chipotle. Cook for 5 to 10 minutes.

3. Stir in corn and mix together well. Add stock and bring to boil. Cook gently for 5 minutes. Stir in spinach and cook for 5 minutes longer, just until wilted. Add pepper, salt and cilantro. Taste and adjust seasonings if necessary.

PER SERVING

Calories	184
g carbohydrate	41
g fibre	6
g total fat	2
g saturated fat	trace
g protein	8

Excellent: vitamin A; vitamin C; folacin
Good: thiamine; niacin; riboflavin; iron; vitamin B$_6$

mg cholesterol	0
mg sodium	178
mg potassium	577

SICILIAN SQUASH

To peel squash more easily, cut it into rounds and then peel each round. You can also use one of those new electric vegetable peelers, which are a great help for arthritis sufferers and work well for squash and other hard-to-peel vegetables, whether you are arthritic or not! You can also buy pieces of squash already peeled.

Makes 4 to 6 servings

2 lb	butternut or other winter squash	1 kg
1 tbsp	olive oil	15 mL
⅓ cup	red wine vinegar	75 mL
1	clove garlic, minced	1
2 tbsp	granulated sugar	25 mL
½ tsp	pepper	2 mL
¼ tsp	salt	1 mL
¼ cup	chopped fresh parsley	50 mL
2 tbsp	chopped fresh mint, or ½ tsp/2 mL dried	25 mL

1. Slice squash into ½-inch/1 cm rounds and peel. Arrange in single layer on non-stick baking sheet or baking sheet lined with parchment paper. Brush with olive oil.

2. Bake squash in preheated 400°F/200°C oven for 30 to 40 minutes, or until tender.

3. Meanwhile, combine vinegar, garlic, sugar, pepper and salt. Stir until sugar and salt dissolve.

4. When squash is tender, transfer to serving dish and pour over vinegar mixture. Sprinkle with parsley and mint.

SQUASH

When a recipe calls for summer squash, it is usually referring to yellow or green zucchini or other soft-seeded squash like patty pan or crookneck. Some winter squashes are butternut, Hubbard, acorn and spaghetti. Butternut is my favourite winter squash because it is sweeter and less watery than most, but it is also the most expensive.

Summer squash does not need peeling, but winter squash does. Instead of peeling it before cooking, you can bake it in the oven or microwave and then scoop out the cooked flesh.

PER SERVING

Calories	153
g carbohydrate	32
g fibre	6
g total fat	4
g saturated fat	1
g protein	2

Good: vitamin C; thiamine; vitamin B$_6$; folacin

mg cholesterol	0
mg sodium	152
mg potassium	750

CREAMY POLENTA WITH CORN AND ROASTED GARLIC

I made this in a Southwest cooking class, and it was a knockout. You could serve it as a side dish or as a main course with a salad.

This dish can be made an hour before serving; keep it warm over a double boiler. If you don't have time to roast the garlic, just add 1 minced clove garlic.

Makes 8 to 10 servings

4	cloves garlic, unpeeled	4
7 cups	water	1.75 L
¾ tsp	salt	4 mL
1 tsp	pepper	5 mL
1½ cups	cornmeal (regular or instant)	375 mL
1 cup	fresh or frozen corn niblets	250 mL
1	4-oz/114 mL tin mild green chiles, rinsed, drained and chopped	1
2 tbsp	chopped fresh cilantro or parsley, optional	25 mL
¾ cup	milk	175 mL

1. Place unpeeled garlic in heavy skillet. On very low heat, shaking pan often, cook for about 40 minutes, or until soft and tender. You can also place garlic on baking sheet and roast in preheated 325°F/160°C oven for about 30 minutes. Cool, peel and mince.

2. Place water in Dutch oven and bring to boil. Add salt and pepper. Whisk in cornmeal slowly, stirring constantly. When mixture bubbles, reduce heat and cook on low heat for 5 minutes for instant cornmeal and 20 to 30 minutes for regular cornmeal. Stir occasionally. If mixture gets too thick, add some boiling water.

3. Add garlic, corn and chiles and cook for about 5 minutes.

4. Stir in cilantro and enough milk to reach consistency of very creamy mashed potatoes. Taste and adjust seasonings if necessary.

POLENTA

When cornmeal is cooked in water, milk or stock, the creamy result is called polenta, a kind of cornmeal porridge. Cook the polenta, stirring often, over low heat (or unattended in a double boiler). Regular cornmeal will take about 30 minutes to become tender. Instant polenta will cook in about 5 minutes.

PER SERVING

Calories	128
g carbohydrate	27
g fibre	2
g total fat	1
g saturated fat	trace
g protein	4
mg cholesterol	2
mg sodium	372
mg potassium	136

SPICY MASHED SWEET POTATOES

Sweet potatoes are so good that I am constantly amazed they aren't cooked by everyone all the time! This is a spicy version, but check the maple variation below if you prefer sweet sweet potatoes.

Makes 6 to 8 servings

6	large sweet potatoes (3 lb/1.5 kg)	6
1	baking potato (½ lb/250 g)	1
3 tbsp	brown sugar or honey	45 mL
½ tsp	pepper	2 mL
½ tsp	cayenne (more or less to taste)	2 mL
pinch	nutmeg	pinch
	Salt to taste	

1. Prick potatoes and place on baking sheet. Bake in preheated 350°F/180°C oven for 1 hour, until very tender when pierced.

2. Spoon potatoes out of their skins into bowl or food mill.

3. Mash potatoes with sugar, pepper, cayenne, nutmeg and salt. Taste and adjust seasonings if necessary.

Maple Mashed Sweet Potatoes: Use maple syrup instead of brown sugar. Omit cayenne. Add ½ tsp/2 mL cinnamon and pinch allspice.

See photo opposite page 161.

BAKED POTATO SKINS
Cut cooked potato skins into thin strips and toss with salt, pepper, seasonings (curry powder, chili powder or other herbs or spices) and a small amount of olive oil if desired. Spread on a baking sheet and bake in a preheated 400°F/200°C oven for 15 to 20 minutes, or until crispy. Stir every 5 minutes. Crumble and sprinkle on soups and salads, or leave in larger pieces and serve as a snack.

PER SERVING

Calories	191
g carbohydrate	46
g fibre	5
g total fat	trace
g saturated fat	0
g protein	3

Excellent: vitamin A; vitamin C; vitamin E
Good: vitamin B_6; folacin

mg cholesterol	0
mg sodium	17
mg potassium	599

See photo opposite page 192.

GARLIC MASHED POTATOES

The nineties will be known as the time when mashed potatoes went from being home cooking to being restaurant fare. You can substitute hot milk for the potato-cooking liquid (always use hot liquid when making mashed potatoes), and use a food mill if you want completely lump-free potatoes. Never mash potatoes in the food processor — you'll end up with glue!

MASHED POTATOES

Fancy mashed potato dishes are now being served in trendy restaurants across North America. Here are some other lower-fat versions to try at home:

- Use buttermilk instead of potato-cooking liquid.
- Use half potatoes and half turnips; add extra liquid only if necessary.
- Stir in a little grated white horseradish and/or Dijon mustard.
- Stir in chopped fresh chives or green onions.

Makes 6 servings

2 lb	baking potatoes, peeled and cut in 2-inch/5 cm chunks	1 kg
6	cloves garlic, peeled	6
1 tbsp	olive oil	15 mL
½ tsp	pepper	2 mL
	Salt to taste	

1. Place potatoes and garlic in large pot or Dutch oven and cover generously with water. Bring to boil and cook until potatoes are tender, 20 to 25 minutes.

2. Lift potatoes and garlic out of water, reserving cooking liquid. Mash potatoes and garlic with potato masher or pass through food mill.

3. Slowly beat in olive oil and some of cooking liquid from potatoes until you reach desired consistency (you'll need about ½ to ¾ cup/125 to 175 mL). Add pepper and salt. Taste and adjust seasonings if necessary.

Smashed Potatoes: Smash cooked potatoes with olive oil, salt and pepper rather than mashing them (so there are still lumps). Add 2 tbsp/25 mL chopped fresh mint or dill, ¼ cup/50 mL chopped fresh chives or green onions and ¼ cup/50 mL chopped fresh basil or parsley. (Sometimes I use red-skinned potatoes, scrubbed but not peeled, in this recipe.)

PER SERVING

Calories	120
g carbohydrate	23
g fibre	2
g total fat	2
g saturated fat	trace
g protein	2

Good: vitamin B_6

mg cholesterol	0
mg sodium	7
mg potassium	376

ROASTED ROSEMARY FRENCH FRIES

These baked potato sticks are very satisfying and, of course, they contain far less fat than the deep-fried version. For children (like mine) who prefer everything basic, omit the rosemary and pepper.

Makes 6 servings

2 lb	baking potatoes	1 kg
1 tbsp	vegetable oil or olive oil	15 mL
½ tsp	salt	2 mL
¼ tsp	pepper	1 mL
1 tbsp	chopped fresh rosemary, or ½ tsp/2 mL dried	15 mL

1. Peel potatoes and cut into French-fry shapes. (Soak in cold water for 30 minutes if you want them extra crispy. Drain well and pat dry.)

2. Toss potatoes with oil. Combine salt, pepper and rosemary and toss with potatoes.

3. Arrange potatoes in single layer on rack set over baking sheet. Bake in preheated 400°F/200°C oven for 40 to 45 minutes, or until cooked and browned.

Curried French Fries: Omit rosemary and add ¼ tsp/1 mL curry powder.

Chili Roasted French Fries: Omit rosemary and add 1 tbsp/ 15 mL chili powder.

Roasted Sweet Potato Fries: Substitute sweet potatoes for the baking potatoes.

POTATOES

There are many different kinds of potatoes. Russets, Idaho, red-skinned potatoes and Yukon Golds are great for mashing or baking (whole or as French fries). Boiling potatoes, such as new potatoes, are good for boiling or steaming and some potato salads. All-purpose or "table" potatoes can be used in all potato dishes.

PER SERVING

Calories	115
g carbohydrate	22
g fibre	2
g total fat	2
g saturated fat	trace
g protein	2

Good: vitamin B$_6$

mg cholesterol	0
mg sodium	197
mg potassium	364

See photo opposite page 161.

ROASTED ROOT VEGETABLES

Sometimes I make this recipe using just potatoes and/or sweet potatoes. You can also cook cauliflower this way; the flavour is very concentrated. Roast the florets for 25 to 30 minutes.

Makes 4 to 6 servings

1 lb	baking potatoes, scrubbed	500 g
1 lb	sweet potatoes, peeled	500 g
1	large carrot, peeled or scrubbed	1
1	parsnip, peeled	1
¼ lb	rutabaga, peeled	125 g
1½ tbsp	olive oil	20 mL
2	cloves garlic, minced	2
2 tbsp	chopped fresh rosemary, or 1 tsp/5 mL dried	25 mL
½ tsp	salt	2 mL
¼ tsp	hot red pepper flakes, optional	1 mL
½ tsp	pepper	2 mL

1. Cut vegetables into 1½-inch/4 cm pieces. Place in cold water if they begin to discolour while you are preparing them. Drain vegetables well and pat dry.

2. Combine oil, garlic, rosemary, salt, hot pepper flakes and pepper. Toss with vegetables.

3. Spread vegetables out in single layer on non-stick baking sheet or baking sheet lined with parchment paper (use two sheets if necessary). Bake in preheated 425°F/220°C oven for 45 to 55 minutes, or until vegetables are browned and tender. Stir twice during cooking.

ORGANIC PRODUCE

In its most narrow sense, organic food is food produced without the use of chemicals. Although many people believe it to be more flavourful, it is often more expensive and hard to find. But if more consumers ask for it, the availability will slowly increase and the price will go down. I don't always buy organic produce because of its high price and lack of availability, but I buy it when I can because I like the taste and want to support farmers who grow things naturally and respect the environment.

PER SERVING

Calories	253
g carbohydrate	49
g fibre	7
g total fat	6
g saturated fat	1
g protein	4

Excellent: vitamin A; vitamin C; vitamin E; vitamin B$_6$
Good: thiamine; folacin

mg cholesterol	0
mg sodium	327
mg potassium	831

BRAISED WHITE BEANS

I like to serve this with lamb or chicken. You can use canned beans instead of dried; use two 19-oz/540 mL tins and rinse the beans to get rid of excess salt. While they aren't as firm as the ones you cook yourself from the dried state, they are still pretty good.

Makes 8 servings

1 lb	dried white beans (white kidney, navy beans, black-eyed peas or a mixture – about 2 cups/500 mL)	500 g
1 tbsp	olive oil	15 mL
¼ tsp	hot red pepper flakes	1 mL
1	large onion, chopped	1
3	cloves garlic, finely chopped	3
1 tsp	chopped fresh rosemary, or ¼ tsp/1 mL dried	5 mL
1 tsp	chopped fresh sage, or pinch dried	5 mL
2 cups	homemade chicken stock (page 59) or water	500 mL
¼ tsp	pepper	1 mL
	Salt to taste	
1 tbsp	lemon juice	15 mL
¼ cup	chopped fresh parsley	50 mL

1. Cover beans with cold water and soak overnight in refrigerator. Or use quick-soak method (page 126).

2. Drain beans. Cover with cold water again, bring to boil, reduce heat and simmer gently for 1 hour, or until almost tender. Rinse and drain.

3. Heat oil in large, deep skillet. Add hot pepper flakes, onion and garlic. Cook gently until fragrant. Add rosemary, sage, stock and drained beans. Cook for 15 to 25 minutes, or until beans are very tender and stock has almost disappeared.

4. Add pepper, salt and lemon juice. Taste and adjust seasonings if necessary. Sprinkle with parsley.

SALT

I use sea salt or kosher salt because they have a wonderful sweet/salty flavour. Kosher salt has a great texture for cooking — it isn't too fine, so you can still pick it up easily with your fingers, but it isn't so coarse that you need a salt-grinder. It is also additive free.

SALT SUBSTITUTES

If you are cutting back on salt in cooking, there are many ways to replace the flavour:

• use very fresh, good-quality ingredients
• use lots of fresh herbs (or add dried herbs discreetly)
• use spices and mustards
• use hot chiles, citrus peel, vinegars, wine and juices

PER SERVING

Calories	225
g carbohydrate	38
g fibre	11
g total fat	3
g saturated fat	1
g protein	13

Excellent: iron; folacin
Good: thiamine; niacin; vitamin B$_6$

mg cholesterol	0
mg sodium	11
mg potassium	588

WHITE BEAN PUREE WITH CUMIN

This is wonderful with roast lamb or chicken. If you wish, you can make it more quickly with two 19-oz/540 mL tins white kidney beans, rinsed and well drained — just reduce the cooking time to 30 minutes. This is actually a perfect use for canned beans because they are pureed.

For extra flavour, add a 2-oz/60 g well-trimmed piece of pancetta or bacon to the beans before cooking. Remove and discard it before pureeing. Or you can add 1 to 2 tbsp/15 to 25 mL olive oil to the puree before serving.

Makes 6 to 8 servings

1 lb	dried white kidney beans	500 g
4	cloves garlic, peeled	4
1 tsp	ground cumin	5 mL
½ tsp	pepper	2 mL
	Salt to taste	

1. Cover beans with plenty of cold water and soak overnight in refrigerator.

2. Rinse and drain beans. Place in large pot and cover generously with cold water. Add garlic, cumin and pepper. Bring to boil, cover and simmer gently until beans are very tender, about 1 to 1½ hours.

3. Drain beans, reserving liquid. Puree beans in batches, using a little cooking liquid in each batch, so consistency is like mashed potatoes. Add salt. Taste and adjust seasonings if necessary.

PER SERVING

Calories	260
g carbohydrate	47
g fibre	19
g total fat	1
g saturated fat	trace
g protein	18

Excellent: thiamine; iron; folacin
Good: niacin; vitamin B$_6$

mg cholesterol	0
mg sodium	5
mg potassium	827

MIDDLE EASTERN COUSCOUS

One of my students, Mary Lou Taylor, gave me this recipe, and I have been making it ever since. Mary Lou, who is a great cook, served the couscous with lamb shanks, but it goes equally well with chicken.

I learned about this method of cooking couscous in Joyce Goldstein's book, The Mediterranean Kitchen, *and it is the most reliable I have ever used.*

For an attractive presentation, lightly oil six individual ramekins and fill with the couscous mixture. You can invert immediately onto serving plates or make ahead and cover with foil. Before serving, place ramekins in a larger baking dish filled with hot water (the water should reach about halfway up the sides of the ramekins) and reheat in a preheated 350°F/180°C oven for 15 to 20 minutes before unmoulding.

Makes 6 to 8 servings

1 cup	couscous	250 mL
1½ cups	boiling water	375 mL
1 tsp	olive oil	5 mL
2	green onions, chopped	2
¾ tsp	ground cumin	4 mL
¼ tsp	turmeric	1 mL
pinch	cinnamon	pinch
1 cup	drained and chopped canned plum tomatoes	250 mL
3 tbsp	raisins	45 mL
2 tbsp	chopped pistachio nuts, optional	25 mL
2 tbsp	chopped fresh parsley	25 mL

1. Place couscous in 8-inch/2 L square baking dish. Add boiling water. Cover tightly with foil and allow to rest for 10 minutes, or until ready to use. Fluff gently with fork.

2. Meanwhile, heat oil in large skillet. Add green onions and cook gently for 2 minutes. Add cumin, turmeric and cinnamon and cook for 30 seconds.

3. Add well-drained tomatoes and cook for a few minutes, until very thick. Add raisins, nuts, parsley and couscous. Combine well. Taste and adjust seasonings if necessary.

QUINOA

Quinoa is an ancient grain that has a high protein content compared to other grains. Be sure to wash it thoroughly before cooking, as it has a slightly bitter covering (saponin) that should be rinsed away. If you like, toast the washed quinoa before cooking. Add it to a dry skillet and cook, stirring, until it colours slightly. This will add a nutty taste without adding fat.

To cook quinoa, rinse 1½ cups/375 mL quinoa in cold water until the water runs clear. Bring 3 cups/750 mL water and 1 tsp/5 mL soy sauce to a boil. Add the quinoa, cover and simmer for 15 minutes. Fluff gently before serving.

Makes 4 to 6 servings.

PER SERVING

Calories	148
g carbohydrate	30
g fibre	2
g total fat	1
g saturated fat	trace
g protein	5
mg cholesterol	0
mg sodium	73
mg potassium	214

See photo opposite page 193.

SHORT-GRAIN RICE

Use short-grain rice when you want the rice to stick together (as in sushi), or when you want the dish to be creamy (as in risottos and rice puddings). Short-grain Italian rice, such as Arborio, is perfect for risotto (which is the name of the dish as well as the technique for cooking the rice). The texture of the finished dish should be creamy, but you should still be able to distinguish each grain in the total creamy mass.

You can use long-grain rice when recipes call for short-grain and vice versa, but the texture will be different.

WEHANI

Wehani is a brown rice that resembles wild rice. It has a firm outside shell and is very chewy and flavourful. Use twice as much water as you would for regular rice, for 40 to 50 minutes, or until tender. Or you can cook it in lots of boiling water like pasta. When tender, drain through a sieve.

PER SERVING

Calories	354
g carbohydrate	64
g fibre	8
g total fat	7
g saturated fat	1
g protein	11

Excellent: vitamin A; vitamin C; niacin; iron
Good: thiamine; vitamin B_6; folacin

mg cholesterol	1
mg sodium	55
mg potassium	561

MIXED GRAIN PILAF

The different grains make this pilaf particularly interesting, but you can use one or two if you cannot find all of them. I got the idea for this from my good friend Mary Risley who owns the Tante Marie School of Cooking in San Francisco.

Makes 4 to 6 servings

2 tsp	vegetable oil	10 mL
1	onion, chopped	1
2	cloves garlic, finely chopped	2
1 tbsp	chili powder	15 mL
¼ tsp	cayenne	1 mL
1 tsp	ground cumin	5 mL
½ cup	long-grain rice, preferably basmati	125 mL
½ cup	pearl barley	125 mL
¼ cup	quinoa, rinsed	50 mL
¼ cup	wehani rice	50 mL
3 cups	homemade chicken stock (page 59), or 1 10-oz/284 mL chicken broth plus water	750 mL
2	sweet red peppers, preferably roasted (page 154), peeled and diced	2
1 tbsp	pine nuts, toasted (page 245)	15 mL
¼ cup	chopped fresh cilantro or parsley	50 mL

1. Heat oil in large saucepan. Add onion and garlic and cook gently until tender. Stir in chili powder, cayenne and cumin. Cook for about 30 seconds, stirring constantly, until very fragrant.

2. Add basmati rice, barley, quinoa and wehani. Stir in well.

3. Add stock and bring to boil. Reduce heat, cover and cook gently for 40 to 45 minutes, until liquid is absorbed and rice is very tender.

4. Stir in peppers, pine nuts and cilantro. Taste and adjust seasonings if necessary.

NAVAJO RICE PILAF

This is a great side dish, but I also serve it as a meatless main course. You can add about ¼ lb/125 g crumbled chèvre or feta and bake it in the oven for about 15 minutes.

Makes 6 to 8 servings

1 cup	long-grain brown rice	250 mL
2¼ cups	water	550 mL
2 tsp	olive oil	10 mL
1	large onion, chopped	1
2	cloves garlic, finely chopped	2
1	zucchini, diced	1
1	sweet red pepper, diced	1
1½ cups	fresh or frozen corn niblets	375 mL
1	4-oz/114 mL tin mild green chiles, rinsed, drained and chopped	1
¼ cup	chopped fresh cilantro or parsley	50 mL
¼ tsp	pepper	1 mL

1. Rinse rice well. Place in saucepan with water and bring to boil. Reduce heat, cover and cook gently for 40 minutes.

2. Meanwhile, heat oil in large, deep skillet or Dutch oven. Add onion and garlic. Cook gently for 5 minutes, or until very tender.

3. Add zucchini and cook for 5 minutes. Add red pepper, corn and chiles and cook for 5 to 10 minutes longer. Stir in cilantro and pepper. Remove from heat.

4. When rice is ready, reheat vegetable mixture and stir in rice. Taste and adjust seasonings if necesssary.

BASMATI RICE

Basmati is a naturally aromatic long-grain rice from India. Before being cooked, the rice should be washed in plenty of cold water until the water runs clear. You can buy brown or white basmati rice, and although both are very good, I find the white more fragrant. Other fragrant rices such as jasmine and Thai-scented are also delicious.

BROWN RICE

Brown rice is more nutritious than white rice, as its outer husk contains bran, fibre and vitamins. But brown rice usually takes twice as long to cook as white rice, and it is more expensive. It also doesn't keep as long as white rice. Buy it in small quantities and/or keep it refrigerated if you are not using it quickly.

PER SERVING

Calories	185
g carbohydrate	38
g fibre	4
g total fat	3
g saturated fat	trace
g protein	5

Excellent: vitamin C
Good: niacin; vitamin B$_6$

mg cholesterol	0
mg sodium	192
mg potassium	280

RICE WITH PASTA AND CHICKPEAS

Although using pasta in a rice pilaf seems unusual, it is quite common in Middle Eastern recipes, and I've learned to love the texture and taste of it.

Makes 4 to 6 servings

2 tsp	olive oil	10 mL
½ cup	broken spaghettini or vermicelli	125 mL
1	onion, chopped	1
1 cup	long-grain rice	250 mL
1½ cups	homemade chicken stock (page 59) or water	375 mL
1	19-oz/540 mL tin chickpeas, rinsed and drained, or 2 cups/ 500 mL cooked chickpeas	1
¼ tsp	pepper	1 mL
	Salt to taste	
2 tbsp	chopped fresh cilantro or parsley	25 mL

1. Heat oil in saucepan. Add pasta and brown slightly. Add onion and cook gently until tender, about 5 minutes.

2. Stir in rice and coat well. Add stock and bring to boil. Reduce heat, cover and simmer gently for 15 minutes.

3. Add chickpeas and cook for 10 minutes longer, still covered, until all liquid has been absorbed. Stir in pepper and salt. Add cilantro. Taste and adjust seasonings if necessary.

CHICKPEAS

Chickpeas are delicious as a side dish, but they are also a great addition to soups, salads and grain dishes. I usually soak dried chickpeas in water overnight in the refrigerator and then cook them for 1½ hours, or until tender. Canned chickpeas are a good substitute; unlike many other canned beans, they retain more of their texture. I always keep a tin in my cupboard for making a last-minute appetizer like hummos (page 37), or to add protein, fibre and flavour to a salad.

PER SERVING

Calories	403
g carbohydrate	74
g fibre	5
g total fat	5
g saturated fat	1
g protein	15

Excellent: vitamin B$_6$; folacin
Good: niacin

mg cholesterol	0
mg sodium	220
mg potassium	308

RISOTTO WITH SQUASH

Risottos are becoming more and more popular, and this is one of my favourites. The colour is lovely and the flavour and texture are rich and complex. For a vegetarian dish, use vegetable broth in place of the chicken stock. You can serve this as a first course, as a main course or as a side dish with roasted or grilled meat or fish.

Cook risotto on medium or medium-high heat. After you begin to add the stock it should take 15 to 18 minutes to reach the perfect consistency. (If the liquid is used up in less than 15 minutes, add more stock and use a lower heat the next time; if the rice is tender and there is still liquid in the pot, raise the heat slightly the next time.)

Makes 6 to 8 servings

1 tbsp	olive oil	15 mL
2	leeks or small onions, trimmed and diced	2
1	clove garlic, finely chopped	1
1½ cups	short-grain rice, preferably Arborio	375 mL
2 cups	diced peeled butternut squash	500 mL
4 cups	homemade chicken stock (page 59), or 1 10-oz/284 mL tin chicken broth plus water, boiling	1 L
½ tsp	pepper	2 mL
	Salt to taste	
2 tbsp	chopped fresh chives or green onions	25 mL

1. Heat oil in Dutch oven. Add leeks and garlic. Cook gently for a few minutes until fragrant and tender but do not brown.

2. Stir in rice and coat well. Add squash and combine well.

3. On medium or medium-high heat, add 1 cup/250 mL stock. Stirring constantly, cook until stock has evaporated. Continue to add stock ½ cup/125 mL at a time. Stirring constantly, cook until each addition is absorbed before adding the next. After 15 minutes, begin tasting risotto to see if it is ready. Season with pepper and salt. Stir in chives. Taste and adjust seasonings if necessary. Serve immediately.

LEEKS

Leeks have a delicate onion-like flavour. Use the white and light-green parts; to avoid wasting all the leek tops, peel away the dark-green outer layers. Inside, the leeks will be light green all the way up.

Leeks catch sand inside their layers and must be cleaned thoroughly. Cut off the root ends and remove the dark-green layers. Wash off any visible dirt. Slice the leeks and swish them around in a large bowl of water. The leeks will rise to the top and the dirt and sand will sink to the bottom. Lift out the leeks gently, leaving the grit and water behind.

PER SERVING

Calories	258
g carbohydrate	49
g fibre	2
g total fat	4
g saturated fat	1
g protein	7

Good: niacin

mg cholesterol	1
mg sodium	27
mg potassium	357

Breakfast Shake *(page 227)*
Cranberry Streusel Muffins *(page 240)*

Lemon Ricotta Pancakes
(page 232)

BREAKFASTS AND BRUNCHES

Grapefruit Calypso

Breakfast Shake

Yogurt Cheese

Breakfast Fruit Crisp

Swiss Muesli

Baked French Toast

Lemon Ricotta Pancakes

Buttermilk Oatmeal Pancakes

Multigrain Griddlecakes

Caramelized Pear Puff Pancake

Chèvre and Fresh Herb Soufflé

Breakfast Pizza

GRAPEFRUIT CALYPSO

This can be served as an appetizer for brunch or lunch, and it also makes a simple but delicious dessert. I like using pink grapefruit, but of course the recipe works equally well with white ones. If you are a little nervous about flambéeing the rum, simply pour it over — the flambé in this case is just for show (pages 262-63).

Makes 6 servings

3	pink grapefruit	3
½ cup	brown sugar	125 mL
½ tsp	cinnamon	2 mL
pinch	nutmeg	pinch
pinch	allspice	pinch
2 tbsp	dark rum, optional	25 mL

1. Cut grapefruit in half and loosen sections with grapefruit knife or serrated knife. Do not remove them from rinds. Place grapefruit on baking sheet.

2. Combine sugar, cinnamon, nutmeg and allspice. Press mixture into surface of grapefruit halves.

3. Just before serving, preheat broiler and broil grapefruit for 3 to 5 minutes, until sugar bubbles and grapefruit is heated.

4. Heat rum gently in small saucepan. When it just bubbles, flambé. Pour over grapefruit, or simply pour rum over grapefruit and serve without flambéeing.

PER SERVING	
Calories	106
g carbohydrate	27
g fibre	2
g total fat	trace
g saturated fat	0
g protein	1

Excellent: vitamin C

mg cholesterol	0
mg sodium	6
mg potassium	222

See photo opposite page 224.

BREAKFAST SHAKE

This is a thick, frothy drink that is especially perfect for anyone who is lactose intolerant but craves a "creamy" shake. You can use any combination of fruit juices, but be sure to include the banana for a velvety texture.

Makes 2 servings

1	ripe banana	1
2 tbsp	frozen orange juice concentrate	25 mL
½ cup	unsweetened pineapple juice, pear nectar or mango juice	125 mL
½ cup	sliced strawberries or other fruit	125 mL
½ cup	crushed ice	125 mL

1. Peel and break up banana and place in blender. Puree with orange juice concentrate.

2. Add juice, strawberries and ice and blend until very frothy. Serve in glasses with straw.

Breakfast Milkshake: Use milk instead of pineapple juice.

CRANBERRY ORANGE COCKTAIL

Here's a wonderful refreshing drink for the hottest summer days. Combine one 9-oz/275 mL tin frozen cranberry juice concentrate and one 12½-oz/355 mL tin frozen orange juice concentrate in a large pitcher. Add 6 cups/ 1.5 L cold soda water and 4 cups/1 L ice cubes.

Makes about 10 cups/2.5 L

PER SERVING

Calories	127
g carbohydrate	32
g fibre	2
g total fat	1
g saturated fat	trace
g protein	1

Excellent: vitamin C; vitamin B$_6$; folacin

mg cholesterol	0
mg sodium	3
mg potassium	493

YOGURT CHEESE

My friend, restaurant reviewer Cynthia Wine, came over when I was making this one day, and she couldn't believe how delicious it was. I said it was something you had to taste to believe, and she agreed, saying, "Some recipes just don't taste good in print!"

Many of my students are surprised how thick and luscious yogurt cheese is, even when it is made with 1 percent low-fat yogurt. It can be used in many recipes instead of sour cream (I think it is much better than light sour cream), whipping cream (it doesn't whip but you can fold it into sauces like lemon custard sauce, page 268). And it doesn't weep the way regular yogurt does in salad dressings. Although you can also use the new thick yogurts, yogurt cheese doesn't contain thickeners or gelatin and has, I think, a much more natural taste and texture. PLEASE TRY IT! Be sure to use natural yogurt containing no stabilizers, gels or thickeners (use the kind that gets watery after you remove some from the container).

(At the time of this printing, some yogurt manufacturers were making pressed yogurt; this can be substituted for our firm yogurt cheese.)

Makes 1¹/₂ cups/375 mL

3 cups	unflavoured low-fat natural yogurt	750 mL

1. Line strainer with cheesecloth, paper towel or coffee filter. Place over bowl.

2. Place yogurt in strainer and cover with plastic wrap. Allow to rest for 3 hours to overnight in refrigerator. After 3 hours, cheese will be medium thick (soft yogurt cheese); if you let it drain overnight, it should be as thick as cream cheese (firm yogurt cheese). Discard liquid (or use it for cooking rice, as is sometimes done in the Middle East) and spoon thickened yogurt cheese into another container. Cover and use as required. Keeps for about 1 week.

SUGGESTIONS FOR USING YOGURT CHEESE:

- use **soft yogurt cheese** in place of sour cream in dips or on baked potatoes, as a garnish in soups, in place of mayonnaise in sandwiches or salad dressings or in place of lightly whipped cream in or on desserts

- use **firm yogurt cheese** in place of cream cheese in spreads or on bagels with smoked salmon

PER TBSP (15 mL)

Calories	15
g carbohydrate	1
g fibre	0
g total fat	trace
g saturated fat	trace
g protein	2
mg cholesterol	2
mg sodium	13
mg potassium	46

HERB CHEESE SPREAD

Combine 1 cup/250 mL firm yogurt cheese with 2 minced cloves garlic, 1 tbsp/15 mL each chopped fresh parsley, chives or green onions and tarragon or dill (if using dried herbs use about ¼ tsp/1 mL of each). Season to taste with salt, pepper and hot red pepper sauce.

Makes about 1 cup/250 mL.

DESSERT TOPPING

Combine 1 cup/250 mL soft yogurt cheese with 2 tbsp/25 mL granulated sugar, 1 tsp/5 mL vanilla and 1 tsp/5 mL grated orange peel. Use in place of whipped cream.

Makes about 1 cup/250 mL.

PER SERVING

Calories	298
g carbohydrate	59
g fibre	7
g total fat	7
g saturated fat	1
g protein	4

Good: iron

mg cholesterol	0
mg sodium	83
mg potassium	470

BREAKFAST FRUIT CRISP

When I was in Ireland, I had one of their world-famous breakfasts that included fabulously creamy oatmeal, wonderful fish dishes, scones and baked goods and an unusual breakfast fruit crisp that they served (like almost everything else!) with clotted cream. Now I make fruit crisp for breakfast and serve it with maple syrup and/or soft yogurt cheese (page 228) or regular yogurt.

I love a combination of fruits in this, but you could simplify the recipe by using four apples and 1 cup/250 mL dried apricots.

Makes 8 to 12 servings

2	apples, peeled and sliced	2
2	pears, peeled and sliced	2
½ cup	pitted prunes	125 mL
½ cup	dried apricots, cut in half	125 mL
½ cup	dried cherries or cranberries	125 mL
2 tbsp	maple syrup	25 mL
¼ cup	apple juice or orange juice	50 mL

Topping:

1 cup	rolled oats	250 mL
½ cup	all-purpose flour	125 mL
⅓ cup	wheat bran	75 mL
½ cup	brown sugar	125 mL
½ tsp	cinnamon	2 mL
¼ cup	soft margarine or unsalted butter, melted	50 mL
⅓ cup	apple juice or orange juice	75 mL

1. Combine apples, pears, prunes, apricots, cherries, maple syrup and ¼ cup/50 mL apple juice. Place in 8-cup/2 L baking dish.

2. For topping, combine rolled oats, flour, bran, brown sugar and cinnamon. Stir in melted margarine or butter and ⅓ cup/75 mL juice. Spoon over fruit.

3. Bake in preheated 350°F/180°C oven for 50 to 60 minutes, or until fruit is very tender and topping is crisp.

SWISS MUESLI

There are two versions of muesli. One version is dry like granola and the other, like this one, is moist and fruity.

I prefer this quite thick, but you can use regular yogurt for a thinner version. This will keep for a few days in the refrigerator.

Makes 6 to 8 servings

1½ cups	rolled oats	375 mL
¾ cup	water	175 mL
1	apple, grated	1
3 tbsp	honey	45 mL
2 cups	mashed fresh or frozen berries	500 mL
1 cup	soft yogurt cheese (page 228) or thick yogurt	250 mL

1. Combine rolled oats with water, apple and honey. Spread over bottom of shallow 3-qt/3 L casserole.

2. Spread mashed fruit over oatmeal mixture. Cover with plastic wrap and refrigerate for a few hours or overnight.

3. Stir yogurt cheese into mixture before serving.

GRANOLA

In large bowl, combine 4 cups/1 L rolled oats, 1 cup/250 mL sliced almonds, ½ cup/125 mL unsweetened coconut, ½ cup/125 mL sunflower seeds, ½ cup/125 mL wheat bran and ½ tsp/2 mL cinnamon.

In saucepan, combine ½ cup/125 mL brown sugar and ⅓ cup/75 mL honey or maple syrup. Bring to boil. Toss with oat mixture. Place granola on large baking sheet lined with parchment paper or lightly oiled foil. Bake in 325°F/160°C oven for 35 to 40 minutes, or until lightly toasted. Place second piece of parchment paper or oiled foil on top of granola and cover with second baking sheet. Turn, remove first baking sheet and paper and bake for 10 to 15 minutes longer.

Break up granola and cool. Stir in 1 cup/250 mL chopped dried fruit. Store in airtight container.

Makes about 6 cups/1.5 L.

PER SERVING

Calories	187
g carbohydrate	35
g fibre	4
g total fat	3
g saturated fat	1
g protein	8

Excellent: vitamin C
Good: thiamine; vitamin B$_{12}$

mg cholesterol	4
mg sodium	38
mg potassium	356

APPLE BUTTER

Use this fat-free spread on its own or with yogurt cheese (page 228) as a spread on toast or bagels.

If you do not have a food mill, core and peel the apples. Puree the cooked mixture in a blender or food processor after cooking.

Wash 6 large apples and cut into chunks (you should have about 8 cups/2 L). In a large saucepan or Dutch oven, combine apples with ¼ lb/125 g dried apple slices (about 1½ cups/375 mL), 2 cups/500 mL apple juice, 1 tbsp/15 mL cinnamon, ¼ tsp/1 mL allspice and ¼ tsp/1 mL ground cloves. Bring to a boil, reduce heat, cover and cook gently for 20 minutes, until thickened. Uncover and cook until very thick (about 2 to 3 cups/500 to 750 mL). Puree through a food mill.

Makes about 2 cups/500 mL.

PER SERVING

Calories	305
g carbohydrate	43
g fibre	2
g total fat	8
g saturated fat	2
g protein	15

Excellent: riboflavin
Good: thiamine; niacin; folacin; vitamin B$_{12}$

mg cholesterol	149
mg sodium	377
mg potassium	331

BAKED FRENCH TOAST

Many people don't know that you don't have to fry French toast; you can bake it. You can make this ahead and soak the bread in the refrigerator overnight, but the recipe works well even after soaking the bread for about 15 minutes.

Serve this with maple syrup, fruit or sweetened soft yogurt cheese (page 228).

Makes 6 servings

4	eggs	4
8	egg whites	8
1½ cups	milk	375 mL
¼ cup	granulated sugar	50 mL
2 tsp	vanilla	10 mL
½ tsp	cinnamon	2 mL
12	½-inch/1 cm slices raisin bread, whole wheat challah (page 252) or whole wheat bread	12
1 tbsp	soft margarine or unsalted butter	15 mL

1. In large flat dish, whisk eggs with egg whites, milk, sugar, vanilla and cinnamon. (Strain mixture if you wish.)

2. Dip bread in egg mixture and turn to coat well. Allow all slices to soak in dish for at least 15 minutes or as long as overnight in refrigerator.

3. Line baking sheet(s) with parchment paper and brush with margarine or butter. Arrange bread in single layer on paper. Dot with any remaining margarine or butter.

4. Bake in preheated 375°F/190°C oven for 25 to 30 minutes, until browned and puffed (you can turn after 15 minutes, if desired).

LEMON RICOTTA PANCAKES

See photo opposite page 225.

The lemon flavour in these pancakes is wonderful to wake up to, but the texture is so light and delicate that they are a treat any time. Dust the pancakes with a little extra sifted icing sugar before serving, if you wish.

Makes 6 servings (about 20 3-inch/7.5 cm pancakes)

1 cup	light ricotta cheese, well drained	250 mL
3	egg yolks	3
½ cup	all-purpose flour	125 mL
¼ cup	granulated sugar	50 mL
2 tsp	grated lemon peel	10 mL
pinch	nutmeg	pinch
1 tbsp	soft margarine or unsalted butter, melted	15 mL
4	egg whites	4
⅓ cup	lemon juice	75 mL
¼ cup	sifted icing sugar	50 mL

1. In large bowl, whisk ricotta with egg yolks, flour, sugar, lemon peel, nutmeg and melted margarine.

2. In separate bowl, beat egg whites until light and fluffy. Stir one-third of whites into ricotta batter. Gently fold in remaining whites.

3. Heat large non-stick skillet to medium-high. Add batter to pan in large spoonfuls, flattening them slightly with back of spoon. Cook for about 2 minutes per side, or until just cooked through.

4. In saucepan, heat lemon juice and stir in icing sugar. Brush lightly over tops of cooked pancakes.

PER SERVING

Calories	194
g carbohydrate	24
g fibre	trace
g total fat	7
g saturated fat	2
g protein	10

Good: riboflavin; vitamin B$_{12}$

mg cholesterol	120
mg sodium	118
mg potassium	120

BUTTERMILK OATMEAL PANCAKES

My children love silver dollar-sized pancakes, but when they were little I used to pipe the batter into the pan through a squirt bottle to make their initials or other shapes. (I liked hearts and other simple shapes, but they preferred things that I had a lot of trouble with, such as tigers and lions and bears!)

Serve these with a drizzle of maple syrup or a light dusting of icing sugar.

Makes about 6 servings (48 small pancakes)

2	eggs	2
1½ cups	buttermilk	375 mL
2 tsp	soft margarine or unsalted butter, melted	10 mL
½ cup	whole wheat flour	125 mL
⅓ cup	all-purpose flour	75 mL
½ cup	rolled oats	125 mL
¾ tsp	baking soda	4 mL
pinch	salt	pinch
3 tbsp	granulated sugar	45 mL

1. Whisk eggs lightly with buttermilk and margarine or butter.

2. In separate bowl, combine whole wheat flour, all-purpose flour, rolled oats, baking soda, salt and sugar. Stir together very well.

3. Whisk egg mixture into flour mixture just until combined.

4. Brush non-stick skillet with small amount of oil and heat. Drop batter by tablespoon for silver dollar pancakes. Cook on one side until bubbles appear and surface changes from shiny to dull. Flip and cook for about 45 seconds on second side.

PER SERVING

Calories	170
g carbohydrate	26
g fibre	2
g total fat	4
g saturated fat	1
g protein	7
mg cholesterol	74
mg sodium	250
mg potassium	185

MULTIGRAIN GRIDDLECAKES

These griddlecakes have an interesting texture, somewhere between an English muffin and a pancake. Serve them with maple syrup or caramelized pears or apples. For thinner pancakes, add a little more buttermilk.

Makes 6 servings (about 24 3-inch/7.5 cm pancakes)

2	eggs	2
2 cups	buttermilk	500 mL
1½ tbsp	soft margarine or unsalted butter, melted	20 mL
1 cup	all-purpose flour	250 mL
½ cup	whole wheat flour	125 mL
½ cup	rolled oats	125 mL
½ cup	cornmeal	125 mL
2 tbsp	granulated sugar	25 mL
1 tsp	baking powder	5 mL
½ tsp	baking soda	2 mL

1. Beat eggs and stir in buttermilk and melted margarine or butter. Reserve.

2. In large bowl, stir together flours with oats, cornmeal, sugar, baking powder and baking soda.

3. Stir in liquid ingredients just until mixed. Batter will be thick.

4. Heat non-stick griddle or two skillets. Brush with small amount of oil and spoon batter onto hot surface in 3-inch/ 7.5 cm rounds. (Cook in batches.) When bubbles appear and surface loses its sheen, flip pancakes and cook second side for about 1 minute.

BACON AND SAUSAGES
If you love high-fat foods such as bacon or sausages, use them as ingredients rather than as a main food. Use a half slice of bacon per person, crisply cooked and well drained, and crumble it into salads. Or cook a small amount of sausage and add it to soups or pasta sauces. You will get the flavour you crave without nearly as much fat.

PER SERVING

Calories	277
g carbohydrate	45
g fibre	3
g total fat	6
g saturated fat	2
g protein	10

Good: thiamine; niacin; riboflavin

mg cholesterol	75
mg sodium	286
mg potassium	251

CARAMELIZED PEAR PUFF PANCAKE

This pancake is so good, you could even serve it for dessert. And it is very quick to make. Serve it hot or cold, and try apples instead of pears for a great variation. If you do not have a non-stick skillet with an ovenproof handle, transfer the pears to a 11 x 7-inch/2 L baking dish and pour the egg mixture on top before baking.

Makes 6 servings

3 tbsp	soft margarine or unsalted butter	45 mL
4	ripe pears, peeled and thinly sliced	4
½ tsp	cinnamon	2 mL
⅓ cup	brown sugar	75 mL
3	eggs	3
2 tbsp	granulated sugar	25 mL
½ cup	milk	125 mL
½ cup	all-purpose flour	125 mL
1 tbsp	sifted icing sugar	15 mL

1. Melt margarine or butter in 10-inch/25 cm non-stick ovenproof skillet. Remove half from skillet and reserve.

2. Add pears, cinnamon and brown sugar to skillet and cook for 5 minutes.

3. Meanwhile, using food processor, blender or whisk, combine reserved margarine or butter, eggs, granulated sugar, milk and flour. Pour batter over pears and bake in preheated 425°F/220°C oven for 20 to 25 minutes, or until browned and puffed.

4. Remove skillet from oven and shake to loosen pears. Invert carefully onto large plate. Sprinkle with icing sugar. Serve in wedges.

PER SERVING

Calories	268
g carbohydrate	43
g fibre	3
g total fat	9
g saturated fat	2
g protein	5
mg cholesterol	109
mg sodium	121
mg potassium	245

Chèvre and Fresh Herb Soufflé

I made this recipe on the Light Gourmet cooking series, and Robin Ward, the host, still says it is the best thing he has ever eaten. You can prepare it ahead and bake it just before serving.

Always wait until your guests are in the house before you put a soufflé in the oven, and serve it right away, before it deflates. (It tastes great deflated, too; it just loses some of its panache!) This is great on its own or with roasted red pepper sauce.

Even if you are usually intimidated by soufflés, you shouldn't be by this one. It is baked in a shallow dish, and although it does rise, because it isn't cooked in the traditional shape, nobody is really sure what it is supposed to look like.

Makes 8 servings

2 cups	cold milk	500 mL
½ cup	all-purpose flour	125 mL
1	clove garlic, minced	1
½ tsp	salt	2 mL
½ tsp	pepper	2 mL
¼ tsp	nutmeg	1 mL
¼ tsp	cayenne	1 mL
1 tbsp	chopped fresh thyme, or ½ tsp/2 mL dried	15 mL
1 tbsp	chopped fresh rosemary, or ½ tsp/2 mL dried	15 mL
2 tbsp	chopped fresh parsley	25 mL
4	egg yolks	4
3 oz	chèvre (goat cheese) or feta cheese, crumbled (scant ½ cup/125 mL)	90 g
2 oz	light ricotta cheese, drained and crumbled (scant ⅓ cup/75 mL)	60 g
7	egg whites	7
1 tbsp	grated Parmesan cheese	15 mL

ROASTED RED PEPPER SAUCE

Serve this sauce with frittatas, meatloaf or roast meats. You can use unroasted peppers, but you may want to puree the sauce through a food mill to remove bits of skin before serving.

In a saucepan, combine 1 minced clove garlic, dash of hot red pepper sauce, 3 roasted, seeded and peeled red peppers (page 154) and 1 cup/250 mL chicken stock. Cook gently for 5 minutes (15 minutes if peppers are not roasted). Puree sauce and heat thoroughly. Season to taste with salt and pepper. (If the sauce is too thick, simply add a bit more stock or water.)

Makes about 2 cups/500 mL.

1. Lightly oil shallow 12 x 8-inch/3 L gratin dish. Preheat oven to 425°F/220°C.

2. In 3-qt/3 L saucepan, whisk milk into flour until smooth. Add garlic and slowly bring to boil, stirring often.

3. Stir in salt, pepper, nutmeg, cayenne, thyme, rosemary and parsley. Remove from heat.

4. Beat egg yolks. Beat a little hot sauce into yolks and then return yolk mixture to saucepan. Stir in chèvre and ricotta. Taste sauce – it should be very well seasoned.

5. In large bowl, beat egg whites until peaks form. Stir one-quarter of whites into sauce base to lighten and then fold in remaining whites gently.

6. Spoon soufflé mixture lightly into gratin dish and sprinkle with Parmesan. Reduce oven temperature to 400°F/200°C. Bake soufflé for 20 to 25 minutes, until browned and puffed. Serve immediately.

CHÈVRE

Chèvre simply means goat cheese, but most recipes that call for it are referring to the soft, creamy goat cheese. This cheese is high in fat, but you can make a lower-fat spread by combining it with low-fat cottage cheese, light ricotta or soft yogurt cheese (page 228). Some people find the taste of goat cheese too strong, but when it is combined with herbs or other foods and warmed, it is irresistible to almost everyone.

PER SERVING

Calories	146
g carbohydrate	11
g fibre	trace
g total fat	7
g saturated fat	4
g protein	10

Excellent: vitamin B$_{12}$
Good: riboflavin; calcium

mg cholesterol	128
mg sodium	372
mg potassium	179

BREAKFAST PIZZA

This is one of the most spectacular brunch dishes I've ever served. It looks stunning and bedazzles my students so much that they rush right home to make it.

There are endless variations to this idea; try thinly sliced prosciutto or smoked trout instead of the smoked salmon, or leave out the eggs altogether. Serve this warm or cold.

Makes 8 servings

1	12-inch/30 cm baked pizza crust or 8 x 15-inch/20 x 38 cm focaccia	1
1 cup	soft yogurt cheese (page 228) or thick yogurt	250 mL
1 tbsp	honey-style mustard	15 mL
¼ cup	chopped fresh chives or green onions, divided	50 mL
2 tbsp	chopped fresh dill or parsley	25 mL
4	eggs	4
6	egg whites	6
¼ cup	water	50 mL
	Salt to taste	
½ tsp	pepper, divided	2 mL
1 tbsp	vegetable oil or unsalted butter	15 mL
6 oz	smoked salmon, thinly sliced	175 g

1. Warm pizza crust in preheated 350°F/180°C oven for 10 minutes.

2. Meanwhile, combine yogurt cheese, mustard, 2 tbsp/25 mL chives and dill. Reserve.

3. Whisk eggs, egg whites, water, salt and ¼ tsp/1 mL pepper until just mixed.

4. Heat oil in large non-stick skillet and add egg mixture. Cook and stir gently until curds form but mixture is still moist.

5. Spread yogurt mixture over warm crust. Spoon eggs on top. Arrange smoked salmon on eggs. Sprinkle with remaining pepper and chives. Cut into wedges or squares. Serve warm or at room temperature.

PER SERVING

Calories	261
g carbohydrate	28
g fibre	1
g total fat	8
g saturated fat	2
g protein	18

Excellent: vitamin B$_{12}$
Good: riboflavin

mg cholesterol	115
mg sodium	558
mg potassium	239

BREADS

Cranberry Streusel Muffins

Oat and Wheat Bran Muffins with Dried Apricots

Apple Cinnamon Muffins

Morning Glory Muffin Bars

Oatmeal Honey Rolls

Double Cornbread with Mild Green Chiles

Buttermilk Black Pepper Biscuits

Buttermilk Oat Scones

Denise Beatty's Potato Scones

Multigrain Yogurt Bread

Spiced Whole Wheat Challah with Honey and Raisins

Red River Cereal Bread

Rosemary Monkey Bread

Irish Soda Bread with Caraway Seeds

CRANBERRY STREUSEL MUFFINS

Cranberries are plump and delicious but tart enough to give a very interesting flavour to baked goods. Blueberries also work well in this recipe.

Makes 12 muffins

2 cups	all-purpose flour	500 mL
1 tbsp	baking powder	15 mL
¼ tsp	salt	1 mL
1	egg	1
⅔ cup	granulated sugar	150 mL
¼ cup	vegetable oil	50 mL
1 cup	milk	250 mL
2 tbsp	grated lemon or orange peel	25 mL
1½ cups	fresh or frozen cranberries	375 mL
¼ cup	brown sugar	50 mL
1 tsp	cinnamon	5 mL

1. Combine flour, baking powder and salt. Reserve.

2. In large bowl, beat together egg, granulated sugar, oil, milk and lemon peel.

3. Combine flour mixture with egg mixture. Stir in cranberries.

4. Scoop batter into 12 large non-stick, oiled or paper-lined muffin cups.

5. Combine brown sugar and cinnamon. Sprinkle over top of muffins. Bake in preheated 400°F/200°C oven for 20 to 25 minutes.

See photo opposite page 224.

CRANBERRIES

Cranberries can be fresh, frozen or dried. If you are using frozen cranberries in baked dishes, add them in the frozen state so that they do not bleed too much of their colour into the batter.

Use cranberries in muffins or cranberry sauce (page 182). Dried cranberries can be eaten as a snack or added like raisins to muffins, breads and pilafs.

PER MUFFIN

Calories	200
g carbohydrate	35
g fibre	1
g total fat	6
g saturated fat	1
g protein	3
mg cholesterol	19
mg sodium	130
mg potassium	88

OAT AND WHEAT BRAN MUFFINS WITH DRIED APRICOTS

Wheat bran is an insoluble fibre that encourages regularity. Oat bran is a soluble fibre that is said to help reduce blood cholesterol. Therefore, don't give up one to have the other — eat them both in this great muffin that includes a variety of tastes and textures.

Makes 12 muffins

¾ cup	all-purpose flour	175 mL
½ cup	whole wheat flour	125 mL
½ cup	wheat bran	125 mL
½ cup	oat bran	125 mL
1 tsp	baking powder	5 mL
1 tsp	baking soda	5 mL
¼ tsp	salt	1 mL
½ tsp	cinnamon	2 mL
pinch	nutmeg	pinch
2	ripe bananas	2
1	egg	1
½ cup	buttermilk or low-fat yogurt	125 mL
¼ cup	vegetable oil	50 mL
½ cup	brown sugar	125 mL
½ cup	chopped dried apricots	125 mL

1. In large bowl, combine all-purpose flour, whole wheat flour, wheat bran, oat bran, baking powder, baking soda, salt, cinnamon and nutmeg. Stir well.

2. In separate bowl, mash bananas and whisk in egg, buttermilk, oil and sugar.

3. Stir liquid ingredients into dry ingredients just until combined. Mix in dried apricots.

4. Spoon batter into 12 non-stick or paper-lined muffin cups and bake in preheated 375°F/190°C oven for 20 to 25 minutes.

MIXING DRY INGREDIENTS

When mixing dry ingredients for quickbreads, muffins or cake mixtures, you can sift all the dry ingredients together, but be sure to mix them thoroughly afterwards. Or you can place just the ingredients that tend to lump (baking soda, baking powder, icing sugar and cocoa) through a small strainer and sift them into the flour and other ingredients.

PER MUFFIN

Calories	177
g carbohydrate	31
g fibre	4
g total fat	6
g saturated fat	1
g protein	4
mg cholesterol	18
mg sodium	187
mg potassium	288

APPLE CINNAMON MUFFINS

Try using an ice-cream scoop to spoon the batter into muffin cups. It will give your muffins nice rounded tops.

Makes 12 muffins

1 cup	whole wheat flour	250 mL
1 cup	all-purpose flour	250 mL
1 tbsp	baking powder	15 mL
½ tsp	baking soda	2 mL
½ tsp	cinnamon	2 mL
pinch	each salt, nutmeg, allspice and ginger	pinch
¼ cup	vegetable oil	50 mL
½ cup	brown sugar	125 mL
1	egg	1
½ cup	low-fat yogurt	125 mL
1 cup	applesauce	250 mL

Topping:

2 tbsp	brown sugar	25 mL
¼ tsp	cinnamon	1 mL
2 tbsp	finely chopped pecans	25 mL

1. Combine flours, baking powder, baking soda, cinnamon, salt, nutmeg, allspice and ginger.

2. In large bowl, combine vegetable oil, brown sugar, egg, yogurt and applesauce.

3. Add dry ingredients to wet ingredients and combine just until blended.

4. Spoon batter into 12 non-stick, oiled or paper-lined muffin cups.

5. Combine ingredients for topping and sprinkle over muffins. Bake in preheated 375°F/190°C oven for 25 minutes.

BAKING SODA

Baking soda makes baked goods rise by reacting with the acid in ingredients like buttermilk, yogurt, sour cream and molasses. It keeps for about a year in an airtight container.

Mix baking soda with the dry ingredients. Combine the dry and wet ingredients just before baking, as the baking soda will lose some of its effectiveness if the mixture is not baked immediately.

Baking soda also has many non-food uses — read the box for more suggestions.

PER MUFFIN

Calories	193
g carbohydrate	32
g fibre	2
g total fat	6
g saturated fat	1
g protein	4
mg cholesterol	18
mg sodium	130
mg potassium	140

MORNING GLORY MUFFIN BARS

We invented these bars for our university survival course. We wanted a healthful, quick breakfast that didn't require any specialized equipment. These bars were a great hit, and they freeze well. Of course, you could also bake them as twelve large muffins.

Makes 24 bars

1½ cups	all-purpose flour	375 mL
1½ cups	bran cereal	375 mL
¼ cup	sesame seeds, toasted (page 34)	50 mL
1 tbsp	baking powder	15 mL
1 tsp	cinnamon	5 mL
1 tsp	allspice, optional	5 mL
½ tsp	baking soda	2 mL
pinch	salt	pinch
1	egg	1
¾ cup	buttermilk or low-fat yogurt	175 mL
½ cup	brown sugar	125 mL
⅓ cup	vegetable oil	75 mL
2 tbsp	molasses or honey	25 mL
1½ cups	grated carrots	375 mL
½ cup	chopped dates or raisins	125 mL

1. In large bowl, combine flour, bran cereal, sesame seeds, baking powder, cinnamon, allspice, baking soda and salt.

2. In separate bowl, whisk egg with buttermilk, brown sugar, oil and molasses.

3. Stir egg mixture into flour mixture just until moistened. Stir in carrots and dates.

4. Spread mixture in oiled 13 x 9-inch (3.5 L) baking dish and bake in preheated 350°F/180°C oven for 25 to 30 minutes, or until centre springs back when gently touched. Cool and cut into bars.

BAKING POWDER
Like baking soda, baking powder helps baked goods to rise. It keeps for about one year (if it fizzes when it is added to boiling water, it is still active). Use about 1 tsp/5 mL for every cup of flour in a recipe and bake immediately after adding it to the wet ingredients. Keep it in a dry place in a tightly sealed container.

PER BAR

Calories	119
g carbohydrate	20
g fibre	3
g total fat	4
g saturated fat	1
g protein	3

Good: vitamin A

mg cholesterol	9
mg sodium	127
mg potassium	164

OATMEAL HONEY ROLLS

I love the muesli rolls from European-style bakeries, which seem to be filled with all kinds of healthful treats. Here's my version. It will fill your home with the aroma of freshly baked bread and make you feel like Mother Earth.

You can also bake the dough in loaves for sandwiches.

Makes 16 rolls

1 tsp	granulated sugar	5 mL
½ cup	warm water	125 mL
1	package dry yeast	1
1½ cups	all-purpose flour (more if necessary)	375 mL
1½ cups	whole wheat flour	375 mL
1 tsp	salt	5 mL
1¼ cups	warm water	300 mL
¼ cup	honey	50 mL
2 tbsp	vegetable oil	25 mL
½ cup	raisins	125 mL
½ cup	rolled oats	125 mL
⅓ cup	chopped walnuts, or pecans	75 mL
⅓ cup	sunflower seeds	75 mL
1 tbsp	sesame seeds	15 mL
1 tsp	caraway seeds	5 mL

Glaze:

1 tbsp	honey	15 mL
1 tbsp	hot water	15 mL
1 tbsp	rolled oats	15 mL

NUTS
Although nuts do not contain cholesterol, most are very high in fat and should be used sparingly. If you do use nuts in cooking, make sure they are fresh. Taste them before buying if possible. Nuts go rancid, so freeze any that you are not using right away. Walnuts go rancid particularly quickly; I use Californian walnuts whenever possible because they are harvested efficiently, kept refrigerated and are well packaged. If I can't find them, I often substitute pecans.

Many people are allergic to nuts, so always warn guests if dishes contain them. If you can't use nuts in cooking or don't want the extra fat, try using crunchy cereals in cookies, etc., or add raisins, dried cherries or dried cranberries.

1. Dissolve sugar in ½ cup/125 mL warm water. Sprinkle yeast over top. Allow to rest for 10 minutes, or until doubled in volume.

2. Meanwhile, combine all-purpose flour, whole wheat flour and salt.

3. In another bowl, combine 1¼ cups/300 mL warm water, ¼ cup/50 mL honey and oil.

4. Stir yeast mixture down and combine with honey water. Stir in flour mixture and then add extra all-purpose flour until very soft dough is formed. Knead for 5 minutes in mixer, 10 minutes by hand or 1 minute in food processor.

5. Stir in raisins, ½ cup/125 mL rolled oats, walnuts, sunflower seeds, sesame seeds and caraway seeds. Add more flour if necessary. Dough should be soft but not sticky.

6. Place dough in large oiled bowl and cover with oiled plastic wrap. Allow to rise in warm spot for 1 hour, or until doubled.

7. Punch dough down and divide in two. Roll each half into rope about 2 inches/5 cm thick and cut into 3-inch/7.5 cm lengths. Place on parchment paper-lined baking sheet. Cover loosely with oiled plastic wrap and allow to rise until doubled, about 45 minutes.

8. To make glaze, combine honey with hot water and brush gently on rolls. Sprinkle rolled oats on top. Bake in preheated 350°F/180°C oven for 20 to 25 minutes. Cool on racks.

TOASTING NUTS

To get the most flavour out of nuts and seeds, toast them before using. Place in a single layer on a baking sheet and bake in a preheated 350°F/180°C oven for 3 to 10 minutes. Watch them closely.

PER ROLL

Calories	182
g carbohydrate	30
g fibre	3
g total fat	6
g saturated fat	1
g protein	5

Good: thiamine; vitamin E; folacin

mg cholesterol	0
mg sodium	147
mg potassium	159

DOUBLE CORNBREAD WITH MILD GREEN CHILES

See photo opposite page 160.

Cornbread is a great homemade quickbread. This easy recipe can be made with or without the cheese, it can be made spicy by adding two chopped jalapeños, and it can be made into muffins by baking the batter for about 20 minutes in twelve non-stick muffin cups.

Makes 16 pieces

1 cup	all-purpose flour	250 mL
1 cup	cornmeal	250 mL
3 tbsp	granulated sugar	45 mL
½ tsp	salt	2 mL
1 tbsp	baking powder	15 mL
¾ cup	grated light Cheddar cheese, optional	175 mL
1 cup	milk	250 mL
2	eggs	2
3 tbsp	vegetable oil	45 mL
1	4-oz/114 mL tin mild green chiles, rinsed, drained and chopped	1
1 cup	fresh or frozen corn niblets	250 mL

1. In large bowl, combine flour, cornmeal, sugar, salt and baking powder. Stir in cheese.

2. In separate bowl, combine milk, eggs, oil and chiles.

3. Stir milk mixture into flour mixture just until combined. Stir in corn.

4. Spoon batter into oiled 8-inch/2 L square baking pan. Bake in preheated 400°F/200°C oven for 25 minutes, or until golden brown.

PER PIECE

Calories	119
g carbohydrate	19
g fibre	1
g total fat	4
g saturated fat	1
g protein	3
mg cholesterol	28
mg sodium	205
mg potassium	80

BUTTERMILK BLACK PEPPER BISCUITS

These biscuits are irresistible. You can serve them with spreads, soups or saucy dishes like barbecued shrimp (page 50). These are wonderful served fresh and warm or at room temperature, but they also freeze well.

Makes about 10 biscuits

2 cups	all-purpose flour	500 mL
2 tbsp	cornmeal	25 mL
1 tbsp	baking powder	15 mL
1 tsp	granulated sugar	5 mL
1 tsp	coarse black pepper	5 mL
½ tsp	salt	2 mL
3 tbsp	soft margarine or unsalted butter, cold	45 mL
⅞ cup	buttermilk	225 mL

Topping:

2 tbsp	buttermilk	25 mL
1 tbsp	cornmeal	15 mL
½ tsp	coarse black pepper	2 mL
pinch	salt	pinch
½ tsp	granulated sugar	2 mL

1. In large bowl, combine flour, 2 tbsp/25 mL cornmeal, baking powder, 1 tsp/5 mL sugar, 1 tsp/5 mL pepper and ½ tsp/2 mL salt.

2. Cut margarine or butter into flour mixture until mixture resembles fresh breadcrumbs.

3. Sprinkle ⅞ cup/225 mL buttermilk over mixture and gather into rough dough. Knead gently for about 5 seconds.

4. Pat dough out gently on floured board to thickness of about ¾ inch/2 cm. Cut into 3-inch/7.5 cm rounds. Place on baking sheet lightly dusted with cornmeal or lined with parchment paper.

5. To prepare topping, brush biscuits lightly with 2 tbsp/25 mL buttermilk. Combine 1 tbsp/15 mL cornmeal, ½ tsp/2 mL pepper, pinch salt and ½ tsp/2 mL sugar. Sprinkle over tops.

6. Bake in preheated 425°F/220°C oven for 15 minutes, or until lightly browned. Cool on racks.

BUTTERMILK

Because of its name and rich texture, many people think buttermilk is high in fat. Traditionally it was the milk left over from making butter and therefore contained very little fat, but now it is commercially made. It has approximately 1 percent fat content. If you do not have buttermilk, substitute yogurt, sour cream or sour milk. To make sour milk, place 1 tbsp/15 mL lemon juice in a measuring cup and add milk to make 1 cup/250 mL. Allow to rest for 10 minutes before using.

PER BISCUIT

Calories	145
g carbohydrate	24
g fibre	1
g total fat	4
g saturated fat	1
g protein	4
mg cholesterol	1
mg sodium	263
mg potassium	76

BUTTERMILK OAT SCONES

When I visited Victoria, B.C., I couldn't believe the size of the scones that were sold in all the tea houses! Each one was large enough to serve four. But I also love dainty little scones like these, and I use the Victoria tea house idea of sprinkling them with icing sugar. Serve these with lightly sweetened soft yogurt cheese (page 228) or yogurt and strawberry jam.

Makes about 12 scones

1½ cups	all-purpose flour	375 mL
3 tbsp	granulated sugar	45 mL
1 tsp	baking powder	5 mL
½ tsp	salt	2 mL
½ tsp	baking soda	2 mL
⅓ cup	soft margarine or unsalted butter, cold	75 mL
1 cup	rolled oats	250 mL
½ cup	currants or raisins	125 mL
½ cup	buttermilk	125 mL
2 tbsp	icing sugar	25 mL

1. In large bowl, sift or stir together flour, sugar, baking powder salt and baking soda.

2. Cut margarine or butter into flour mixture until it is in tiny bits.

3. Stir in oats and currants. Drizzle buttermilk over all and gather dough into ball. Do not overknead.

4. Pat dough out on floured surface to thickness of about 1 inch/2.5 cm. Cut out 2-inch/5 cm rounds. Pat extra dough together gently and continue cutting out rounds until all dough is used.

5. Place scones on baking sheet lined with parchment paper. Bake in preheated 375°F/190°C oven for 15 to 20 minutes, or until puffed and golden. Cool on racks. Sift icing sugar over baked scones.

MARGARINE OR BUTTER?

A minimal amount of fat is used in the recipes in this book, because the key to healthy eating is to eat less total fat, especially less saturated fat. Some of the recipes list butter as an option to soft margarine. Although many people, myself included, prefer the taste of butter, if you choose to use butter instead of margarine, you should know that the amount of fat will be the same but the type of fat will vary.

For example, in a 2 tsp/ 10 mL serving:

	soft margarine	butter
Calories (kcal)	70	70
Total fat (g)	8	8
Saturates (g)	2	5

For more information on food fats, see Appendix page 288.

PER SCONE

Calories	165
g carbohydrate	26
g fibre	2
g total fat	6
g saturated fat	1
g protein	3

mg cholesterol	0
mg sodium	245
mg potassium	111

DENISE BEATTY'S POTATO SCONES

Actually, these are Denise's mother's scones. Helen Glendenning gave Denise this recipe for a Toronto Star Mother's Day article, and that's when I had the opportunity to taste them. They were so good that even though this book was going to print, I knew I had to get them in! By the way, if you haven't already read Denise's introduction to this book, please do. It is packed with healthful information.

Makes 8 large scones

1½ cups	all-purpose flour	375 mL
¼ cup	granulated sugar	50 mL
1 tbsp	baking powder	15 mL
½ tsp	salt	2 mL
3 tbsp	soft margarine, shortening or unsalted butter, cold, cut into bits	45 mL
½ cup	leftover mashed potatoes, or 1 potato, peeled, cooked, mashed and cooled	125 mL
¼ cup	raisins	50 mL
1	egg, beaten	1
¼ cup	milk	50 mL
1 tbsp	granulated sugar	15 mL

1. Sift together flour, ¼ cup/50 mL sugar, baking powder and salt.

2. Rub in margarine, shortening or butter until it is in tiny bits and mixture resembles coarse meal. Using your fingertips, rub mashed potatoes into flour mixture just until well combined. Stir in raisins.

3. Combine egg and milk. Reserve about 1 tbsp/15 mL. Stir remaining mixture into flour and gather together gently into ball.

4. Knead dough 8 to 10 times on lightly floured surface and shape into 7-inch/18 cm flattened round. Score top into 8 wedges. Brush with reserved egg mixture and sprinkle lightly with 1 tbsp/15 mL sugar.

5. Transfer to lightly oiled or parchment paper-lined baking sheet. Bake in preheated 400°F/200°C oven for 25 to 30 minutes, or until golden brown.

PER SCONE

Calories	197
g carbohydrate	34
g fibre	1
g total fat	5
g saturated fat	1
g protein	4
mg cholesterol	27
mg sodium	310
mg potassium	142

MULTIGRAIN YOGURT BREAD

If you love different flavours and textures in breads, try this one. I really enjoy the very subtle taste and aroma of licorice from the anise. This dough makes great toast bread and is also wonderful baked as hot dog or hamburger buns (bake for about 25 to 34 minutes).

Makes 2 loaves

½ cup	rolled oats	125 mL
½ cup	cornmeal	125 mL
1½ cups	boiling water	375 mL
¼ cup	honey or brown sugar	50 mL
1 tbsp	vegetable oil	15 mL
1½ tsp	salt	7 mL
½ tsp	ground or whole anise seeds, optional	2 mL
2 tsp	granulated sugar	10 mL
½ cup	warm water	125 mL
2	packages dry yeast	2
2 cups	all-purpose flour (more if necessary)	500 mL
2 cups	whole wheat flour	500 mL
½ cup	wheat bran	125 mL
½ cup	oat bran	125 mL
1 cup	low-fat yogurt	250 mL

Glaze:

2 tbsp	beaten egg	25 mL
¼ tsp	salt	1 mL

YEAST
Yeast is a living organism, and that's probably why so many people are afraid to bake bread with it. After all, you could kill it! Yeast loves warm cosy places, and that's the best way to judge how to handle it, the temperature of the water to dissolve it in and where to put the bread dough to rise.

Yeast is available in two forms, dry and cake. Dry yeast can be regular or instant-dissolving. One package of yeast is a scant tablespoon and will be enough for about 5 cups/ 1.25 L flour in a bread recipe. I prefer cake yeast if available, because it rises a bit faster and I think has a slightly nicer flavour. But it can be hard to find and is very perishable. When I find it I buy extra and freeze it. Always dissolve it in warm water before using.

1. In large bowl, combine rolled oats and cornmeal. Stir in boiling water, honey, oil, 1½ tsp/7 mL salt and anise. Stir to dissolve honey and salt. Allow mixture to cool for 20 minutes or until lukewarm.

2. Dissolve sugar in warm water. Sprinkle yeast over top. Allow mixture to rest for 10 minutes, or until volume doubles and mixture has bubbled up.

3. In separate bowl, combine all-purpose flour, whole wheat flour, wheat bran and oat bran.

4. When yeast mixture has risen, stir down and add to rolled oats mixture. Stir in yogurt and dry ingredients. Add more all-purpose flour if necessary to form soft but manageable dough that does not stick to your fingers.

5. Knead dough for 10 minutes by hand, 5 minutes with electric dough mixer or in large food processor for 1 minute.

6. Place dough in oiled bowl and turn so that it is completely oiled. Cover with oiled plastic wrap and allow to rise in warm spot for about 1 hour, or until dough has doubled in bulk.

7. Punch dough down and divide in half. Shape to fit two 9 x 5-inch/2 L loaf pans. Oil pans and line with parchment paper. Place dough in pans. Cover loosely with oiled plastic wrap and allow to rise for 45 to 60 minutes, or until doubled again.

8. Combine egg and salt and brush breads with this mixture. Bake in preheated 400°F/200°C oven for 45 to 55 minutes. Remove from pans immediately and cool on racks.

PER SLICE (1/16 loaf)

Calories	93
g carbohydrate	19
g fibre	2
g total fat	1
g saturated fat	trace
g protein	3
mg cholesterol	5
mg sodium	134
mg potassium	97

SPICED WHOLE WHEAT CHALLAH WITH HONEY AND RAISINS

My grandmother Jenny Soltz was a great bread-baker. She had eleven children and not much money, so she entered her challah breads in country fair bake-offs each year and always won enough flour to keep her family in bread through the winter. She used to make two braids and bake them side by side in a deep square pan — the top would rise over the edge in a beautiful ornate bubble.

Challah is a special-occasion bread in Jewish homes, but when you serve it, it is an occasion in itself! This lightly spiced variation makes the house smell wonderful.

Makes 1 large loaf

1 cup	warm water	250 mL
1 tbsp	granulated sugar	15 mL
1	package dry yeast	1
1	egg	1
¼ cup	honey	50 mL
2 tbsp	vegetable oil	25 mL
1 tsp	salt	5 mL
2 cups	whole wheat flour	500 mL
1 cup	all-purpose flour (more if necessary)	250 mL
½ tsp	cinnamon	2 mL
pinch	nutmeg	pinch
pinch	ground cloves	pinch
pinch	ground ginger	pinch
¼ cup	raisins, optional	50 mL

Glaze:

2 tbsp	beaten egg	25 mL
pinch	salt	pinch
1 tbsp	sesame seeds	15 mL

Place ropes as shown.

Bring top rope down,
bottom rope up.

Bring right rope over left and
left over right.

Repeat in the same order until
braid is formed.

1. In small bowl, combine warm water and sugar. Sprinkle yeast over water and allow to rest for 10 minutes. Mixture should bubble up and double in volume.

2. Meanwhile, in separate bowl, combine egg, honey, oil and salt.

3. Place whole wheat flour, all-purpose flour, cinnamon, nutmeg, cloves and ginger in large bowl and stir together well.

4. When yeast mixture has doubled, stir down and combine with egg mixture. Add to flour and mix until sticky dough forms. Add more all-purpose flour until dough comes together into ball and can be kneaded. (Do not add too much flour or bread will be hard and dry.) Knead dough on floured surface for about 10 minutes. (Knead dough in heavy mixer for 5 minutes or in food processor for 1 minute.)

5. Place dough in oiled bowl, cover with oiled plastic wrap and put in warm place to rise. Allow to double in bulk – about 1 hour.

6. Punch dough down and knead in raisins. To shape dough into crown, roll into rope about 24 inches/60 cm long. Holding one end in place, wind rest of dough around it in fairly tight spiral that is slightly higher in centre. To braid dough, cut into three equal pieces, roll each piece into rope about 12 inches/30 cm long, pinch three ends together and braid ropes together. Or for a four-strand braid, divide dough in half, roll into two very long ropes and braid as shown.

7. For freeform loaf, place dough on baking sheet that has been oiled or lined with parchment paper. Cover loosely with oiled plastic wrap and allow to rise in warm place until doubled – about 45 minutes. (You can also bake dough in loaf pan if you want to use bread primarily in sandwiches.)

8. For glaze, combine 2 tbsp/25 mL egg with pinch salt and brush gently over bread. Sprinkle with sesame seeds.

9. Bake in preheated 350°F/180°C oven for 25 minutes. Reduce heat to 325°F/160°C and continue baking for 25 minutes longer.

PER SLICE ($\frac{1}{16}$ loaf)

Calories	126
g carbohydrate	22
g fibre	2
g total fat	3
g saturated fat	trace
g protein	4
mg cholesterol	22
mg sodium	152
mg potassium	91

RED RIVER CEREAL BREAD

I always feel very patriotic when I make this bread, since Red River cereal truly is a wonderful Canadian product. You can also use five-grain cereal or rolled oats in this recipe.

This bread is hearty and somewhat heavy, so do not have light and fluffy expectations!

Makes 2 loaves

1 cup	Red River cereal	250 mL
2 cups	boiling water	500 mL
3 tbsp	honey	45 mL
1 tbsp	vegetable oil	15 mL
1 tsp	salt	5 mL
1 tbsp	granulated sugar	15 mL
½ cup	warm water	125 mL
2	packages dry yeast	2
3 cups	all-purpose flour (more if necessary)	750 mL
1½ cups	whole wheat flour	375 mL
½ cup	wheat bran	125 mL

1. Combine cereal, boiling water, honey, oil and salt. Allow to rest for 20 minutes, or until lukewarm.

2. Dissolve sugar in warm water and sprinkle yeast over top. Allow to rest for 10 minutes, or until doubled in volume.

3. In large bowl, combine 2½ cups/625 mL all-purpose flour with whole wheat flour and bran. Stir well.

4. Stir yeast down and add to cereal mixture. Stir into flour mixture. If dough is too sticky, add extra all-purpose flour until dough is still very soft but does not stick badly to your fingers. Knead for 10 minutes by hand, 5 minutes in mixer or 1 minute in food processor.

5. Place dough in oiled bowl and turn so it is oiled on all sides. Cover with oiled plastic wrap and allow to double in size in warm place – about 1½ hours.

6. Punch dough down, divide in half and shape into two loaves. Place in two oiled 9 x 5-inch/2 L loaf pans and cover loosely with oiled plastic wrap. Allow to rise until doubled, about 1 hour.

7. Bake in preheated 400°F/200°C oven for 35 to 45 minutes. Cool on racks.

PER SLICE (¹⁄₁₆ loaf)

Calories	93
g carbohydrate	19
g fibre	2
g total fat	1
g saturated fat	trace
g protein	3
mg cholesterol	0
mg sodium	74
mg potassium	58

See photo opposite page 32.

ROSEMARY MONKEY BREAD

In this recipe, bread dough is formed into balls, rolled in a blend of rosemary and pepper and then baked together in a loaf pan. When the bread is done, you pull the balls apart. You can also use this idea with frozen bread dough. You can, of course, bake the dough as a regular loaf, with or without the herb mixture. (It also makes a great pizza dough.) For a swirled loaf, roll out the dough and sprinkle it with the herb mixture. Roll up tightly and bake in a loaf pan.

Makes 12 servings

1½ cups	warm water	375 mL
1 tbsp	granulated sugar	15 mL
1	package dry yeast	1
3 cups	all-purpose flour (more if necessary)	750 mL
¾ cup	cornmeal	175 mL
1½ tsp	salt	7 mL
4 tbsp	olive oil, divided	60 mL
2 tbsp	chopped fresh rosemary, or 1 tsp/5 mL dried	25 mL
1 tsp	coarse black pepper	5 mL
1	clove garlic, minced	1

1. Place warm water in small bowl and stir in sugar. Sprinkle yeast over top and allow to rest for 10 minutes, or until bubbly.

2. In large bowl, combine flour, cornmeal and salt.

3. Stir yeast mixture down and add 1 tbsp/15 mL oil. Stir into flour. Add extra flour if necessary to form smooth dough. Knead for 10 minutes. Place dough in oiled bowl and cover. Allow to rise in warm spot for 1 to 1½ hours, or until doubled in bulk.

4. Divide dough into about 12 balls. Combine 3 tbsp/45 mL olive oil with rosemary, pepper and garlic. Roll balls in herb mixture.

5. Line large loaf pan with parchment paper and place balls in pan. Cover and allow to rise in warm spot for about 1 hour, or until doubled in bulk. Bake in preheated 375°F/190°C oven for 40 to 50 minutes, or until puffed and golden.

PER SERVING

Calories	192
g carbohydrate	32
g fibre	2
g total fat	5
g saturated fat	1
g protein	4
mg cholesterol	0
mg sodium	289
mg potassium	65

IRISH SODA BREAD WITH CARAWAY SEEDS

This quickbread is perfect to serve with a meal or as a snack at tea time. You can add 1 tsp/5 mL dried rosemary, cumin seeds or anise seeds instead of the caraway seeds.

Makes 16 servings

1½ cups	all-purpose flour	375 mL
1 cup	whole wheat flour	250 mL
2 tbsp	granulated sugar	25 mL
1½ tsp	baking powder	7 mL
½ tsp	baking soda	2 mL
½ tsp	salt	2 mL
⅓ cup	currants or raisins	75 mL
1 tbsp	caraway seeds	15 mL
1	egg	1
1¼ cups	buttermilk	300 mL
3 tbsp	vegetable oil	45 mL

1. In large bowl, combine all-purpose flour, whole wheat flour, sugar, baking powder, baking soda and salt. Stir together well.

2. Stir currants and caraway seeds into flour mixture.

3. In separate bowl, combine egg, buttermilk and oil. Pour liquid ingredients over flour mixture and very lightly combine together into rough dough.

4. Place dough in 9-inch/2.5 L springform pan lined with parchment paper. Bake in preheated 350°F/180°C oven for 50 to 55 minutes. Remove from pan and cool on rack.

DRIED FRUITS

Although dried fruits are high in calories, they contain no fat and can add a lot of taste to dishes because of their concentrated flavour. They are great in muffins, breads and pilafs.

Dried fruits include prunes, apricots, raisins, dates, figs and newly available kinds like cherries, cranberries, blueberries, apples and pears.

PER SERVING

Calories	119
g carbohydrate	19
g fibre	2
g total fat	3
g saturated fat	trace
g protein	4
mg cholesterol	14
mg sodium	157
mg potassium	108

Anna's Angel Food Cake with Berry Berry Sauce
(page 274)

Nick Malgieri's Honey Almond Biscotti *(page 282)*
Fruit Yogurt Dip and Peach Salsa *(page 263)*

DESSERTS

Strawberries with Balsamic Vinegar

Pears Poached in Spiced Red Wine

Caramelized Winter Fruit Compote

Baked Apples Amaretti

Bananas Flambé

Fruit Yogurt Dip and Peach Salsa

Dessert Fruit Curry

Creamy Rice Pudding

Floating Island

Upside-down Lemon Meringues

Blueberry Grunt

Plum Crisp

Rhubarb and Strawberry Cobbler

Apple Strudel Pie

Quick Apple Cake

Anna's Angel Food Cake with Berry Berry Sauce

Chocolate Angel Food Cake with Chocolate Sauce

Old-fashioned Cheesecake

Strawberry Meringue Shortcakes

Mocha Meringue Kisses

Nick Malgieri's Honey Almond Biscotti

Matrimonial Squares (Date Squares)

Oatmeal and Raisin Spice Cookie Squares

STRAWBERRIES WITH BALSAMIC VINEGAR

I never get tired of eating these strawberries with their mysterious ingredient — balsamic vinegar. And you certainly cannot get tired of making this dessert, as it only takes a minute! (Be sure to use a good-quality aged balsamic vinegar.)

This recipe also works well with raspberry vinegar or lemon juice. Serve this as is or in a small cantaloupe half.

Makes 6 servings

4 cups	strawberries	1 L
3 tbsp	granulated sugar	45 mL
3 tbsp	balsamic vinegar	45 mL

1. Rinse strawberries and pat dry. Trim and halve or quarter berries, depending on their size.

2. Sprinkle berries with sugar and vinegar. Stir gently and allow to marinate for about 10 minutes before serving.

BERRIES

Fresh berries must be handled gently. Buy berries that are uniform in colour and make sure the packages are not soiled. Use the fresh berries quickly, as they will not ripen once picked. Store them in flat, wide containers rather than deep ones to avoid crushing. Overripe berries lose their pectin or thickening potential, so do not use them in jams. Instead, poach or bake them, or use them in sauces.

To freeze berries, place them in a single layer on a waxed paper-lined baking sheet, freeze and then pack into bags or containers. This way the berries will stay separate and can be removed as you wish. Frozen berries lose their texture when they are defrosted, so only use them if the berries are going to be cooked or pureed into a sauce. You can buy berries frozen in syrup, but I prefer the individual quick-frozen berries.

PER SERVING

Calories	55
g carbohydrate	14
g fibre	2
g total fat	trace
g saturated fat	0
g protein	1

Excellent: vitamin C

mg cholesterol	0
mg sodium	1
mg potassium	173

PEARS POACHED IN SPICED RED WINE

This is one of the most popular desserts I make in my Italian cooking classes. You can serve these as is, in meringue cups or over sorbet. You can even puree the cooked pears with the reduced and strained juices and freeze it in an ice-cream machine for a fabulous sorbet!

Star anise is a licorice-tasting spice available in Asian grocery stores.

Makes 8 servings

1	*bottle dry red Italian wine	1
1 cup	*Port or orange juice	250 mL
2 cups	water	500 mL
½ cup	granulated sugar	125 mL
	Peel of one orange, cut in chunks	
	Peel of one lemon, cut in chunks	
1	cinnamon stick, broken	1
2	star anise, optional	2
8	ripe pears	8
	Sprigs of fresh mint	

1. Place wine, Port, water, sugar, orange and lemon peel, cinnamon stick and star anise in saucepan and bring to boil.

2. Peel pears, cut in half and remove cores neatly with melon baller. Place pears in liquid and poach for 20 to 30 minutes until tender. If you wish, to make sure pears stay submerged in liquid during cooking, place clean tea towel or upside-down plate directly on surface of liquid to weigh pears down.

3. Remove pears to serving dish. Reduce liquid to about 2 cups/500 mL. Strain and spoon liquid over pears. Garnish with fresh mint.

* *If this recipe is used in the Passover menu (page 31), use dry, kosher red wine and orange juice.*

PEARS

Pears, like bananas, are one of the few fruits that ripen after they have been picked. I always try to cook with ripe pears (I prefer Bartlett or Bosc), as unripe ones have little flavour.

You can use pears in almost all recipes that call for apples. Try pear sauce or pear crisp for something a little different.

PER SERVING

Calories	201
g carbohydrate	43
g fibre	3
g total fat	1
g saturated fat	0
g protein	1
mg cholesterol	0
mg sodium	9
mg potassium	324

CARAMELIZED WINTER FRUIT COMPOTE

This is a comforting dessert to serve with angel food cake (page 274), scones (page 248) or on its own. Try to buy Californian figs, as they are more tender and cook faster than other varieties.

You could simplify this by using just apples; it will still taste great, but I love the different tastes and textures of a combination of fruits.

Makes 8 servings

1 cup	granulated sugar	250 mL
¼ cup	water	50 mL
2	apples, peeled and thickly sliced	2
2	pears, peeled and thickly sliced	2
½ cup	apricot nectar, orange juice or apple juice	125 mL
1 cup	pitted prunes	250 mL
1 cup	dried apricots	250 mL
1 cup	dried figs	250 mL
2 tbsp	cognac or brandy, optional	25 mL
½ cup	soft yogurt cheese (page 228) or thick yogurt, optional	125 mL

1. Place sugar and water in large saucepan or Dutch oven. Heat, stirring, until sugar dissolves. Brush down sides of saucepan with pastry brush dipped in cold water to dissolve any undissolved sugar. Allow mixture to boil, without any stirring, for about 5 minutes, or until sauce turns deep caramel colour. Do not leave stove for a minute, as it could burn, but do not stir!

2. Carefully add apples, pears and apricot nectar gently, standing well out of way in case of splattering. Cook, stirring, for about 5 minutes, until fruit starts to soften.

3. Add prunes, apricots, figs and cognac. Cook for 5 to 10 minutes, until all fruit is tender and sauce has thickened. Serve warm or cold. Serve with spoonful of soft yogurt cheese.

LOW-FAT COOKING AIDS

- Pastry brush: Use it to brush a thin layer of oil onto the bottom of a skillet or baking sheet.

- Parchment paper: Sometimes called non-stick paper or baking paper, this paper is coated with silicon to prevent food from sticking. Use it to line pans without having to oil them. You can reuse the paper by wiping it clean if it is not too dirty.

- Meatloaf pans: These pans have a false perforated bottom that allows excess fat to drain out.

PER SERVING

Calories	292
g carbohydrate	75
g fibre	9
g total fat	1
g saturated fat	trace
g protein	2

Good: vitamin A

mg cholesterol	0
mg sodium	6
mg potassium	631

BAKED APPLES AMARETTI

Although I grew up eating baked apples, none of them tasted as good as this Italian version. Pears also work well in this recipe, and gingersnaps can be used instead of the Amaretti biscuits (which can be found in Italian delicatessens, bakeries or supermarkets).

Serve the apples garnished with mint sprigs or with a dollop of sweetened yogurt or soft yogurt cheese (page 228) in the centre.

Makes 6 servings

6	apples	6
2 tbsp	honey	25 mL
1 cup	crushed Amaretti biscuits (about 20 biscuits, or 3 oz/90 g)	250 mL
½ cup	dry Marsala wine or orange juice	125 mL
½ cup	water	125 mL

1. Starting at top of apple, remove core without cutting all the way through to bottom, leaving base on apple. Pierce skin in a few places.

2. Combine honey and crushed biscuits and stuff into apples. Arrange apples in baking dish, open side up.

3. Combine wine with water and pour over apples.

4. Bake in preheated 400°F/200°C oven for 40 to 45 minutes, or until apples are tender and cooked through. Serve whole or cut in quarters.

COOKING WITH WINES AND LIQUEURS

Wines and liqueurs can be great seasonings in cooking. On hand, I like to have brandy or cognac; dark rum; orange liqueur to use when any fruit liqueur is called for; and a reasonably priced dry red and white wine.

Brandy, cognac, rum and liqueurs do not have to be refrigerated after opening, but wines will oxidize and go off quickly once they have been opened. Keep opened bottles in the refrigerator and use them within a day or two or, if you plan to use the wine only for cooking, pour a tablespoon or two of olive oil into the bottle. The oil floats on the surface and blocks off the air (the wine should keep, refrigerated, for a month or two).

PER SERVING

Calories	180
g carbohydrate	38
g fibre	4
g total fat	4
g saturated fat	2
g protein	1
mg cholesterol	0
mg sodium	7
mg potassium	227

BANANAS FLAMBÉ

There are many versions of this dessert, but the cinnamon, nutmeg and allspice make this my favourite. I serve it a lot when people drop over on the spur of the moment, because I always have the ingredients on hand. (Bananas seem to be one of the few things everyone in our house loves!)

Serve this over vanilla frozen yogurt or with sweetened soft yogurt cheese (page 228) or thick yogurt if you wish, but it is also great on its own. If you can find the tiny finger bananas, use them whole — they look adorable in this dish.

Makes 6 to 8 servings

½ cup	brown sugar	125 mL
⅓ cup	pineapple juice	75 mL
½ tsp	cinnamon	2 mL
¼ tsp	nutmeg	1 mL
¼ tsp	allspice	1 mL
8	bananas	8
¼ cup	dark rum	50 mL

1. In deep skillet, place brown sugar, pineapple juice, cinnamon, nutmeg and allspice. Stir well and heat until mixture is boiling and smooth.

2. Peel bananas and cut lengthwise into halves or quarters. Add to sugar mixture in skillet. Cook for about 3 minutes, until hot.

3. Add rum. When mixture begins to sizzle, flambé it (see sidebars). If it does not flambé, do not worry – it will still taste great.

FLAMBÉEING

Food is flambéed for three reasons. First, flambéeing burns off most of the alcohol in a dish, making the result sweeter and less harsh-tasting. (If the flambé doesn't work, the alcohol will evaporate when the mixture comes to a boil anyway, so don't worry.)

Another reason to flambé is to lightly singe the top of the food to seal in flavour and make a crust.

The third reason to flambé is for show. If it doesn't work, the show is over (don't try to flambé something more than once or twice, or the dish will become too boozy).

FLAMBÉEING TIPS

- Turn off your smoke alarm.
- Tie back long hair.
- Never pour alcohol directly from the bottle. Pour the amount you need into a glass first, and keep the bottle away from the heat.
- The alcohol doesn't always ignite right away, so continue to stand back while you are flambéeing.
- Make sure no alcohol is spilled, otherwise you may have "table flambé"!

PER SERVING

Calories	234
g carbohydrate	56
g fibre	3
g total fat	1
g saturated fat	trace
g protein	2

Excellent: vitamin B$_6$

mg cholesterol	0
mg sodium	7
mg potassium	689

See photo opposite page 257.

FRUIT YOGURT DIP AND PEACH SALSA

I love serving fruit platters for dessert, but often look for something to make them a little more special. Serve an array of fresh fruit with one or two dipping sauces — one made with yogurt cheese and the other made with fruit. Be sure to use ripe fruit for the best flavour. This yogurt dip is a great topping for other desserts, too.

For an extra treat, you can dip biscotti (page 282) in either of these along with the fruit.

Makes 1 cup/250 mL dip; 2 cups/500 mL salsa

Fruit Yogurt Dip:

1 cup	soft yogurt cheese (page 228) or thick yogurt	250 mL
2 tbsp	brown sugar	25 mL
1 tbsp	rum or orange liqueur, optional	15 mL
1 tsp	vanilla	5 mL

Peach Salsa:

2	large ripe peaches, plums or mangos, peeled and diced	2
6	strawberries, trimmed and diced, or ½ cup/125 mL raspberries	6
2 tbsp	orange marmalade	25 mL
1 tbsp	rum or orange liqueur, optional	15 mL
1 tbsp	chopped fresh mint, optional	15 mL
pinch	each cinnamon, allspice, ground ginger and nutmeg	pinch

1. For fruit yogurt dip, combine yogurt cheese, brown sugar, rum and vanilla and whisk. (Pureeing may make it watery.)

2. For peach salsa, combine peaches, strawberries, marmalade, rum, mint and spices. Mash lightly with potato masher until mixture is moist enough to hold together.

HOW TO FLAMBÉ

Method 1: Heat alcohol in a small pot. Standing back, light a long match and hold it over the pot until the evaporating fumes ignite the alcohol. Pour the flaming alcohol over the dish.
Method 2: If the food is cooking, drain off any fat. Pour the alcohol on top of the hot food and, standing back, light it with a long match. The hot alcohol should ignite in 2 to 10 seconds.

PER TBSP (15 mL)
(Fruit Dip)

Calories	22
g carbohydrate	3
g fibre	0
g total fat	trace
g saturated fat	trace
g protein	2
mg cholesterol	2
mg sodium	14
mg potassium	52

PER TBSP (15 mL)
(Peach Salsa)

Calories	8
g carbohydrate	2
g fibre	trace
g total fat	0
g saturated fat	0
g protein	trace
mg cholesterol	0
mg sodium	0
mg potassium	24

DESSERT FRUIT CURRY

Although people do not usually associate curries with dessert, a curry is really just a mixture of spices, and here sweet spices are used in the blend. This idea originally came from Margaret Carson, a Halifax cooking teacher whom I met when taping a Dini Petty show in the Maritimes. If peaches are not in season, use an apple, a pear and a kiwi or other fruits (cook apples and pears in the brown sugar mixture for about 5 minutes before adding the rum). I do not peel the peaches or plums, but I do peel the apples and pears.

Serve this as is or with raspberry sorbet, sweetened soft yogurt cheese (page 228) or over angel food cake (page 274). If there is any fruit curry left over, I sometimes put a crisp topping on it (page 270) and bake it for 30 minutes.

Makes 6 to 8 servings

⅓ cup	brown sugar	75 mL
1 tsp	cinnamon	5 mL
1 tsp	ground ginger	5 mL
¼ tsp	nutmeg	1 mL
¼ tsp	ground cardamom	1 mL
¼ tsp	ground coriander	1 mL
¼ cup	orange juice	50 mL
¼ cup	orange liqueur or rum, optional	50 mL
2 tbsp	lemon juice	25 mL
2	peaches, pitted and sliced	2
1	pineapple, peeled, cored and cut in chunks	1
3	plums, pitted and cut in quarters	3
1 cup	mixed berries	250 mL
1	banana, sliced thickly on diagonal	1

1. In large skillet, combine sugar, cinnamon, ginger, nutmeg, cardamom, coriander and orange juice. Cook for a few minutes until sugar melts and becomes syrupy. Add orange liqueur and lemon juice and bring to boil.

2. Add peaches, pineapple and plums to syrup and cook for a few minutes.

3. Add berries and banana and cook for 1 minute, just until heated.

WINE SUBSTITUTES

In a recipe, there is always something you can substitute for an alcoholic product. Remember, though, that different substitutes are used in different recipes, and that a substitute will never give you exactly the same taste as the original.

- white wine: substitute chicken stock or vegetable juice in savory dishes and light-coloured fruit juices (apple, orange or pineapple) in desserts
- red wine: substitute beef stock or tomato juice in savory recipes and red fruit juices in desserts
- Marsala, Madeira or port: substitute stock or vegetable juice in savory recipes and fruit juice concentrates in dessert recipes
- fruit liqueurs: substitute fruit juice concentrate, citrus peel or pure vanilla extract
- cognac, brandy or rum: fruit juice concentrates or concentrated stocks in savory recipes or fruit purees or concentrated juices in desserts

PER SERVING

Calories	151
g carbohydrate	38
g fibre	3
g total fat	1
g saturated fat	trace
g protein	1

Good: vitamin C

mg cholesterol	0
mg sodium	7
mg potassium	370

CREAMY RICE PUDDING

I never would have dreamed how popular a rice pudding recipe could be. After this recipe was first published, people wrote that it had even saved their marriages! But I guess that's what comfort food is for.

Use a large heavy saucepan for this and don't worry — even with all the liquid it will eventually thicken! Although this pudding works with all kinds of rices, short-grain white rice gives you the creamiest texture, and that's what I always use (see page 221).

If you love crème brûlée, place chilled rice pudding in a flat, ovenproof dish and sprinkle with sifted brown sugar. Place under the broiler until the sugar melts (watch it closely).

Makes 8 servings

½ cup	rice (preferably short-grain)	125 mL
1 cup	boiling water	250 mL
⅓ cup	granulated sugar	75 mL
1 tsp	cornstarch	5 mL
pinch	salt	pinch
5 cups	milk	1.25 L
pinch	nutmeg	pinch
¼ cup	raisins	50 mL
1 tsp	vanilla	5 mL
1 tbsp	cinnamon	15 mL

1. Combine rice with boiling water in large saucepan. Cover. Bring to boil, reduce heat and simmer gently for 15 minutes, or until water is absorbed.

2. Combine sugar with cornstarch and salt. Whisk in 1 cup/250 mL milk. Stir until smooth.

3. Add sugar mixture and remaining milk to rice. Combine well. Add nutmeg and raisins. Stirring, bring to boil.

4. Cover, reduce heat to barest simmer and cook for 1 to 1½ hours, or until mixture is very creamy. Stir occasionally.

5. Stir in vanilla. Transfer pudding to serving bowl and sprinkle with cinnamon. Serve hot or cold.

PER SERVING

Calories	173
g carbohydrate	31
g fibre	1
g total fat	3
g saturated fat	2
g protein	6

Good: riboflavin; calcium

mg cholesterol	11
mg sodium	77
mg potassium	288

FLOATING ISLAND

This classic dessert is as light and airy as a cloud! I bake it like an angel food cake in a tube pan, but it can also be baked in muffin cups or in a loaf pan. If you are using a pan with a removable bottom, wrap the outside tightly with foil to prevent the water bath from leaking into the batter.

This meringue is baked in a water bath so the texture will be spongy and moist rather than dry and crisp. A water bath is like a double boiler but used in the oven. To make one, put a large roasting pan in the oven and pour in water to come halfway up the sides of the meringue pan. Allow the water to heat while the oven is preheating. When you are ready to bake the meringue, place the meringue pan gently in the water bath.

Instead of using the custard sauce, you could serve this in a pool of raspberry sauce (see sidebar), chocolate sauce (page 276) or lemon custard sauce (page 268).

Makes 6 to 8 servings

8	egg whites	8
½ tsp	cream of tartar	2 mL
¾ cup	granulated sugar or superfine sugar (page 268)	175 mL
1 tsp	vanilla	5 mL

Custard Sauce:

2	eggs	2
¼ cup	granulated sugar	50 mL
1 tbsp	all-purpose flour	15 mL
2 cups	milk, hot	500 mL
1 tsp	vanilla	5 mL

Caramel Sauce:

½ cup	granulated sugar	125 mL
2 tbsp	cold water	25 mL
½ cup	boiling water	125 mL

RASPBERRY SAUCE
Use this sauce with fruit desserts, chocolate desserts and just about everything in between.

Thaw two 10-oz/300 g packages frozen raspberries and drain, reserving juices. Puree with 2 tbsp/25 mL granulated sugar. Strain out the seeds if you wish. Stir in 2 tbsp/25 mL orange or raspberry liqueur (or 1 tbsp/ 15 mL frozen orange juice concentrate) and enough reserved juice to make a sauce. (If you use sweetened berries, omit the sugar and/or add a little lemon juice.)

Makes about 2 cups/500 mL.

DRIZZLING

This is a lovely, easy way to garnish soups, salads, appetizers and desserts. The easiest method is to put yogurt or a sauce in a plastic squeeze bottle. If you don't have a squeeze bottle, put the sauce in a small, heavy-duty plastic bag and cut out a tiny piece of one corner. Then use it as a piping tube. Drizzle the mixture back and forth over the dish.

SPIDER WEB GARNISH

To make a spider web design on a soup or sauce, make concentric circles with a contrasting sauce (e.g., yogurt or fruit puree). Pull the tip of a knife from the outside edge into the centre at 12, 3, 6 and 9 o'clock. Then go from the centre to the outside edge at 1:30, 4:30, 7:30 and 10:30. Or, simply swirl the circles with the tip of a knife.

PER SERVING

Calories	288
g carbohydrate	56
g fibre	0
g total fat	3
g saturated fat	2
g protein	10

Good: riboflavin; vitamin B$_{12}$

mg cholesterol	78
mg sodium	135
mg potassium	211

1. Oil 8- to 10-cup/2 to 2.5 L angel food cake pan (preferably without removable bottom) and dust lightly with sugar. Preheat oven to 350°F/180°C. Put water bath pan in oven (see introduction).

2. Beat egg whites with cream of tartar for about 10 seconds. On medium-high speed, beat whites until opaque. Add sugar gradually and continue beating until firm. Add vanilla.

3. Spoon meringue into prepared pan and smooth surface. Bake in water bath for 30 minutes. Cool. Run knife around edge of pan and invert meringue onto•plate. Chill (but do not cover with plastic wrap).

4. For custard sauce, beat eggs with sugar and flour. Beat in hot milk and bring to boil. Reduce heat and cook, stirring constantly, for about 1 minute. Remove from heat and stir in vanilla. Cool.

5. For caramel sauce, combine sugar with cold water in heavy medium saucepan. Stirring, bring to boil. Using pastry brush dipped in cold water, brush any undissolved sugar crystals down sides of pan. Without stirring, cook mixture until it is golden and caramel coloured. Standing back, add boiling water. Stir well and cool.

6. To serve, spoon about ⅓ cup/75 mL custard sauce onto serving plate. Place slice of meringue on top of sauce. Drizzle about 2 tbsp/25 mL caramel sauce over and around "island."

UPSIDE-DOWN LEMON MERINGUES

In this recipe, a butter-laden crust is replaced with a fat-free meringue, giving you a beautiful, delicious and carefree dessert. Serve these immediately if you like your meringues crispy.

Makes 8 servings

Meringues:

2	egg whites	2
pinch	cream of tartar	pinch
½ cup	granulated sugar or superfine sugar (see sidebar)	125 mL
¼ tsp	vanilla	1 mL

Lemon Custard Sauce:

3 tbsp	cornstarch	45 mL
¾ cup	granulated sugar	175 mL
1	egg	1
½ cup	lemon juice	125 mL
⅓ cup	orange juice	75 mL
1 tbsp	grated lemon peel	15 mL
1 cup	soft yogurt cheese (page 228) or thick yogurt	250 mL
2 cups	strawberries	500 mL
8	sprigs fresh mint	8

1. For meringues, beat egg whites with cream of tartar until light. Beat in ½ cup/125 mL sugar gradually until stiff peaks form. Beat in vanilla.

2. Trace 8 3-inch/7.5 cm circles on parchment paper–lined baking sheet. Spread egg whites inside circles. Bake in preheated 300°F/150°C oven for 30 to 40 minutes, or until completely dry. Freeze if not using right away.

3. To prepare lemon custard sauce, in small saucepan stir cornstarch and ¾ cup/175 mL sugar together. Whisk in egg, lemon juice, orange juice and peel. Bring to boil and cook for 1 minute. Cool.

4. To serve, fold yogurt cheese into lemon mixture. Place meringue on each serving plate. Spoon sauce on top. Arrange strawberries around meringues and garnish with mint.

SUPERFINE SUGAR
Superfine or instant dissolving sugar is sometimes called fruit sugar or bar sugar. It is finer than regular sugar and dissolves more easily in cold drinks, meringues, caramel mixtures and syrups. You can buy it, or make your own by processing regular granulated sugar in the food processor for about 30 seconds.

PER SERVING

Calories	195
g carbohydrate	42
g fibre	1
g total fat	2
g saturated fat	1
g protein	5

Excellent: vitamin C
Good: vitamin B$_{12}$

mg cholesterol	30
mg sodium	49
mg potassium	214

BLUEBERRY GRUNT

This old-fashioned dessert is delicious despite its unlikely name. It tastes like sweet dumplings in a spiced blueberry sauce. If fresh blueberries are not in season, use frozen.

Serve this as is or with a bit of frozen vanilla yogurt or sweetened soft yogurt cheese (page 228).

Makes 4 to 5 servings

4 cups	fresh or frozen blueberries	1 L
1/3 cup	granulated sugar	75 mL
1/2 tsp	cinnamon	2 mL
pinch	allspice	pinch
1/2 cup	orange or grape juice	125 mL

Topping:

3/4 cup	all-purpose flour	175 mL
1/4 cup	granulated sugar	50 mL
1 1/2 tsp	baking powder	7 mL
pinch	salt	pinch
1 tbsp	soft margarine or unsalted butter, cold, cut in bits	15 mL
1	egg white	1
1/4 cup	milk	50 mL
1/2 tsp	vanilla	2 mL

1. Place blueberries, 1/3 cup/75 mL sugar, cinnamon, allspice and juice in deep 10-inch/25 cm skillet and cook for about 5 minutes, or until blueberries are soft and juicy. Remove from heat.

2. In bowl, combine flour with 1/4 cup/50 mL sugar, baking powder and salt. Add margarine or butter and rub into flour with your fingers.

3. Combine egg white with milk and vanilla. Stir into flour.

4. Drop batter by spoonful on top of blueberries but not too close to edge of pan. Cover and cook over medium-low heat for about 15 minutes, or until biscuits are cooked through.

PER SERVING

Calories	333
g carbohydrate	72
g fibre	5
g total fat	4
g saturated fat	1
g protein	5

Good: vitamin C

mg cholesterol	1
mg sodium	166
mg potassium	253

PLUM CRISP

I love apple crisp because it is warm and comforting and reminds me of my childhood. But I love plum crisp because it is new, exciting and delicious! You can actually make a crisp with any of your favourite fruits — apples, pears, peaches, berries or rhubarb. This crisp is a little tart (not unlike rhubarb), so add a bit more sugar if you like things sweet or serve it with some sweetened soft yogurt cheese (page 228).

I like to use a mixture of purple, red and yellow plums, but this tastes great even when made with just one variety. Serve it warm or cold.

Makes 10 servings

2 lb	plums (7 to 8 large)	1 kg
½ cup	all-purpose flour	125 mL
½ cup	brown sugar	125 mL
½ tsp	cinnamon	2 mL
pinch	nutmeg, optional	pinch
¼ cup	soft margarine or unsalted butter, melted	50 mL
½ cup	rolled oats	125 mL

1. Halve plums, remove pits and cut in quarters if they are large. Place in bottom of oiled 9-inch/2.5 L square baking dish.

2. Combine flour, sugar, cinnamon and nutmeg. Drizzle margarine or butter over mixture and combine. Stir in oats.

3. Sprinkle topping evenly over plums. Bake in preheated 350°F/180°C oven for 45 to 50 minutes, or until plums are very tender and topping is crisp.

BUYING FRESH FRUIT
- Look for fruit that has a fragrant aroma and is firm but not hard. Buy fruit that is not prepackaged so that you can inspect each piece.
- When buying melons, look for ones that seem heavy for their size (weigh a few that look the same size) and ones that smell sweet at the stem end.
- Bananas and pears ripen after picking, but most fruits, like berries and grapes, only get worse. Most immature, green fruits will never ripen or become sweet, so do not mistake rotting for ripening.

STORING FRUIT
- If a fruit needs ripening, store it at room temperature but not in direct sunlight (which can cause uneven ripening).
- For faster ripening, store fruit in a perforated paper bag.
- Store ripe fruit in the refrigerator to prevent rotting.

PER SERVING

Calories	167
g carbohydrate	29
g fibre	2
g total fat	5
g saturated fat	1
g protein	2
mg cholesterol	0
mg sodium	64
mg potassium	193

RHUBARB AND STRAWBERRY COBBLER

The cake-like topping on the fruit is a little different from the biscuit-like dough in most cobblers. This idea originally came from pastry chef, cookbook author and teacher Jim Dodge. I use different fruits depending on the season, but so far this is my favourite combination. Serve the cobbler warm or at room temperature with sorbet or sweetened soft yogurt cheese (page 228).

Makes 10 servings

8 cups	mixed fresh strawberries and rhubarb, cut in bite-sized pieces	2 L
½ cup	granulated sugar	125 mL
3 tbsp	all-purpose flour	45 mL
pinch	cinnamon or nutmeg	pinch

Topping:

⅓ cup	soft margarine or unsalted butter	75 mL
¾ cup	granulated sugar	175 mL
1	egg	1
1½ cups	all-purpose flour	375 mL
1 tsp	baking powder	5 mL
½ tsp	baking soda	2 mL
¼ tsp	salt	1 mL
⅔ cup	buttermilk	150 mL

1. Toss strawberries and rhubarb with ½ cup/125 mL sugar, 3 tbsp/45 mL flour and cinnamon. Place in bottom of oiled 13 x 9-inch/3.5 L baking dish. Press down gently.

2. To make topping, in large bowl, cream margarine or butter with ¾ cup/175 mL sugar until very light. Beat in egg.

3. In separate bowl, sift together 1½ cups/375 mL flour, baking powder, baking soda and salt. Mix together well. Add flour mixture to batter alternately with buttermilk in three or four additions.

4. Smooth batter over fruit, leaving 1-inch/2.5 cm space between batter and edge of dish. Bake in preheated 375°F/190°C oven for 45 to 50 minutes, or until topping springs back when pressed in centre (the centre tends to take longer to cook).

PER SERVING

Calories	269
g carbohydrate	48
g fibre	3
g total fat	7
g saturated fat	1
g protein	4

Good: vitamin C; vitamin B$_6$

mg cholesterol	22
mg sodium	249
mg potassium	273

APPLE STRUDEL PIE

This pie looks and tastes sensational, and it is perfect for anyone who has a fear of traditional pastry. I find that Krinos brand, available at most supermarkets, is an easy brand to work with. This dish is also wonderful made with pears.

Makes 10 to 12 servings

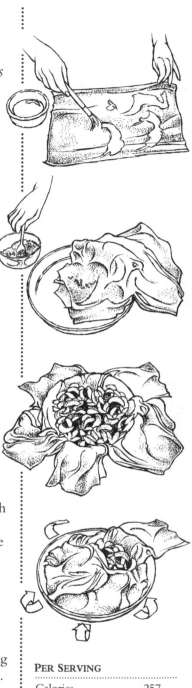

6	apples (about 3 lb/1.5 kg), peeled, cored and sliced	6
½ cup	brown sugar	125 mL
½ tsp	cinnamon	2 mL
¼ cup	all-purpose flour	50 mL
pinch	nutmeg	pinch
¼ cup	dry breadcrumbs	50 mL
2 tbsp	granulated sugar	25 mL
10	sheets phyllo pastry	10
⅓ cup	soft margarine or unsalted butter, melted	75 mL
2 tbsp	icing sugar	25 mL

1. Combine apples, brown sugar, cinnamon, flour and nutmeg. Reserve.

2. Have 10-inch/3 L springform pan at hand. In small bowl, combine breadcrumbs with granulated sugar.

3. Working with one sheet of phyllo at a time (keep remaining sheets covered with damp tea towel), brush pastry lightly with melted margarine or butter and dust with breadcrumb mixture. Fold pastry in half lengthwise and brush again. Place pastry in pan with one short end in centre of pan and other end hanging over edge. Sprinkle with breadcrumb mixture.

4. Repeat with remaining sheets, overlapping each slightly when arranged in pan. Leave a lot of pastry hanging over edge. Bottom of pan should be covered.

5. Spoon filling into pastry. Fold pastry back over filling so filling is completely covered and pastry is somewhat ragged looking. Brush top of pie with remaining margarine or butter.

6. Bake in preheated 400°F/200°C oven for 15 minutes. Reduce heat to 350°F/180°C and bake for 50 to 55 minutes longer, or until apples are tender when pie is pierced with sharp knife. Cool for at least 15 minutes before removing from pan. Dust with icing sugar before serving.

PER SERVING

Calories	257
g carbohydrate	47
g fibre	3
g total fat	7
g saturated fat	1
g protein	3
mg cholesterol	0
mg sodium	267
mg potassium	186

QUICK APPLE CAKE

Although cakes are usually time-consuming, this one is quick enough for a last-minute dessert. Make it first, and by the time you have prepared the rest of the meal and eaten, the cake will be ready to serve.

This is a dense cake with great flavour.

Makes 12 pieces

1	egg	1
½ cup	granulated sugar	125 mL
⅓ cup	vegetable oil	75 mL
3 tbsp	orange juice or apple juice	45 mL
1 tsp	vanilla	5 mL
¾ cup	all-purpose flour	175 mL
1 tsp	baking powder	5 mL
pinch	salt	pinch
⅓ cup	brown sugar	75 mL
1 tsp	cinnamon	5 mL
3	apples, peeled and sliced	3

1. Beat egg with sugar until thick and light. Beat in oil, juice and vanilla.

2. In separate bowl, combine flour, baking powder and salt. Stir into egg mixture and combine only until blended.

3. Combine brown sugar and cinnamon.

4. Arrange apples in bottom of oiled 8-inch/2 L square baking dish. Sprinkle with half the brown sugar mixture. Smooth batter on top. Sprinkle with remaining brown sugar mixture.

5. Bake in preheated 350°F/180°C oven for 35 to 40 minutes, or until cake comes away from sides of pan slightly. Cool for 10 minutes before serving.

APPLES

Some apples are crisp and tart, some are softer but have a strong apple flavour. Often my favourite eating apples are not my favourite in cooking. I like to eat McIntosh apples, but they turn into mush when cooked. For cooking I like Spy, Ida Red, Royal Gala, Golden Delicious and Empire.

PER PIECE

Calories	165
g carbohydrate	26
g fibre	1
g total fat	7
g saturated fat	1
g protein	1
mg cholesterol	18
mg sodium	29
mg potassium	76

ANNA'S ANGEL FOOD CAKE WITH BERRY BERRY SAUCE

See photo opposite page 256.

This is my daughter's very favourite cake; she loves to make it as well as eat it.

Angel food cake is old-fashioned and delicious, yet it contains virtually no fat. The cake freezes well, and you can serve it with the berry sauce or with plain fresh fruit, sweetened soft yogurt cheese (page 228) or sorbet. You should use a traditional tube or angel food cake pan, and remember that the whole trick to making a high, light angel cake is to beat the egg whites properly (see sidebar).

The berry sauce makes a fabulous dessert as well as a sauce — just use more berries. You can serve it with meringues (page 268) or in bowls with a bit of sweetened yogurt cheese on top. I often use frozen raspberries for pureeing, as fresh ones are so precious that I'd rather eat them whole. A food mill (a relatively inexpensive old-fashioned gadget) will puree the raspberries and strain out the seeds at the same time. If you puree the raspberries in a blender or food processor, you will have to strain the mixture afterwards if you want to remove the seeds.

If you use unsweetened frozen berries, you may have to add about 1 tbsp/15 mL sugar to the sauce.

Makes 12 to 16 servings

1½ cups	granulated sugar, divided	375 mL
1 cup	cake and pastry flour	250 mL
2 cups	egg whites (12 to 16 whites)	500 mL
1 tsp	cream of tartar	5 mL
1 tbsp	lemon juice or frozen orange juice concentrate	15 mL
1 tsp	vanilla	5 mL
1 tsp	grated lemon or orange peel	5 mL

BEATING EGG WHITES

To beat egg whites properly, the bowl and the beaters must be completely free of fat and grease. When you separate the eggs, make sure no egg yolk gets into the whites. (If you do get a bit of yolk in the whites, try scooping it out using half an egg shell; it seems to work like a magnet to attract the yolk.)

It is best to separate each egg in a clean bowl, adding yolks to yolks and whites to whites after they are separate. Add 1 tsp/5 mL lemon juice or ¼ tsp/1 mL cream of tartar for every 4 egg whites. If you are adding sugar, beat it in slowly just after the egg whites turn opaque.

Berry Berry Sauce:

1	10-oz/300 g package frozen raspberries	1
2 tbsp	orange or raspberry liqueur, optional	25 mL
2 cups	fresh strawberries, trimmed and quartered	500 mL
1 cup	fresh raspberries	250 mL
1 cup	fresh blueberries	250 mL

1. Sift ¾ cup/175 mL sugar with flour twice. Reserve.

2. With electric mixer, beat egg whites with cream of tartar and lemon juice on medium speed until "loosened." Continue to beat at medium-high until light. Slowly add remaining ¾ cup/175 mL sugar, beating constantly. Egg whites should be very light and stiff. Beat in vanilla. Stir in peel.

3. Gently mix or fold in flour mixture in three additions. Do not overfold so as not to deflate egg whites.

4. Very delicately spoon or pour batter into 10-inch/4 L tube pan. Bake cake in preheated 375°F/190°C oven for 35 to 45 minutes, or until cake tester comes out clean and dry and top of cake springs back when lightly touched.

5. To make sauce, defrost frozen raspberries. If they come in syrup, strain them. Reserve juices and puree berries through food mill or in blender or food processor. Add enough reserved juices to make medium-thick sauce. Add liqueur and gently stir in fresh berries.

6. Cool cake in pan upside down (if pan does not have little feet to act as rack, invert cake and pan onto rack so air can circulate underneath).

7. To remove cake from pan, use long, thin knife to loosen edges. If pan has removable bottom, remove sides and then loosen bottom with knife. If you are using a one-piece pan, use spatula or knife to loosen bottom. Do not worry if cake seems crushed – it usually springs back into shape. Serve cake with berry sauce.

Cappuccino Angel Food Cake: Add 1½ tbsp/20 mL crushed instant coffee powder and ¼ tsp/1 mL cinnamon to flour mixture. Add ¼ tsp/1 mL almond extract with vanilla.

Per Serving

Calories	185
g carbohydrate	41
g fibre	1
g total fat	trace
g saturated fat	0
g protein	6

Good: vitamin C

mg cholesterol	0
mg sodium	68
mg potassium	154

CHOCOLATE ANGEL FOOD CAKE WITH CHOCOLATE SAUCE

This cake has a light but very satisfying chocolate flavour. Serve it with or without the sauce. It can also be served with raspberry sauce (page 266), custard sauce (page 266) or lemon custard sauce (page 268). For a mocha-flavoured cake, add 1 tbsp/15 mL crushed instant coffee powder to the flour mixture.

Makes 12 to 16 servings

1¾ cups	granulated sugar, divided	425 mL
1 cup	cake and pastry flour	250 mL
⅓ cup	cocoa	75 mL
2 cups	egg whites (12 to 16 whites)	500 mL
1 tsp	cream of tartar	5 mL
pinch	salt	pinch
1 tsp	vanilla	5 mL

Chocolate Sauce:

6 oz	bittersweet or semisweet chocolate, chopped	175 g
2 tbsp	cocoa	25 mL
3 tbsp	corn syrup	45 mL
½ cup	water	125 mL
1 tsp	vanilla	5 mL

COCOA
Cocoa is unsweetened powdered chocolate with much of the cocoa butter removed. While it can't be substituted for regular chocolate in all cases, in some recipes it can add a strong, satisfying chocolate flavour, with only a small amount of fat.

1. Sift ¾ cup/175 mL sugar with flour and cocoa three times. Stir well. Reserve.

2. In large bowl, beat egg whites with cream of tartar and salt until light and opaque. Slowly beat in remaining 1 cup/ 250 mL sugar. Beat until stiff. Beat in vanilla.

3. Fold reserved flour mixture into egg whites in three additions. Do not overfold, but make sure there are no pockets of flour in batter.

4. Gently turn batter into 10-inch/4 L tube pan. Bake in preheated 325°F/160°C oven for 45 to 50 minutes.

5. To make chocolate sauce, combine chocolate, cocoa, corn syrup and water in saucepan and cook gently until smooth. Remove from heat and stir in vanilla. Cool.

6. Invert cake pan on rack and allow to cool for 1 hour. Remove gently from pan by running knife around inside edge of pan and centre tube. Slice cake and serve drizzled with sauce.

Chocolate Angel Food Cake with a Tunnel of Raspberry:
After cake has been cooled and removed from pan, cut ½-inch/1 cm slice from top of cake. Gently scoop out centre part of cake, leaving ½ inch border at bottom and sides. Cut pieces of scooped-out cake into ½-inch/1 cm pieces and fold into 4 cups/1 L softened raspberry sorbet (you could also use other flavours of sorbet or frozen yogurt). Fill tunnel with sorbet mixture. Replace top and freeze cake. Serve with or without chocolate sauce.

PER SERVING	
Calories	260
g carbohydrate	49
g fibre	2
g total fat	7
g saturated fat	4
g protein	7
mg cholesterol	0
mg sodium	97
mg potassium	179

OLD-FASHIONED CHEESECAKE

In the past ten years most people have become used to rich and creamy cheesecakes, but this version is similar to the cheesecake my mom made when I was growing up. It is very clean-tasting, not too sweet or dense, and I love it.

I think any cheesecake is too heavy to serve after a meal, but I do love it for a snack or treat. I can even convince myself that it is good for breakfast! If you prefer, bake it in a 9-inch/2.5 L springform pan and cut it into thin wedges. To cut the cake easily, dip a knife into very hot water and wipe dry before slicing.

Makes about 35 squares

Crust:

1¼ cups	Graham cracker crumbs	300 mL
¼ tsp	cinnamon, optional	1 mL
3 tbsp	soft margarine or unsalted butter, melted	45 mL

Filling:

1½ lb	low-fat pressed cottage cheese	750 g
1 cup	granulated sugar	250 mL
3	eggs	3
1 tsp	vanilla	5 mL
½ cup	soft yogurt cheese (page 228) or thick yogurt	125 mL
2 tbsp	all-purpose flour	25 mL

Topping:

1 cup	soft yogurt cheese or thick yogurt	250 mL
2 tbsp	granulated sugar	25 mL
1 tsp	vanilla	5 mL
20	strawberries, halved	20

1. Combine Graham cracker crumbs with cinnamon and melted margarine or butter. Press into bottom of a 12 x 8-inch/3 L baking dish.

2. For filling, if cottage cheese seems at all watery, drain it in strainer set over bowl for 1 hour. Discard any liquid.

3. Beat cottage cheese with 1 cup/250 mL sugar. Whisk in eggs one at a time, beating well after each addition. Whisk in 1 tsp/5 mL vanilla, ½ cup/125 mL yogurt cheese and flour. Pour over crust.

4. Bake in preheated 350°F/180°C oven for 45 to 50 minutes, or until just set when gently shaken.

5. For topping, combine 1 cup/250 mL yogurt cheese with 2 tbsp/25 mL sugar and 1 tsp/5 mL vanilla. Spread over hot cheesecake. Bake for 5 minutes longer. Chill thoroughly.

6. To slice, trim edges. Cut cake into squares and serve with strawberries.

Lemon Cheesecake: Add 1 tbsp/15 mL grated lemon peel to filling.

Ginger Cheesecake: Use gingersnap crumbs instead of Graham cracker crumbs. Add ½ cup/125 mL chopped candied ginger to filling.

Banana Cheesecake: Add 1 ripe pureed banana to filling instead of yogurt cheese.

PER SQUARE

Calories	86
g carbohydrate	12
g fibre	trace
g total fat	2
g saturated fat	1
g protein	5

Good: vitamin B_{12}

mg cholesterol	21
mg sodium	56
mg potassium	74

STRAWBERRY MERINGUE SHORTCAKES

Meringues can be fussy to make on the best of days. Perfect meringues are supposed to be crisp and crunchy. But this dish actually works better when the meringues are slightly chewy.

Makes 6 servings

Meringues:

3	egg whites	3
¼ tsp	cream of tartar	1 mL
½ cup	granulated sugar or superfine sugar (page 268)	125 mL
½ tsp	vanilla	2 mL

Filling:

2 cups	sliced strawberries	500 mL
3 tbsp	granulated sugar, divided	45 mL
1½ cups	soft yogurt cheese (page 228), thick yogurt or raspberry sorbet	375 mL
1 tbsp	orange liqueur or rum, optional	15 mL
2 tbsp	sifted icing sugar	25 mL

Garnish:

6	whole strawberries	6
6	sprigs of fresh mint	6

1. Preheat oven to 375°F/190°C. For meringues, beat egg whites with cream of tartar until light. Beat in ½ cup/125 mL sugar gradually until stiff peaks form. Beat in vanilla.

2. Trace 12 3-inch/7.5 cm circles on parchment paper-lined baking sheets. Spread meringue inside circles.

3. Place meringues in oven and turn off heat immediately. Allow to rest in oven for 6 hours or overnight. Freeze if not using right away.

4. For filling, combine sliced berries with 1 tbsp/15 mL sugar and allow to marinate for 30 to 60 minutes.

5. Combine yogurt cheese with remaining 2 tbsp/25 mL sugar and liqueur just before using.

6. Set one meringue on each of 6 serving plates. Top with berries. Spoon yogurt cheese on top. Place remaining meringues on top and dust with icing sugar. Garnish with whole berries and fresh mint. Serve immediately.

PER SERVING

Calories	185
g carbohydrate	35
g fibre	1
g total fat	2
g saturated fat	1
g protein	8

Excellent: vitamin C; vitamin B$_{12}$
Good: riboflavin; calcium

mg cholesterol	6
mg sodium	80
mg potassium	318

MOCHA MERINGUE KISSES

These meringues should turn out dry and crisp. But, if you want chewy meringues, try the following technique I learnt from one of my staff, Rhonda Caplan. Preheat the oven to 375°F/190°C. Place meringues in preheated oven and turn off heat immediately. Allow to rest in closed oven for 6 hours or overnight.

This works well for Upside-Down Lemon Meringues (page 268) and Strawberry Meringue Shortcakes (page 280) as well as these cookies.

Makes about 60 cookies

3	egg whites	3
¼ tsp	cream of tartar	1 mL
⅔ cup	granulated sugar or superfine sugar, divided	150 mL
½ tsp	vanilla	2 mL
2 tsp	★cornstarch	10 mL
1 tbsp	crushed instant coffee powder	15 mL
¼ cup	finely chopped toasted hazelnuts or almonds	50 mL

1. Beat egg whites with cream of tartar until frothy. Gradually add ⅓ cup/75 mL sugar and beat until stiff. Beat in vanilla.

2. Combine remaining ⅓ cup/75 mL sugar with cornstarch, coffee powder and nuts. Fold into beaten egg whites.

3. Line two baking sheets with parchment paper. Spoon meringue mixture onto sheets or transfer mixture into large piping tube fitted with star nozzle and pipe in 1½-inch/4 cm mounds.

4. Bake in preheated 300°F/150°C oven until dry, about 25 to 30 minutes. Turn off oven and allow cookies to cool in oven. Tops should be dry and only slightly browned.

★ *If you use this recipe in the Passover menu (page 31), omit the cornstarch.*

COPPER BOWLS

Although you do not need a copper bowl (I seldom use one), copper works well for egg whites because it reacts with the beater to stabilize the whites. Be sure to clean the inside of the bowl with a little vinegar or lemon juice and salt just before you use it. If you do not have a copper bowl, use glass or stainless steel, as plastic bowls can trap grease. You can add ¼ tsp/1 mL cream of tartar or 1 tsp/5 mL lemon juice for every 4 unbeaten egg whites to simulate the results from using a copper bowl.

PER COOKIE

Calories	13
g carbohydrate	2
g fibre	0
g total fat	trace
g saturated fat	0
g protein	trace
mg cholesterol	0
mg sodium	3
mg potassium	8

NICK MALGIERI'S HONEY ALMOND BISCOTTI

See photo opposite page 257.

Biscotti are "twice-baked" cookies that are quite dry and hard but very flavourful. These are easy to make, very in vogue, absolutely delicious and remarkably low in fat! They are meant to be dipped in tea, coffee or the traditional vin santo, a sweet Italian dessert wine.

Nick Malgieri is a wonderful teacher and has a devoted following at my school. His book on Italian desserts is excellent, and we have on occasion taken students to New York to attend his classes at Peter Kump's New York Cooking School.

Makes about 60 cookies

2 cups	all-purpose flour	500 mL
¾ cup	granulated sugar	175 mL
¾ cup	almonds, finely ground	175 mL
½ tsp	baking powder	2 mL
½ tsp	baking soda	2 mL
½ tsp	cinnamon	2 mL
¾ cup	whole unblanched almonds	175 mL
⅓ cup	honey	75 mL
⅓ cup	water	75 mL

1. Combine flour, sugar, ground almonds, baking powder, baking soda, cinnamon and whole almonds. Stir together well.

2. Add honey and water. Stir until stiff dough forms.

3. Divide dough in half. Roll each half into log about 15 inches/ 38 cm long.

4. Line baking sheet with parchment paper (to help prevent burning, use a double baking sheet if you can). Place logs, well apart, on paper. Bake in preheated 350°F/180°C oven for about 30 minutes, until well risen, firm and golden. Be sure to bake fully.

5. Cool logs slightly and place on cutting board. Cut, on diagonal, into ½-inch/1 cm slices. Return cookies to pan, cut side down, and bake for 15 minutes longer until dry and lightly coloured.

PER COOKIE

Calories	47
g carbohydrate	8
g fibre	trace
g total fat	2
g saturated fat	trace
g protein	1
mg cholesterol	0
mg sodium	12
mg potassium	27

MATRIMONIAL SQUARES (DATE SQUARES)

Wonderful old-fashioned treats like these are making a big comeback. They freeze perfectly, so don't think you have to eat them all at once!

The easiest way to chop dates is to cut them up with kitchen scissors.

Makes 25 squares

Filling:

1 lb	dates, chopped (about 3 cups/ 750 mL)	500 g
¼ cup	granulated sugar	50 mL
1½ cups	water	375 mL
1 tbsp	lemon juice	15 mL

Base and Topping:

½ cup	soft margarine or unsalted butter	125 mL
¾ cup	brown sugar	175 mL
3 tbsp	granulated sugar	45 mL
1 cup	all-purpose flour	250 mL
¼ tsp	baking soda	1 mL
1 cup	rolled oats	250 mL

1. To make filling, in saucepan, combine dates, ¼ cup/50 mL granulated sugar, water and lemon juice. Bring to boil. Reduce heat and simmer gently, stirring often, until thickened – 10 to 15 minutes. Cool.

2. For base and topping, cream margarine or butter. Add brown sugar and 3 tbsp/45 mL granulated sugar. Beat well.

3. Combine flour, baking soda and oats and stir well. Stir flour mixture into margarine or butter mixture. Mixture should be a little crumbly.

4. Pat two-thirds of flour mixture into bottom of 9-inch/2.5 L baking dish that has been oiled or lined with parchment paper. Spread date mixture on top. Sprinkle with remaining flour mixture.

5. Bake in preheated 350°F/180°C oven for 25 to 30 minutes, or until top is browned lightly. Cool and cut into squares.

PER SQUARE

Calories	151
g carbohydrate	29
g fibre	2
g total fat	4
g saturated fat	1
g protein	1
mg cholesterol	0
mg sodium	63
mg potassium	160

OATMEAL AND RAISIN SPICE COOKIE SQUARES

You can make this dough into individual cookies (bake them for only 10 to 12 minutes), but I think they are easier to make when they are baked in a large pan and then cut into squares. Instead of raisins, try using dried cherries, cranberries or chopped apricots, or a mixture.

Makes about 30 cookies

½ cup	soft margarine or unsalted butter	125 mL
½ cup	brown sugar	125 mL
⅓ cup	granulated sugar	75 mL
1	egg	1
½ tsp	vanilla	2 mL
¾ cup	all-purpose flour	175 mL
¼ tsp	baking powder	1 mL
½ tsp	cinnamon	2 mL
¼ tsp	allspice	1 mL
¼ tsp	ground ginger	1 mL
1½ cups	rolled oats	375 mL
¾ cup	raisins	175 mL

1. Brush 13 x 9-inch/3.5 L baking dish with oil and then line with parchment paper or foil, pressing paper down firmly so it stays in place.

2. In large bowl, cream margarine or butter until light. Gradually beat in sugars until smooth. Add egg and vanilla and mix in well.

3. In separate bowl, combine flour, baking powder, cinnamon, allspice and ginger. Stir together well. Add to batter and mix in. Stir in rolled oats and raisins.

4. Press dough evenly into baking dish. Flatten gently. Bake in preheated 350°F/180°C oven for 15 to 18 minutes, or until brown. (Less time for chewy; more for crispy.) Allow to rest for 2 or 3 minutes and then lift cookies out of pan on parchment paper. Cool slightly and cut into squares.

PER COOKIE

Calories	91
g carbohydrate	14
g fibre	1
g total fat	4
g saturated fat	1
g protein	1
mg cholesterol	7
mg sodium	46
mg potassium	65

APPENDICES

The recipes in this book have been developed with the average, healthy person in mind, the person who wants to reduce the risk of heart disease and other nutrition-related diseases, and adopt a healthy way of eating. However, if you or a member of your family has elevated blood cholesterol or high blood pressure, you may need to pay more careful attention to what you eat, especially to fat and sodium.

Salt or Sodium

There are many sources of sodium. One main source is salt. Salt is a chemical compound made up of 40% sodium and 60% chloride. There is approximately 575 mg sodium in every one-quarter teaspoon of salt. Other sources include: baking powder, baking soda and other compounds used in food processing.

WAYS TO FURTHER REDUCE SODIUM

- Salt added at the table and used in the preparation of foods is the major source of sodium in the diet. Use of the salt shaker at the table should be eliminated and salt added in food preparation should be limited.
- Many processed and convenience foods contain sodium. Check the labels and compare: some are higher in sodium than others.
- Avoid high sodium foods such as: cured and luncheon meats (ham, bacon, sausages), canned or smoked fish, canned or dried soups, condiments such as pickles, ketchup, prepared mustard, soy sauce★, many snack foods (potato chips, pretzels, salted top crackers, salted popcorn and peanuts), processed cheese. Note also that many of these high sodium, processed foods are also high in fat.
- Take-out and fast foods are frequently high in sodium and fat and should be consumed in moderation.
- Thoroughly rinse canned beans or lentils in cold water, and drain before using.
- Don't add salt to water when cooking vegetables, pasta or rice.
- Make ahead and freeze your own homemade soup stocks (reuse plastic food containers to pre-portion). Try the recipes on pages 53, 59 and 62.
- Instead of using canned tomatoes and vegetables, freeze your own. Commercially frozen vegetables are also lower in sodium.
- Use spices and herbs to flavour foods. Be creative, pepper is not the only spice that you can use. See Bonnie's suggestions for salt substitutes page 218.

★ Soy sauce is used in some recipes in this book. To reduce sodium from this source, use half the amount of soy sauce as stated in recipes and replace the other half with water, or use sodium-reduced soy sauce.

CANNED VS DRIED LEGUMES, WHAT'S THE DIFFERENCE?

Beans, peas and lentils, either canned or cooked from dried, are excellent sources of dietary fibre. Canned legumes are convenient alternatives when dried legumes are not available. However, beware of the sodium content. Canned legumes should be rinsed well and drained.

One 19 oz can of red kidney beans, drained of the liquid, contains about 1236 mg sodium. An equivalent amount of cooked kidney beans (2 cups), prepared from dried without added salt, contains only 7 mg sodium. Both the canned and the cooked red kidney beans provide 33 g dietary fibre.

SODIUM CONTENT IN BREADS

Type of Bread	Sodium (mg)
white, 1 slice (30 g)	152
whole wheat, 1 slice (30 g)	159
rye, light, 1 slice (30 g)	167
rye, pumpernickel, 1 slice (30 g)	170
foccacia/flatbread (30 g)	222
Italian bread, 1 slice (30 g)	175
bagel, 1 whole (85 g)	707
flour tortilla, 8", 1 whole	162
pita, 1 whole (60 g)	204
bread crumbs, dry, grated, 1 cup	801

WAYS TO FURTHER REDUCE FAT

- Choose dairy products that are the lowest in % b.f. or % m.f. (butter fat, milk fat), i.e., skim milk and lower-fat cheeses (<15% m.f.).
- When using the recipes in this book (except for recipes for baked goods) try reducing the margarine, oil, or butter by cutting it in half.
- Other ingredients which contribute fat may also be reduced by half; for example, cheeses, nuts and seeds, and mayonnaise. Low-fat yogurt can be used to replace half or all of mayonnaise.
- Often water, homemade stock or apple juice can replace the oil used in cooking. Substitute with the same amount and reduce cooking heat.
- In recipes, use:
  - low-fat milk (1% or skim)
  - lower-fat and skim milk cheeses (<15%)
  - low-fat yogurt instead of sour cream or mayonnaise
  - extra lean ground meat or ground chicken breast
  - egg whites instead of whole eggs (2 whites = 1 whole)

FAT CONTENT IN MILK

	g total fat *(per 1 cup/250 mL)*
whole	8
2% b.f.	5
1% b.f.	2
skim	trace

How much fat do you save by changing to a lower-fat milk?

Switch from 2% milk to 1% milk and save 3 grams of fat for every cup you drink. If you go from 2% milk to skim milk you will save 5 grams of fat.

- Use non-stick cookware and specially designed tools, such as a fat strainer, and low-fat cooking methods, such as steaming, broiling, poaching. Use paper towels to absorb surface fat.
- Use lean cuts of meat. Trim fat from within, if possible, and around meat. Remove skin from chicken before cooking.

Cholesterol

Cholesterol is a waxy, fatty substance made by the body and found in foods from animal sources. It is essential in forming cell membranes, in producing various hormones and is a part of bile acids which are necessary for fat absorption.

WHERE IS CHOLESTEROL FOUND?

There are two types of cholesterol: dietary cholesterol and blood cholesterol. Dietary cholesterol is cholesterol from the foods that we eat. Sources of dietary cholesterol include all animal products, such as eggs, milk products, meat, fish and poultry. Plants do not produce cholesterol, so fruits, vegetables, vegetable oils and grains are cholesterol-free. Although coconut and palm oils are cholesterol-free, they are high in saturated fat (see section on Food Fats). These oils and foods made with them should be consumed in moderation.

Serum or blood cholesterol is the cholesterol circulating in the blood. High circulating blood cholesterol is a risk factor for heart disease. Cholesterol can deposit on the inside of artery walls and cause them to narrow and become blocked. It is now known that dietary cholesterol is not the only culprit for high blood cholesterol. High dietary fat consumption, especially saturated fat, appears to be more closely associated with elevated blood cholesterol.

There are two main types of blood cholesterol: high density or HDL-cholesterol and low density or LDL-cholesterol.

- HDL-cholesterol is often referred to as "good" cholesterol because it helps carry excess cholesterol back to the liver to be excreted by the body, preventing its build-up in arteries. HDL is primarily influenced by exercise, weight loss, smoking and genetics.
- LDL-cholesterol is often referred to as "bad" cholesterol because it carries cholesterol through the blood to tissues, potentially causing build-up. LDL can be affected by dietary fat intake.

Food Fats and Heart Health

The fat in food is usually a mixture of different types of fat:

SATURATED FAT

Saturated fats tend to raise LDL-cholesterol in blood. LDL-cholesterol is a harmful form of blood cholesterol, closely linked to heart disease.

Key sources: meat and poultry, all milk products (except skim milk products), butter, lard, tropical oils (palm, palm kernel and coconut) often found in foods such as cookies, cakes, crackers and other convenience foods.

MONOUNSATURATED FAT

This type of fat appears to lower LDL-cholesterol and may also raise HDL-cholesterol. HDL-cholesterol, sometimes referred to as the "good" blood cholesterol, is protective against heart disease.

Key sources: olive and canola oil and soft margarines made from these oils; avocado; nuts such as filberts, almonds, pistachios, pecans and cashews.

POLYUNSATURATED FAT

Polyunsaturated fat helps lower harmful LDL-cholesterol.

Key sources: safflower, sunflower, corn, soybean, sesame seed and most nut oils, soft margarines made with these oils; nuts such as walnuts, pinenuts, brazil and chestnuts; seeds such as sesame and sunflower.

OMEGA-3 FAT

This is a type of polyunsaturated fat found primarily in fatty fish such as salmon and trout. It promotes heart health by reducing the stickiness or clotting tendencies of blood.

TRANS FAT

Trans fat is primarily a man-made form of unsaturated fat. It is created during the process of hydrogenation, used to turn a liquid oil into a solid fat product. Although it is technically unsaturated, it acts more like a saturated fat by raising blood levels of LDL-cholesterol.

Key sources: vegetable shortening and foods made with vegetable shortening such as cookies, crackers and other packaged foods; some peanut butter; many but not all margarines.

Facts on Fibre

Dietary fibre comes from the parts of plants that cannot be broken down by the human digestive system. It is a mixture of cellulose, hemicellulose, pectin, lignin and gums. Fibre is divided into two groups according to whether or not they can dissolve in water, called soluble and insoluble.

SOLUBLE FIBRE

Soluble fibre may help in lowering blood cholesterol levels and in controlling blood sugar levels.

Sources of soluble fibre: oat bran, oatmeal, legumes (dried beans, peas and lentils), pectin-rich fruits (apples, strawberries and citrus fruits).

INSOLUBLE FIBRE

Insoluble fibre, or roughage, with its water-retaining capacity, increases bulk and helps prevent and control bowel problems. It may be important in the prevention of certain cancers.

Sources of insoluble fibre: wheat bran, wheat bran cereals, whole grain foods like whole wheat bread, fruit and vegetables, including skins and seeds.

What Nutrition Claims Really Mean:

What the label says:	*What the label means:*
Fat free	• almost no fat
Low in fat	• less than 3 g of fat per serving (less than a tsp of fat)
Reduced in fat	• must contain at least 25% less fat and at least 1.5 g less fat per serving than the regular product • not necessarily low in fat
Light or Lite	• may contain less fat and less energy • may contain less salt, e.g., "light" soy sauce • may contain less alcohol, e.g., "light" beer • may not be nutrition-related, i.e., light in colour or in taste
Cholesterol free, or No cholesterol	• hardly any cholesterol (no more than 3 mg per 100 g), and • little saturated fat (no more than 2 g per serving, and no more than 15% of total energy)
Low cholesterol, or Low in cholesterol	• small amount of cholesterol (no more than 20 mg per 100 g and per serving) • little saturated fat (no more than 2 g per serving, and no more than 15% of total energy)

Adapted from: Label Smart, an educational program on nutrition labelling developed by the National Institute of Nutrition, January 1994.

ANTIOXIDANT VITAMINS

Dietary Sources of Antioxidant Vitamins

Vitamin C (ascorbic acid):

- vegetables such as broccoli, Brussels sprouts, cauliflower, cabbage, green peppers, kale, snow peas and sweet potatoes
- fruits such as cantaloupes, grapefruits, honeydew melons, oranges, tangerines, and strawberries

B-carotene (plant form of Vitamin A):

- dark green leafy vegetables such as collard greens, kale, mustard greens, peppers, spinach, turnip greens and Swiss chard
- yellow-orange vegetables such as carrots, pumpkins, sweet potatoes and winter squash
- yellow-orange fruits such as apricots, cantaloupes, mangos, papayas and peaches

Vitamin E (tocopherols and tocotrienols):

- almonds, hazelnuts
- peanut butter
- salad/vegetable oils
- sunflower seeds
- wheat germ

CANADIAN DIABETES ASSOCIATION FOOD CHOICE SYSTEM

The following CDA Food Choice Values have been assigned to the recipes in this book in accordance with the Good Health Eating Guide (1994) which is used for meal planning by people with diabetes. The Food Choice Value for a certain serving size has been calculated for each recipe to make it easy to fit into a personalized meal plan. Servings must be measured carefully, since changing the serving size will increase or decrease the Food Choice Value assigned. Some recipes may include an inappropriate portion of a certain food group for a person with diabetes. For these recipes, it is recommended that the portions that are in excess be reduced to include them in a meal plan.

The Good Health Eating Guide (1994) has recently been revised to reflect the Canadian Diabetes Association's position on the intake of sugar by people with diabetes. Current research does not support the traditional recommendation to people with diabetes to strictly avoid simple sugars. This means that simple sugars can be incorporated into a meal plan according to the information in the new Good Health Eating Guide (1994) and with the help of a dietitian-nutritionist.

The Food Choice System used in the Good Health Eating Guide (1994) is based on Canada's Food Guide To Healthy Eating. For more information on diabetes and the complete Good Health Eating Guide (1994), write to the National Office, Canadian Diabetes Association, 15 Toronto Street, Suite 1001, Toronto, Ontario, M5C 2E3 and your letter will be forwarded to the provincial Division Office nearest you.

FOOD CHOICE VALUE PER SERVING

PG	RECIPE (PORTION SIZE)	STARCH □	FRUITS & VEGETABLES ◨	2% MILK ◈	PROTEIN ⊘	FATS & OILS ▲	EXTRA ❖❖	SUGARS ❖
34	Eggplant Spread with Tahini (1 tbsp/15 mL)						1	
35	Refried Black Bean Dip (1 tbsp/15 mL)						1	
36	White Bean Spread with Greens (1 tbsp/15 mL)						1	
37	Hummos with Sesame (1 tbsp/15 mL)		½					
38	Guacamole (1 tbsp/15 mL)						1	
39	Tzatziki (1 tbsp/15 mL)						1	
40	Caponata (1 tbsp/15 mL)						1	
41	Chèvre Dip with Potatoes (¹⁄₃₂ of recipe)		½		½			
42	Ricotta Bruschetta (¹⁄₂₄ of recipe)	½			1			
43	Grilled Bread with Tomato, Pepper and Basil Salsa (1/16 of recipe)	½				½		
44	Provence-style Herb Onion Toasts (⅛ of recipe)	1½				½	1	
45	Pesto Pizza (¹⁄₃₂ of recipe)		½					
46	Smoked Salmon Tortilla Spirals (¹⁄₃₂ of recipe)		½		½			
47	Polenta Bites (¹⁄₃₂ of recipe)		½					
48	Chicken Dumplings with Sweet and Sour Sauce (¹⁄₃₂ of recipe)				½		1	
50	Louisiana Barbecued Shrimp (⅛ of recipe)		½		1			
52	Seafood Soup with Ginger Broth (⅛ of recipe)		½		1			
53	Hot and Sour Soup (⅙ of recipe)		1½		2			
54	Apple and Squash Soup (⅙ of recipe)		2		½			

PG	RECIPE (PORTION SIZE)	STARCH	FRUITS & VEGETABLES	2% MILK	PROTEIN	FATS & OILS	EXTRA	SUGARS
55	Cabbage Borscht (¹⁄₁₂ of recipe)		1		1			
56	Green Minestrone with Cheese Croutons (⅛ of recipe)		1½		1½	½		
57	Potato and Garlic Soup with Pesto Swirls (⅛ of recipe)	1	½		½	½		
58	Leek and Potato Soup (⅛ of recipe) *No Food Choice Value included for variation*	1			½			
59	Chicken and Seafood Gumbo (⅛ of recipe)	1	1		1			
60	"Cream" of Fennel, Leek and Carrot Soup (⅛ of recipe)	1			½	½	1	
61	Chickpea and Spinach Soup (⅙ of recipe)	2			1		1	
62	White Bean Soup with Salad Salsa (⅛ of recipe)	1½	½		1			
64	Lentil Vegetable Soup (⅙ of recipe)	1½			1½			
65	Mushroom, Bean and Barley Soup (¹⁄₁₂ of recipe)	1	½		1			
66	Moroccan Lentil Soup with Pasta (⅛ of recipe)	2	½		2		1	
68	Black Bean Soup with Yogurt and Spicy Salsa (⅛ of recipe)	2			2		1	
70	Split Pea Soup with Dill (⅛ of recipe)	2	1		1½			
72	Tabbouleh Salad (⅛ of recipe)	1	½		½	½		
73	Mixed Grain Salad (⅛ of recipe) (no chickpeas)	2½				1½		
74	Black Bean, Corn and Rice Salad (⅛ of recipe)	2½			½	1	1	
75	Sushi Salad (⅙ of recipe)	2½	½			½		
76	Tomato and Cucumber Salad (⅙ of recipe)		½					½
77	Asian Coleslaw (⅙ of recipe)		1			½		1
78	Salad Niçoise (⅙ of recipe)	1½	½		2			
79	Beet Salad (¼ of recipe)		1					
80	Potato Salad (⅙ of recipe)	1½	½			1		
81	Grilled Bread and Cherry Tomato Salad (⅙ of recipe)	1	½			1		
82	Spaghettini with Salad Greens (⅛ of recipe)	2½	½		½	½		
83	Spaghetti Salad with Tuna (⅙ of recipe)	2½	½		2½			
84	Thai Chicken and Noodle Salad (⅛ of recipe)	2½			2½			½
86	Grilled Chicken Salad with Peanut Sauce (⅙ of recipe)	½	1		4½			1
88	Chopped Grilled Chicken Salad (⅙ of recipe)	½	2		3			
90	Letty's Noodle Salad (⅙ of recipe)	4	½		2	½		
91	Balsamic Spa Dressing (1 tbsp/15 mL) (no honey)						1	
92	Mustard Pepper Dressing (1 tbsp/15 mL)					½	1	
93	Roasted Garlic Dressing (1 tbsp/15 mL)		½			½		
94	Citrus Vinaigrette (1 tbsp/15 mL)					½		
95	Sesame Ginger Dressing (1 tbsp/15 mL)							½
96	Roasted Red Pepper Dressing (1 tbsp/15 mL)						1	
98	Pasta with Red Peppers and Eggplant (⅙ of recipe)	3	2½		1	1		
99	Penne Arrabbiata (⅙ of recipe)	3½	½		1	1		
100	Penne with Potatoes and Rapini (⅙ of recipe)	4			½	1½		
101	Spaghetti Puttanesca (⅙ of recipe)	3½	½		½	½		
102	Mark's Spaghetti with Tomato Sauce (⅙ of recipe)	3½	½		1	½		

		STARCH	FRUITS & VEGETABLES	2% MILK	PROTEIN	FATS & OILS	EXTRA	SUGARS
PG	RECIPE (PORTION SIZE)	▯	▱	◆	⬦	▲	⬛	✳
103	Spaghettini with Corn (⅙ of recipe)	5	½		1			
104	Pasta with Tomatoes and Beans (⅙ of recipe)	4	1		1½			
105	Curried Tofu and Noodles (⅙ of recipe)	4	½		1½			
106	Pasta with Tomato Sauce and Ricotta (⅙ of recipe) (no pancetta or bacon)	3½	1		1½	½		
107	Noodles with Vegetables and Peanut Sauce (⅛ of recipe)	3	½		1	1		
108	Linguine with Tomatoes and Scallops (⅙ of recipe)	3½	1		2			
109	Spaghettini with Clam Sauce (⅙ of recipe)	4			1			
110	Pasta with Grilled Salmon and Stir-fried Vegetables (⅙ of recipe)	3½	1		2½			½
112	Linguine with Grilled Seafood and Pesto Tomato Sauce (⅙ of recipe)	3½	1		2½			
113	Rigatoni with Tuna, Peppers and Tomato Sauce (⅙ of recipe)	4	½		1½		1	
114	Spaghetti with Meatballs (⅙ of recipe)	3½	1		2	1		
116	Vegetable Paella (⅛ of recipe)	2½	1½			½		
117	Vegetarian Muffuletta (⅛ of recipe)	3½	1		1			
118	Stir-fried Tofu with Vegetables (¼ of recipe)	½	1		2½			
120	Black Bean Chèvre Quesadillas (⅙ of recipe)	2½			2	1		
121	Mixed Bean Chili (⅛ of recipe)	1½	½		1			
122	Baked Polenta Casserole (⅛ of recipe)	1½	½		1	½		
124	Sweet and Sour Vegetable Stew (⅙ of recipe)	2½	3		½	½		1
126	"Cassoulet" of Onions (⅛ of recipe)	2	1½		1½			
128	Springtime Stir-fried Rice and Vegetables (⅙ of recipe)	3	1			½		
129	Quickbread Pizza (⅛ of recipe)	3		½	1	1½		
130	Falafel Vegetable Burgers (⅛ of recipe)	2			1	½		
132	Potato and Broccoli Egg White Frittata (⅙ of recipe)	1			1			
134	Ribollita (⅛ of recipe)	2	1½		1½		1	
136	Grilled Tofu Kebabs (¼ of recipe)	½	1½		2½			½
138	Sesame-crusted Salmon on Greens (⅙ of recipe)		½		3½		1	½
139	Roasted Salmon with Lentils (⅙ of recipe)	1½	½		4			
140	Steamed Salmon with Korean Dressing (¼ of recipe)	1½	½		3			
142	Oven-poached Halibut with Herb Vinaigrette (⅙ of recipe)		½		3½			
144	Hoisin-glazed Sea Bass or Salmon (¼ of recipe)				3		1	
145	Asian Tuna or Swordfish Burgers (⅙ of recipe)	2½			3			
146	Seared Tuna with Japanese Noodle Salad (⅙ of recipe)	1½	1		3			
148	Baked Red Snapper with Hot Chiles (⅛ of recipe)				3		1	
149	Oven-baked Fish and Chips (⅙ of recipe)	3½			3			
150	Sweet and Sour Swordfish (⅛ of recipe)		1		3			
151	Swordfish Teriyaki (⅙ of recipe)				3			1
152	Gefilte Fish with Beet Horseradish Salad (1/16 of recipe)		½		2½			
154	Provençal Fish Stew with Rouille (⅛ of recipe) (no mayonnaise)	1	1		3½			

PG	RECIPE (PORTION SIZE)	STARCH	FRUITS & VEGETABLES	2% MILK	PROTEIN	FATS & OILS	EXTRA	SUGARS
156	Mussels with Black Bean Sauce ($\frac{1}{6}$ of recipe)		1		1½			
158	Risotto with Seafood and Peppers ($\frac{1}{6}$ of recipe)	3			2	½	1	
160	Fish Fillets with Rosemary ($\frac{1}{4}$ of recipe)				3			
162	Moroccan Chicken ($\frac{1}{6}$ of recipe)				4			1½
163	Asian Chicken Chili ($\frac{1}{8}$ of recipe)	1			3	1		
164	Chicken Pot Pie ($\frac{1}{8}$ of recipe)	1½	½		4			
166	Chicken Burgers Teriyaki ($\frac{1}{6}$ of recipe)	2½			3			
	Lemon Ginger Teriyaki Sauce (1 tbsp/15 mL)							1
167	Breaded Chicken Fingers ($\frac{1}{4}$ of recipe)	2			4			
168	Caribbean Vegetable and Chicken Curry ($\frac{1}{8}$ of recipe)	1½	1½		3			
170	Barbecued Chicken Fingers ($\frac{1}{4}$ of recipe)				3½			½
171	Chicken Fajitas ($\frac{1}{8}$ of recipe)	2	1		3			½
172	Chicken Breasts with Black Bean Sauce ($\frac{1}{6}$ of recipe)				4		1	
173	St. Lucia Barbecued Chicken ($\frac{1}{8}$ of recipe)		½		4½			1
174	Stir-fried Chicken and Vegetables ($\frac{1}{4}$ of recipe)		1½		4½			
176	Skewered Chicken on a Bun ($\frac{1}{4}$ of recipe)	2			3½			
177	Chicken with Forty Cloves of Garlic ($\frac{1}{6}$ of recipe) (no shallots)		½		3½			
178	Chicken with Raspberry Vinegar ($\frac{1}{4}$ of recipe)		1		4			
179	Roast Chicken with Bulgur Stuffing							
	Bulgur Stuffing ($\frac{1}{6}$ of recipe)	1	1		½	½		
	Roast Chicken with Skin and Stuffing ($\frac{1}{6}$ of recipe)	1	1		4½	½		
	Roast Chicken with No Skin and Stuffing ($\frac{1}{6}$ of recipe)	1	1		4			
180	Linda Stephen's Grilled Cilantro Chicken with Pad Thai ($\frac{1}{6}$ of recipe)	2	½		4½			½
182	Roast Turkey Breast with Rosemary and Garlic ($\frac{1}{8}$ of recipe)				5			½
184	Moroccan Meatballs with Chickpeas and Couscous ($\frac{1}{6}$ of recipe)	3	½		2	½		
186	Meatloaf with Irish Mashed Potatoes ($\frac{1}{8}$ of recipe)	2	½		3	½		
188	Stir-fried Barbecued Beef and Noodles ($\frac{1}{8}$ of recipe)	1½	½		2½			
190	Middle Eastern Burgers with Yogurt Mint Sauce ($\frac{1}{6}$ of recipe)	3			2½	½		
191	Aunt Pearl's Tzimmes (Carrot Stew) ($\frac{1}{12}$ of recipe)	½	2		1½	½		½
192	Texas Chili ($\frac{1}{12}$ of recipe)	1	½		4½			
193	Beef Sukiyaki ($\frac{1}{6}$ of recipe)	1	1		3			
194	Korean Flank Steak ($\frac{1}{4}$ of recipe)				4			1
195	Sirloin Steak with Mustard Pepper Crust ($\frac{1}{6}$ of recipe)				4			
196	Veal Cutlets in Tomato Sauce Casserole ($\frac{1}{6}$ of recipe)	1	1		3			
198	Cantonese-style Grilled Leg of Lamb ($\frac{1}{8}$ of recipe)				4			½
199	Roast Lamb with Rosemary and Potatoes ($\frac{1}{10}$ of recipe)	1½			3½			
200	Pork Tenderloin with Apricot Glaze ($\frac{1}{6}$ of recipe)				3½			1½
201	Southern Barbecued Pork Roast ($\frac{1}{10}$ of recipe)				3½			4

PG	RECIPE (PORTION SIZE)	STARCH	FRUITS & VEGETABLES	2% MILK	PROTEIN	FATS & OILS	EXTRA	SUGARS
202	Stir-fried Pork (¼ of recipe)		1½		3			
204	Broccoli or Rapini with Raisins and Pine Nuts (¼ of recipe)		1½		½			
205	Glazed Cumin Carrots (¼ of recipe)		1½		½	½		½
206	Asparagus with Ginger (⅙ of recipe)		½					
207	Roasted Red Onions with Balsamic Vinegar (⅛ of recipe)		2					
208	Caramelized Beets and Onions (¼ of recipe)		1½					1
209	Corn with Garlic and Chives (¼ of recipe)	2				½		
210	Herb Barbecued Corn on the Cob (⅙ of recipe)	2						
211	Spicy Corn Ragout (⅛ of recipe)	2	½		½			
212	Sicilian Squash (¼ of recipe)		2			1		½
213	Creamy Polenta with Corn and Roasted Garlic (⅛ of recipe)	1½					1	
214	Spicy Mashed Sweet Potatoes (⅙ of recipe)	2½						½
215	Garlic Mashed Potatoes (⅙ of recipe)	1½				½		
216	Roasted Rosemary French Fries (⅙ of recipe)	1½				½		
217	Roasted Root Vegetables (¼ of recipe)	2	1			1	1	
218	Braised White Beans (⅛ of recipe)	2			1½			
219	White Bean Puree with Cumin (⅙ of recipe)	2			2			
220	Middle Eastern Couscous (⅙ of recipe)	1½	½					
221	Mixed Grain Pilaf (¼ of recipe)	3½	½		½	1		
222	Navajo Rice Pilaf (⅙ of recipe)	2	½			½		
223	Rice with Pasta and Chickpeas (¼ of recipe)	4½			1	½	1	
224	Risotto with Squash (⅙ of recipe)	2½	1			½		
226	Grapefruit Calypso (⅙ of recipe)		1					1½
227	Breakfast Shake (½ of recipe)		3					
228	Yogurt Cheese (1 tbsp/15 mL)						1	
229	Breakfast Fruit Crisp (⅛ of recipe)	1/2	3			1½		1½
230	Swiss Muesli (⅙ of recipe)	1	½	½	½			1
231	Baked French Toast (⅙ of recipe)	2			1½	1		1
232	Lemon Ricotta Pancakes (⅙ of recipe)	1			1	½		1
233	Buttermilk Oatmeal Pancakes (⅙ of recipe)	1		½	½	½		1
234	Multigrain Griddlecakes (⅙ of recipe)	2½		½	½	1		
235	Caramelized Pear Puff Pancake (⅙ of recipe)	½	1½		½	1½		1½
236	Chèvre and Fresh Herb Soufflé (⅛ of recipe)	½		½	1	1		
238	Breakfast Pizza (⅛ of recipe)	2			2	½		
240	Cranberry Streusel Muffins (1/12 of recipe)	1	½			1		1½
241	Oat and Wheat Bran Muffins with Dried Apricots (1/12 of recipe)	½	1			1		1
242	Apple Cinnamon Muffins (1/12 of recipe)	1	½			1½		1
243	Morning Glory Muffin Bars (1/24 of recipe)	1				1		½
244	Oatmeal Honey Rolls (1/16 of recipe)	1½				1		½
246	Double Cornbread with Mild Green Chiles (1/16 of recipe)	1				½	1	

PG	RECIPE (PORTION SIZE)	STARCH	FRUITS & VEGETABLES	2% MILK	PROTEIN	FATS & OILS	EXTRA	SUGARS
247	Buttermilk Black Pepper Biscuits (1/10 of recipe)	1½				1		
248	Buttermilk Oat Scones (1/12 of recipe)	1	½			1		½
249	Denise Beatty's Potato Scones (1/8 of recipe)	1	1			1		1
250	Multigrain Yogurt Bread (1/32 of recipe)	1						
252	Spiced Whole Wheat Challah with Honey and Raisins (1/16 of recipe)	1				½		½
254	Red River Cereal Bread (1/32 of recipe)	1						
255	Rosemary Monkey Bread (1/12 of recipe)	2				1		
256	Irish Soda Bread with Caraway Seeds (1/16 of recipe)	1				½	1	
258	Strawberries with Balsamic Vinegar (1/6 of recipe)		½					½
259	Pears Poached in Spiced Red Wine (1/8 of recipe)		2½					1½
260	Caramelized Winter Fruit Compote (1/8 of recipe) (no cognac or yogurt cheese)		4					2½
261	Baked Apples Amaretti (1/6 of recipe)		2½			½		1
262	Bananas Flambé (1/6 of recipe)		3½			½		2
263	Fruit Yogurt Dip and Peach Salsa (1/16 of recipe) (no liqueur)			½				
264	Dessert Fruit Curry (1/6 of recipe) (no liqueur)		2½					1
265	Creamy Rice Pudding (1/8 of recipe)	½	½	1				1
266	Floating Island (1/6 of recipe)			½	1			5
268	Upside-down Lemon Meringues (1/8 of recipe)		1	½				3
269	Blueberry Grunt (1/4 of recipe)	1	2½			1		3
270	Plum Crisp (1/10 of recipe)	½	1			1		1
271	Rhubarb and Strawberry Cobbler (1/10 of recipe)	1	½			1½		2½
272	Apple Strudel Pie (1/10 of recipe)	1	1½			1½		1½
273	Quick Apple Cake (1/12 of recipe)		1			1½		1½
274	Anna's Angel Food Cake with Berry Berry Sauce (1/12 of recipe) (no liqueur)	½	½		½			2½
276	Chocolate Angel Food Cake with Chocolate Sauce (1/12 of recipe)	1			½	1		3½
278	Old-fashioned Cheesecake (1/35 of recipe)				1		1	1
280	Strawberry Meringue Shortcakes (1/6 of recipe)		½	1	½			2½
281	Mocha Meringue Kisses (1/60 of recipe)						1	
282	Nick Malgieri's Honey Almond Biscotti (1/20 of recipe) (3 cookies)	1				1		1
283	Matrimonial Squares (Date Squares) (1/25 of recipe)	½	1			1		1
284	Oatmeal and Raisin Spice Cookie Squares (1/30 of recipe)	½				1		½

INDEX